THE LOST
COUSINS
OF COUNTY
ARMAGH

JANNIS DEGRAW BUHR

ACKNOWLEDGEMENTS

Special Thanks:

To my wonderful husband and high school sweetheart, Mark Buhr.

To my precise editor, Lucie Winborne.

To my thorough beta readers, Dan Buhr, Julie Childs & Jessica Jagod.

And to my sweet Scottish connection, Heather Waddell Byrne.

I could not have accomplished this without all of your help!

And, many thanks to my Lord and Savior, Jesus Christ, for His guidance at every step of the way in this journey of writing, publishing and promoting The MacCauley Trilogy.

Thank you, readers, for waiting so patiently for this final story of the MacCauley saga. Enjoy.

**This book is dedicated to
Jeanne McElroy DeGraw.**

Everyone needs that one cheerleader:
That person who pushes you on
through the good and the bad times,
who praises your first attempts at anything you try,
who reads every single manuscript you write—good or bad,
and finds the good in it,
giving you the energy
and the strength
to keep on going
despite your own critical self!

Mom, you are and have been that to me, and I'll never forget it.
Saying this one "thank you" doesn't feel like enough.
But know that it has a thousand "thank yous" behind it.
I hope I can pay it forward to others who cross my path in life like you have
done for me.
I love you.

"CHRIST WITH ME

CHRIST BEFORE ME

CHRIST BEHIND ME

CHRIST IN ME

CHRIST BENEATH ME

CHRIST ABOVE ME

CHRIST ON MY RIGHT

CHRIST ON MY LEFT

CHRIST WHEN I LIE DOWN

CHRIST WHEN I SIT DOWN

CHRIST WHEN I ARISE

CHRIST IN THE HEART OF EVERYONE WHO THINKS OF ME

CHRIST IN THE MOUTH OF EVERYONE WHO SPEAKS OF ME

CHRIST IN EVERY EYE THAT SEES ME

CHRIST IN EVERY EAR THAT HEARS ME."

— ST. PATRICK

List of Names and Pronunciations

Book One:

From the United States:

Robert & Phyllis Beckett and their daughter, Haley

Henry and Martha Beckett (Robert's parents) and their daughters: Margaret, Susanna and Ruth

Fred & Alma Wagner and their children: Edward, Keith and Peggy

Haley Beckett's friends: Tonya Miller, Penny Baumann and Carrie

Troublemaking "Townies": Scott and Steve Brannen

Detectives: Uncle Bobby Hanford and Drew Carter

From Northern Ireland:

Ian (**Ee** yan) & Anna MacCauley (Ma **Caw** ley) and their sons, Eoin (**O** wen) and Gareth

RUC (Royal Ulster Constabulary) Sean (Shawn) Fergus Collins

New in Book Two:

From Scotland:

Dave McGilroy (Mc **Gil** roy) and his son, Johnny

From Northern Ireland (natives of Scotland):

George and Margaret McGilroy

From the United States:

Gareth and Haley MacCauley's children: Annie, Fiahd (**Fee** yah) and Bobby

Scott and Penny Brannen's children: Jonathan and Angie

Keith and Carrie Wagner's children: Katie (who died at birth) and Benny

<u>New pronounciations in Book Three</u>:

Armagh: Aar-**maa**

Callum: **Cahl**-um

Brodie: **Broh**-dee

Maisie: **May**-zie

Liam: **Lee**-um

Seamus: **Shay**-mus

Siobhan: Shi-**von**

* The dates and facts of the historical events, many of the tragedies of Northern Ireland, and the polical events in this book are real; however, many of the names have been changed.

* In the back of this book there is a glossary for vocabulary, a pronunciation guide for Irish and Scottish brogues, and a list of political names, acronyms and initialisms.

PROLOGUE: LATE SUMMER. 1974 NORTHERN IRELAND

Sean MacCauley pushed away from the table and crossed his arms, deep in thought. Normally he would be satisfied with the cottage pie his wife, Erin, had made, but at the moment he was filled with no small amount of worry. A few weeks ago his brother, Ian, came over with the news that his wife, Anna, and eldest son, Eoin, didn't come home to their cottage close by, just south of Lurgan. There was no word from them or anyone who knew them and the police couldn't help. The amount of violence and protests on the streets kept them too busy to help with a small missing persons claim.

It wasn't until Gareth came biking frantically to Sean MacCauley's house today with two pieces of Anna's Samsonite luggage tied to his fender that they learned about everything else. When they could get Gareth to stop talking so fast and take a breath, he explained that his da, Ian, was carted off as a political prisoner to Long Kesh—something about being associated with the IRA? The Irish Republican Army? Sean and Erin had no idea that Gareth had been hiding out in his home alone for a few days, packing up his stuff. Then, today, when three men in balaclavas barged into his home, he snuck out his bedroom window and hid behind the house, watching the men carefully through a back window. After the intruders rummaged through his home, they lit it on fire. That's when Gareth took off on his bike to his uncle's place.

What was going on?

"Boys-a-dear," Erin said sadly as she took a dish from the table. "Did ya see the worried look in his eyes?"

"Aye. I don' blame him, ya know?"

"Gareth put his luggage in the barn in case he has ta run again." Erin put the dirty dish in the sink and returned to the table, worried. "Sure and the lad knows more than us of what's goin' on. I hate ta speak in this manner, but, is it a danger ta keep him with us, Sean? Ought we ta take him in ta the police?"

Sean shook his head, appalled his wife would suggest such a thing. "Ah, sit yer ground! How can ya say such a thing? They wouldn't help us find Anna and Eoin!"

"Away off and feel yer head!" Erin laughed sardonically. "Amn't I in with ya on this?"

"Besides, Ian and Anna would want us ta keep him safe with family! There's no option."

Erin stepped behind her husband's chair and rubbed his shoulders. "But we have ta think of the whole family. Sure and we should report this."

"So we do." Sean put his hand on his wife's. "Don' know what good it will do, but tomorrow I'll go."

Gareth, twelve years old and short for his age, leaned against a post in his uncle's barn, dark curls falling over closed eyes. He counted while his cousins hid—well, with one eye closed and one eye on the door of the barn facing the house. Would those men come here and destroy his uncle's house, too? He was afraid. He was angry. He was a lot of things at the moment.

Maisie, seven years old and tiny, shut herself up in an old wooden storage box in the loft of the barn while Gareth counted. She was still bothered by her cousin trying to help her by suggesting good places to hide. "I don' need no mollycoddlin'!" she had shouted in his face. She let out one last quiet harrumph as she snuggled into the box, her long, thick, strawberry-blond hair—with bits of hay tangled in—creating a nice cushion for her head. They had just been fed a dinner of comfort foods in the house and now she began to relax and breathe deep in her hide-out.

Brodie, eleven, perched himself up on a beam and hung like a monkey, his dark curls swinging freely. Callum, fourteen and gangly with a shock of black hair like a badly stooked haystack, ran out into the field with large feet flying. When Gareth reached the count of fifty, he started the search. Of course, Brodie was the first to be spotted and Gareth laughed at his cousin's silliness. He was the crazy one of the brothers with an extra dose of adrenalin at times and surely the most daring. Brodie swung down and pointed to the back door of the barn. Smiling deviously, Gareth ran with him out into the field to search for Callum. It felt good to run and play, and for a minute Gareth was able to forget his misery. Meanwhile, Maisie, tired of waiting for what seemed to be an eternity, drifted off into a peaceful slumber, her freckled face buried in a pillow of fairy hair.

Brodie and Gareth pounced on Callum tucked down behind an apple tree, but he slipped away from them with a yell and took chase, swerving between the trees in the neighbor's orchard. Gareth was unusually quick today, his adrenalin rush encouraged by recent events. He cut Callum off and whipped him to the ground.

"How'd ya do that, cousin?" Brodie marveled.

"Sure an' he gets crazy in the head like ya at times, that's how he does it!" Callum said, feeling defeated. The boys ran back toward the barn to search for Maisie. She was a clever girl and was known to outwit her big brothers and cousins often, much to their dismay.

Just as they entered the barn from the back, they heard men's voices. Rushing past the stalls and toward the front double doors, they pulled back quickly when they saw three men in balaclavas. Shots went off and made them jump. Callum and Gareth peered around the edge of the door and watched as the men lit up the thatched roof of the house. Brodie peeked through the crack between the barn door and the door frame and let out a gasp. The men turned and the boys disappeared immediately. Seeing an empty barn from where they stood, the men figured it was nothing and went back to their work. Gareth motioned for his cousins to stay put. When he peered out again and got a better look, he saw Sean and Erin lying helpless on the ground, dying, the blood pooling around them. His own blood boiled. He was angry and suddenly he didn't care what happened to him. Everyone he loved, every adult he depended on in this world, had been taken from him in a few short days. He grabbed the shotgun in the corner of the barn.

"What are ya doin'?" Callum said in a half whisper, alarmed at the fire in his cousin's eyes. Gareth ignored him, ran boldly to the entrance of the barn, and yelled angrily, "Saunter away or I'll knock yer pan in and bust yer dial, ya bad eggs!" Then he fired the gun. One man fell. The other men stopped in their tracks as they watched their comrade go down. They looked toward the barn again.

"Everybody run!" Gareth shouted to his cousins as he dropped the gun. The boys bolted and hid out in the orchard, hoping Maisie would stay hidden, hoping they could find her in the evening after it grew dark.

Hearing the first rounds of gunshots, Maisie started to wake up. Then she jerked with the sound of another gunshot blast close by. She whimpered quietly. She heard Gareth yell something. Afraid to come out of her safe hiding place, she waited. When things grew quiet, she pushed the lid up slightly and listened. She heard footsteps, and, thinking it was the boys, she stepped out of the box. Her nostrils filled with the scent of smoke coming from the house. Suddenly a gruff voice broke the silence. "Where are ye, lads? Ye have no place ta go!" She had seen men like this on the streets of Lurgan and knew they were dangerous. Shivering with fright, she laid down flat on her belly, holding back a cry, watching, listening carefully to their conversation. Smoke began to fill the barn and the men vanished from her sight.

      After it grew quiet, Maisie called softly, "Callum? Brodie? Gareth? Where are ya?" No answer. She stepped down off the ladder and moved beneath the haze toward the entrance of the barn. Her foot kicked something; she picked it up and put it in her pocket as she continued to move a little closer to the house. "Ma? Da? Why is the house burnin'?! Sure an' yer all hidin' from me?" She put a hand before her eyes to try to see better. Her feet stopped at a large lump on the ground and she squatted down to see what it was. She screamed, turned from it immediately, and ran down the road crying hysterically, tears streaking down her soot-covered face.

      Surely her whole family was dead.

      Surely she was left alone in all of County Armagh, Northern Ireland.

CHAPTER 1

1993. Belfast, Northern Ireland.

Maisie O'Leary finished tying her four-year-old daughter's runners and tried to lift the girl to her feet. The child suddenly became twice as heavy and as wobbly as a rag doll. It was always like this on the mornings they had to rush out to catch the bus.

"We've no much time left, Erin!" Maisie said in frustration.

"I wanna stay home and play, so I do!"

"Ya have ta go ta preschool while I work ta buy food, so it is!"

Erin began to wail.

"Catch yerself on and calm down," Maisie said, all the while talking to herself. Breathe. What good would it do to tell her child to settle down if she were screaming too? She took a deep breath. "There are worse things in life, lassie. Stop the tears and get movin'."

Maisie took her daughter's hand and they stepped out the door of their damp, two-up-two-down, terraced house on the smog-ridden streets of Belfast. They passed a British soldier leaning against the door of an abandoned shop having a smoke, his eyes constantly on the movements of the people rushing to bus stops, trying to get to work or to a shop. Civilians carefully avoided eye contact with him as well as the other soldiers who stood at their posts down the street. There had been too many protests and riots, and too many shootings and car bombs in this city for the past twenty years for Britain to call their soldiers back to their homeland. It wasn't a job many of them had signed on for and now the morale was low. In the last few years they had been issued plastic bullets to just "hurt" the rioting crowds, but some had actually penetrated and mortally wounded not just the troublemakers, but innocent civilians—even children. Thus, the hatred for the British soldiers along with the Royal Ulster Constabulary—who by now donned flak jackets for protection—had grown deeper amongst the Irish.

Maisie hurried Erin to the bus stop designated Protestant. There was a Catholic bus stop closer to their home but the harassment they'd suffer wasn't worth the convenience. Erin sat close to her ma on the bus as Maisie combed her fingers through her daughter's tangled mess of dark curls. Hair just like her da and Brodie. She pushed the last picture of her father away—that final horrible day—and thought only of the day she remembered him stepping into the kitchen, his wet curls pulling straight, dripping down his face. Maisie was sitting at the table having a warm cup of tea with her ma. Her da smiled through the mess and said, "Nice day for ducks," and her ma said, "Ach, it's a grand soft day, God bless it." And then her da kissed her ma on the head and the two of them laughed. That was her favorite memory and she kept it close to her heart. She didn't have too many. She was young when she lost her family. Too young to lose her da. *And* her ma. She looked down at Erin, named after the Nana she'd never know. Maisie didn't want to be so hard on her wee daughter, but it was better to learn early that life was one big disappointment after another.

At least, that's what she knew of things. After losing her family so young, Maisie was placed in an orphanage run by the Sisters of Bethlehem. It was a Catholic institution and, even though she was raised Presbyterian, it was the only option at the time. As a child she didn't see much difference than her own upbringing except for the statues, and those were fascinating. She was especially enamored of the statue of Mary holding baby Jesus that always stood in the foyer of the church. It reminded her of Christmastime when her ma would get out the crèche and set up the small figures of Mary, Joseph, and baby Jesus. Maisie always wondered where the rest of the manger scene was in the Catholic church and why they didn't put out Joseph, the shepherds, the wisemen, the camels and the sheep.

It wasn't until ten years later that her brothers found her at the orphanage just before she was old enough to leave. She thought her brothers were dead and they had assumed the same about her. The reunion was emotional. By then, Callum was married to Molly and they had started a family. Brodie, still a bachelor, took her in and she soon discovered he was involved in a loyalist paramilitary group, the Ulster Volunteer Force. After what happened to his family, Brodie couldn't get past the urge to fight against the Provisional Irish Republican Army. The PIRA, informally called Provos, was a split off the original IRA and became dominant during the Troubles. Brodie hated them with a passion. Maisie and Callum begged him to leave the UVF, but he couldn't.

It was one of his UVF friends, Michael O'Leary, with whom she fell in love. She'd never forget the first time she saw him marching with his gang down the street: black polo-neck jumper, black trousers, black leather jacket with well-polished boots, sunglasses, and a cap like the commandos wore in WWII. She asked Brodie to introduce him to her and Michael took her out that night. They fell in love quickly and, against Callum's wishes, she married Michael. Soon, they were able to afford a decent flat near the Shankill Road.

The years with Michael were good at first, but when things got intense in the neighborhoods, he was gone late into the nights. Maisie wished he'd leave the gang, but that wasn't in the mix. It was too dangerous to leave. And then one night, he didn't come home. Maisie waited up for him that night. She was excited to tell him the news—that she was pregnant. When 5 a.m. rolled around she started to suspect something was amiss. Then Brodie came knocking on her door. She knew immediately by the look on his face something had happened. Brodie explained that Michael had told the leader of the organization, Joe Campbell, this was his last time fighting. Then Brodie hung his head. He didn't need to say anymore. Maisie knew what it meant. Joe had pulled out his gun and Michael was shot immediately. That's what often happened if one pulled out of the paramilitary.

She never got to tell Michael about Erin.

Maisie couldn't afford to continue the mortgage on their flat after he died, so she moved to a tenement house further down the Shankill, close to the Catholic neighborhoods. Her brothers weren't happy. But what could she do? She didn't earn much as a waitress and she refused to be on the bru, which meant getting government help. It was a constant struggle, being a single mom, living in a volatile city. But she had no choice. At least Erin brought her a piece of sunshine she hadn't felt since before the attack on her family in 1974.

Erin was old enough to understand what today was. As soon as she woke up she bounded off her mattress on the floor, put her shoes on, sat on her mama's mattress and bounced as she chanted loudly, "It's Saturn-day, Ma, it's Saturn-day!"

Maisie turned over in her bed and smiled sleepily. "Sa-*turr*-day, so it is." She observed the pajamas coupled with the shoes and laughed. "An' where would ya be goin' without a bell on yer bike?"

"Down the town! Down the town!"

"Is that where ye want ta go?"

"Aye, it is, ta get treats and fish-and-chippies!"

Maisie laughed. "Food. That's all ye can think of, then?"

"Fish-and-chippies! Fish-and-chippies! And ta go see Mr. Murphy!"

"Aye, is that because he always gives ya extra chippies?"

"So it is! So it is!"

Maisie was as excited as her daughter to go to the fish-and-chip shop. It was fun to look through the window at the white-coated workers taking their wire scoops, lifting out the crisply battered haddocks and laying them out to drain by the delicious golden piles of chips. Maisie had wonderful memories as a young child of walking down the street from the chip shop with her hot fish-and-chips wrapped in newspaper, the smell of vinegar on her fingers. After she had been placed in the orphanage that pleasure came to an end, but now, with her own daughter, she could enjoy it again.

Maisie showered quickly, put on a pair of jeans and a blouse, and pulled her auburn hair back in a ponytail. She found Erin standing by the door completely dressed and ready to go. What a difference in her energy level now that it was Saturday. They stepped out of the tenement building and walked along the Shankill Road. It was a beautiful day as the sun worked hard to send rays through the smog. The street swarmed with people unconcerned about fashion like the people strutting on London streets. Instead, these folk were concerned about shopping, taking a stroll, or excited to line up at a machine dispenser outside a shop for soft ice cream on cones. Buskers—street entertainers—were out staking their territories with their guitars, mandolins, and saxophones. Even the soldiers along the streets looked a bit more relaxed on a day like today.

This part of the Shankill was a loyalist part of town and the Ulster flag was draped plentifully from shops and tenement windows. One would think a Protestant could feel safe here, but the fact of the matter was, there was no guarantee of safety anywhere—not for Catholics *or* Protestants, in any part of town. A random bomb from the enemy, a riot of some sort, a shooting—all of the above—could happen from the "enemy," at any time. But, just like everyone else out on this beautiful day, Maisie treated this time with Erin like it was an ordinary day, a day filled with sunshine and being out together. She needed to give her daughter some semblance of normalcy. And Maisie prayed this would be just that, a normal day.

After picking up some wool to knit Erin a new scarf, and some sweets for later, they headed to Murphy's Fish Shop, singing while swinging arms and shopping bags. "Ho, ro, the rattlin' bog, the bog down in the valley-o, real bog, the rattlin' bog—"

They were just a few blocks down from their destination when a loud explosion made them cut their song short and fall to the ground as their packages went flying everywhere. Maisie instinctively covered her daughter's body to protect her. Erin wiggled under her mother's grasp and began to cry. Maisie looked up and saw a plume of smoke rising in the air as dust coated everyone. People were yelling and screaming. Some were running away from the explosion and some were running toward it. Maisie could hear the word "Murphy's" repeatedly in the mayhem and she wanted to cry out, "Not Murphy's!" but she refrained for her daughter's sake. Why Murphy's? Mr. Murphy and his daughter were always good to the people in town. Why would someone bomb their store? The sound of sirens filled their ears as Maisie retrieved what she could of their scattered bags and pulled Erin in the opposite direction.

"Ma, what happened? I want chippies. It's *this* way." Erin fought to go back the other way. "Ya said we're goin' ta get some!"

"Not today, me bonny lass," Maisie said as she kept both hands strongly around her daughter and pushed through the crowds. She had to think quickly. "How about we go ta Beatties Chippy and get pasties instead?"

"Why not Murphy's? Was that a bomb?" Erin yanked out of Maisie's grasp and started off toward the shop again. "I want fish-and-chippies, Ma!"

"Erin! Stop!" She grabbed her daughter's arm and held on tight.

"That hurts!"

"Come with me."

"I want ta go ta Murphy's, I do!" Erin stomped her foot.

A woman heard her. She stopped and said, "Sure an' he didn't survive—"

"Please," Maisie said to the woman. The woman looked at Erin and then mouthed the word *"sorry."*

"We can't get fish-and-chippies today, me wee bairn. Maybe another time."

"Did the bomb blow up the chippies shop?"

"Sure and I haven't a clue."

"Were bodies blown up?"

"Don' ask that! And we're not goin' ta go that way ta find out!"

"Why not?"

"It's not safe!"

Maisie's voice almost broke as they hurried down the sidewalk. Angry tears trickled down her cheeks. Her daughter was four and she already knew what a bomb could do. Other children in other countries surely didn't experience this kind of life. She wished she could get away from Belfast and Northern Ireland altogether! She used to think about moving to London, but the IRA were there, too. The Republic of Ireland was poorer than Northern Ireland, but it was safer. Would she be welcome there? Her "Protestantism" was obvious and people on this island could sniff out one's religion in a heartbeat. She knew to keep her mouth shut living with the Catholic sisters all those years and to go along with what they taught, but once she left them, she felt free to hold strongly to what her parents had taught her at such a young age. That could be trouble, living on a day-to-day basis in the Republic of

Ireland. America sounded lovely, but moving there was beyond her wildest dreams. Besides, it was too expensive and too foreign. This awful bloodstained place was what she knew. Tears ran down her face. Tears for Erin. Tears for herself. Tears for the sweet people at Murphy's Fish Shop who were badly injured and possibly dead—innocent lives just hoping for some fish-and-chips today. It could've been her daughter and herself in that store. *Thank you, God, for keepin' us away and protectin' us one more time, so ya have. But, if I might ask, can we just get away from here completely?*

After Maisie put Erin to bed the following night, she sat on the edge of the sofa with a cup of tea and turned on the telly to watch the news. They were calling the explosion at the fish shop the Shankill Road bombing. The Provos had aimed to assassinate the leader of the Ulster Defense Association, a loyalist paramilitary group, who was supposed to be attending a meeting above Murphy's Fish Shop.

The day of the bombing, at 1 p.m., two nineteen-year-old Provos, disguised as deliverymen, entered the shop with a bomb in a backpack. To their unfortunate demise, it detonated early. One of the young men died instantly and the other was hospitalized. Ten people died in that explosion, including Mr. Murphy, his daughter, one UDA member, and two children. Fifty-seven were wounded. The bomb was personal to those who lived on the Shankill and was a direct attack on the community. The UDA leader wasn't even in the shop! Hatred for the Provos grew.

"Two young boys like Michael, fightin' fer what, Lord? Sure and they killed innocent civilians that they didn't even know," Maisie said aloud. There were no adults here for her to talk to so it was often that she directed her words to God. "They've no respect fer the law. But can they help it when the British soldiers pin them up against a wall and kick their legs apart? The Brits have no clue what they've started." Maisie sunk back, pulled out her Bible and let it fall open to the Psalms. But she was too upset to read.

A part of the UVF that Brodie belonged to met in an abandoned cottage just past the Glencairn Estates. There were twenty-one of them, waiting in anticipation for their leader, Joseph Campbell, to arrive. Joe was in his early forties and had scars that he wore as trophies of his battles against the Provisional IRA.

"Dis one was when we was cornered by t'e Provos on one side and t'e police on t'e uhter." He pointed to a long scar on his arm. "Dis was from a plastic bullet dat took a piece of me flesh and nearly kilt me!" He pointed to the side of his neck. And on and on he'd go to impress the newer members of the gang.

These young Protestant/Loyalist men had nothing better to do than get into fights with the enemy. And the mentality amongst them wasn't unique to their side. Catholics/Republicans were just the same. There was nothing at the time, nothing in the whole of Northern Irish culture that taught a creative way to work out a problem between them. In their minds someone won and someone lost. End of story. Most of the young men were "school leavers"—drop outs—and were living on the dole—English unemployment rolls—traditionally called the bru in Northern Ireland.

The men sat on crates and broken-down furniture with plastic cups of cheap whiskey or soda, while some puffed away at cigarettes. Brodie MacCauley sat by a window to avoid inhaling the smoke but it was always futile. He straightened the old scally cap on his head, munched on his bag of crisps, and took a swig of Fanta. Unlike so many others here, Brodie didn't drink and worked for a living at the docks. It had been years since his parents had any influence on him, but there were some morals that remained, including to be a hard worker, avoid spending good money on the drink and not to take charity from the government. Would they be happy he had joined up with a paramilitary group? He couldn't answer that question, but he felt that someone had to take up the cause and get justice for what the enemy did to his parents.

When he and Callum fled from the scene of his parents' murder, they lived in barns and abandoned houses until Joe found them and took them under his wing. When they were old enough, he pushed them to join his paramilitary group. Callum refused. He was caught up in the Mod scene—a culture that originated in London and focused on fashion, music and motor scooters— and was in love with a girl named Molly. But Brodie had nothing else to live for and he burned inside with hatred for those who killed his parents and split up his family. When he met William and Paul, two brothers who had joined before him, he felt like he'd found a new home.

"Hey, William, are ye gettin' enough on t'e bru fer yer new wee bairn?" a red-headed lad asked.

"We got our stipend yesterday," William said.

"An' it's enough, is it?" Redhead asked.

"We get by with housin', furniture, health care—it's all covered."

The younger lads listened with interest.

"Brodie, lad, ya oughta quit workin' fer Harland and Wolff and get government help," William said.

"Why should I when I can work at the shipyard with me own two hands?"

"Eejit," Paul scoffed.

"Rumors are sayin' t'e shipyard is closin' soon." A thirty-something lad with a cigarette hanging from his mouth joined the conversation.

"Well, lads—" Brodie took a casual sip of his Fanta. "I'll work there till it closes, so I will." The others shook their heads.

"Yer as mad as a box o' frogs," Cigarette lad said.

"Ach, that's what me sister always says." Brodie took off his cap, pushed his curls back, and put his cap back on. What he didn't say was that Maisie's insult was directed toward him being here with these paras, hungry for revenge.

Joseph pushed the door open and walked in as if he owned the place—he most likely did—and the men and boys grew quiet.

"Did ya all hear of t'e bombin' on da Shankill t'e uhder day?" Everyone nodded. "It was an attack by t'e Provos against t'e UDA." Joe lit up a cigarette and took in a long pull. "Dem UDA laloos are off der heads, but it doesn't mean we're lettin' it go!" The group yelled and cheered. "T'ere's a shipment of weapons comin' for t'e Provisional IRA via t'e Crumlin road. We can't let it get ta 'em first."

"The Crumlin road?" Brodie sat up. "That's a very hostile area of West Belfast, Joe, so it is."

"Ya didn' have ta tell me dat. T'ey'll certainly be opposition from t'e uhder side."

"An' the UDA'll be dere, ya know?" Paul said, looking warily at his brother and Brodie.

"Ta be sure, they'll be dere and I'll need all of ya out dere fightin'."

Brodie's heart sank. There hadn't been a fight in a while and he'd hoped to avoid any more of it. He had to keep in front of him the reason he'd joined in the first place—to avenge his parents and the ruination of his family's humble and quiet life. He originally felt that his da would be proud of him— fighting for justice—but seeing so many useless killings made him think otherwise.

The arrangements and the strategy were confirmed.

"All right, time ta go spit on yer own grates, men."

Some grumbled, not anxious at all to head back to the reality of their homes full of hungry, poorly clothed children and nagging wives. But Brodie was happy to leave this place that was becoming more and more dangerous and unpredictable.

Everyone pushed up from their seats and meandered out the door a few at a time so as not to look obvious to the neighbors. They left the place trashed with empty bottles of Coke and beer, food wrappers and cigarette butts.

Callum MacCauley stood in the middle of the sitting room with his hands on his hips. He'd just come home from a tough day of work at the docks and as he entered the door of his home he learned from his wife, Molly, that his eight-year-old son got in a fight with some Catholic boys. He wasn't pleased with Tommy, who sat very still on the sofa with his head tipped up while Molly wiped his bloody nose with a cold cloth. Shannon, ten, looked on.

"Youse stupid wee eejit!" Callum said.

"Callum! Yer words!" Molly said.

"Youse should be locked up fer the week, so ya should!"

Callum looked at his wife, who was shaking her head in disapproval. He drew in a long breath. How could this be happening all over again? Another generation of Protestant and Catholic children fighting, imitating the adults in this useless conflict!

Tommy looked over at his father. "Da—"

"Tommy, keep yer head up like I said," Molly instructed.

Tommy followed his mother's instructions and turned his head back. "I had ta, Da. The Catholic boys was pickin' on Will—"

"Ah, poor wee Willy!" Shannon stepped forward. "Da, he's so puny—sure an' it's not fair!"

"Shannon, stay out of this, please," Callum said in a low, firm voice. Shannon knew that particular tone of her father's was not one to argue with. She stepped back and leaned against the wall.

"Were ya stickin' ta the routes we designated ta be safe?"

"Aye, Da, no lies, we was. They was hidin' out. They musta seen us go that route the other day. Willy was ahead o' me and they grabbed him. There was no way I could walk off and leave 'im ta suffer."

"Ya couldn't get help, could ya then?"

"They was punchin' him from both sides. I had ta save him right then and there."

Callum looked at his wife. Molly had the softest expressions ever a woman could give to make a man melt. It didn't help that her short dark hair fell in soft wisps about her gentle face as she cared for their son. She looked up at Callum with a plea for mercy for her brave little boy who tried to rescue one weaker than himself and suffered a bloody nose for it.

"All right, well, go on and mind yerself, lad. And mind that ya never see the likes o' those lads again."

Tommy sighed with relief. "I'll do just that. I promise."

Shannon smiled at her father.

"Go on yerself, lassie." Callum winked. Shannon gave him a quick hug and went off to her room.

Molly put on the tea and sat with Callum at the small table in their snug kitchen at the Glencairn Estates, a newer housing development built exclusively for Protestants. The homes, called Maisonettes, were connected side by side with individual front doors and it cut into the hillside with a great view of Belfast, overlooking Forthriver Road—the main thoroughfare in and out of Glencairn.

"He was bein' noble, that he was," Molly said, as she poured a cup of tea for Callum and a cup for herself.

"He was this time but I can't help thinkin' he aggravates these encounters."

"Callum, sure and ya don' remember when we were in school how many different paths we took ta avoid the Catholic kids? An' didn't ya do some aggravatin' yerself against the other side?"

"Nay. All I remember is watchin' ya at yer desk. Ya were pure beauty ta this poor orphaned boy, sittin' there so bonny, workin' so seriously on yer books."

Molly smiled. "I couldn't believe that Callum MacCauley—the tall, quiet lad in the back row, so mod with his long-sleeved polo shirts, trousers, loafers, and perfectly straight sideburns— had his eye on me. I'll ne'er ferget the other lassies bein' a wee jealous. But when ya started askin' me out, me da wasn't so happy. Especially when I got me hair cut short and wore short skirts ta complement me boyfriend's style!" Molly laughed.

"I liked the look on ya. Ya had a bright orange dress that I always liked. It showed off yer—"

"Callum! Mind yer words!" Molly blushed as she looked toward the stairs leading to the second floor.

"Wha'? The children are in their room."

"Well, havin' the babes ended that style fer me, so it did."

"Yer still me bonny lass. An' ya still don' need makeup."

"I'll ne'er ferget the day when Da learnt ya were livin' with the notorious Joe Campbell."

Callum laughed. "It were yer da that helped me break away from livin' there and kept me from joinin' up with Joe's gang."

"Sure and ya had no choice if ya wanted me ta yerself." Molly laughed and Callum put his hand over hers.

"Ya saved me, sweet Molly. I only wish me broder had someone ta do the same fer himself."

"We can keep prayin' God will take Brodie away from the violence," Molly said.

"How can God do that?"

"Nothin' is impossible with God, is it, me dear?"

"Sure an' yer always right, lass."

"Ya still doubt it at times, though, don' ya?"

"I have minutes of doubt."

"Because of yer folks?"

"Aye. It's a wee bit hard ta understand why God let it all happen? Why did me parents and me uncle's family all have ta die? Why did Auntie Anna disappear? Why did we all get split up? And why can't we escape the fightin' still?"

"Da says God is all sovereign and He has it all in control—He has a plan."

"I wish I had yer faith and yer da's faith, Molly. I want ta believe it, surely I do."

CHAPTER 2

1994. Watertown, Wisconsin.

Annie, five, and Fiahd, three, skipped down the aisle of the Baptist church keeping perfect time with the organist's rendition of Purcell's "Trumpet Tune." The skirts of their pink chiffon dresses bounced about their knees while flower petals were released in tiny handfuls at random intervals, floating around them like fairy dust. To everyone's amusement, Bobby MacCauley, a miniature but chubby version of his daddy, Gareth, dressed in a little black tux with dark curls framing his round face, toddled behind his sisters, his stubby legs no match for their spindly long limbs. The children finally made their way up to the front to join the bridal party consisting of Ian MacCauley's sons, Eoin and Gareth, and their wives, Tonya and Haley.

And then the more serious part of Phyllis and Ian's June wedding commenced as Phyllis walked down the aisle on the arm of her old neighbor friend, Fred Wagner. Phyllis's hair was in an innocent updo and after Alma Wagner's pleas, she had allowed a bit of makeup on her face. The effect was stunning and Ian's heart leapt as his new bride came down the aisle. Phyllis could barely keep her composure, but found that when she locked eyes with Ian, all was right in the world.

Many knew the story of the groom—that Ian lost his family more than two decades ago while cooped up unjustly in a prison cell, Long Kesh, in

Northern Ireland. It was a blessing to eventually be reunited with his two sons: Gareth, who had been sent off to America at twelve years old, and Eoin, who had disappeared at fourteen along with Ian's wife, Anna. Unbeknownst to Ian and Gareth, Eoin's missing years had been spent in Scotland. When Eoin resurfaced in 1987, he revealed the sad news of Anna's death, and after her body had been discovered on Waterfoot Beach, in County Antrim, Northern Ireland, the church in Watertown gave her an honorable funeral.

Of course, people in Watertown knew Phyllis's husband, Robert Beckett, a longtime member of the Wisconsin Dairyman's Association and a third-generation farmstead owner in southern Wisconsin. Many had bargained and dickered with him at the farmer's market, or discussed farm business in the old feed store on Water Street. These people, along with the members of his church, shared in the grieving process with Phyllis when he passed away.

During the bleakness of this past winter, many homes were warmed with the happy announcement of an engagement between Robert's widow and this new Irishman who built and sold wonderful unique furniture in a shop downtown. For months, the ceremony was carefully planned and talked about.

Pastor Keith Wagner stood on the platform with several more pounds added to his stature—a result of sitting at a desk every day, but with the same farmer's appetite to which he was accustomed. Consequently, today he performed the ceremony in a newer, better-fitting suit. Retired Pastor Sutton stood by his side. It was a short but beautiful ceremony, and there weren't many dry eyes in the end. The day provided a moment to relish God's blessings upon the handsome, middle-aged couple, strong and ready to face a new era. It was a story of hope and encouragement that there was still life after great loss and getting older!

Tonya and Eoin couldn't sit down fast enough with their servings of white wedding cake and creamy white frosting. Haley and Gareth followed and sat across from them. Eoin's fork was in the cake before anyone else's.

"You girls both look so beautiful today," Gareth said as he admired his wife's sleek dark hair pulled up at the sides with bejeweled barrettes. "Don't you think so, broder?" Eoin didn't answer. He was too focused on the dessert before him. Tonya nudged him.

"Ya don' have ta ask *me* if I wanted ta stare at me own wife through the entirety of the weddin'!" Eoin stuffed another big bite of cake into his mouth and the girls laughed.

"Mrs. Wagner tried to curl my hair but it just kept going straight. Sometimes I envy you, Tonya. Your curls are performing gorgeously today!"

"You know I have always envied your straight hair, and now I love your shorter cut. I could never do that! I would look like Bozo the Clown." Tonya laughed.

"But you can do the curly style around your face that most women have to perm their hair for."

"Yeah, I tried it but I think it makes me look like an old lady. I have such a baby face. I like it longer anyway. It's easier to manage and I can tie it up when I want!"

"I like how you pull it up with combs on both sides," Haley said. "And you guys cleaned up well. Such handsome MacCauley men!" She turned to Gareth. "I love to see you in a suit and tie."

"Right? Aren't they handsome brothers? Such nice haircuts." Tonya reached over and combed her fingers through Eoin's hair—cut above his collar but long on top. He smiled and leaned over to kiss her cheek.

"After today that dress isn't going to disappear in our closet, is it, Haley girl?" Gareth said, wistfully.

"Not if you take me out somewhere special on our anniversary!" Haley winked and Gareth nodded.

"Your mom looks so radiant—so beautiful, Haley," Tonya said.

"I agree." Gareth nodded. "And what about Da?"

"He's such a stunning, handsome man, just like his sons," Haley said.

"I haven't seen Da so happy in donkey's years," Eoin commented with a mouth full of moist cake and rich frosting.

"What did he say?" Haley asked.

The others laughed.

"It's so amazing that my momma's your mom-in-law now!" Haley smiled at her friend.

Tonya put her hand to her heart. "I love that."

"It's strange—they act just like a young couple!" Haley said.

"True love! It makes one young and alive again!"

"Tonya, where did you get that from? A movie?"

"Well, Gareth, maybe I did."

"Won't it be strange to have Da moving back into the big house with you all?"

Eoin pushed his plate away. "Aye, broder, and a married man at that!"

"Ach, I can't even think about what that means," Gareth said.

"Don't then." Eoin smirked and turned to Tonya. "Are ya going ta finish yer cake?"

"No," She pushed her plate toward him. "I don't dare eat anymore if I want to wear this dress ever again. It's not fair you can eat so much and stay in such good shape."

"Are you still considering moving back to Northern Ireland, Eoin?"

"*Every day,* Haley."

"Eoin would pick us up and move us tomorrow if he could."

"What about you, Tonya?"

"I'm ready when he says it's time."

Eoin tapped his fork on his plate. "She's a right blessin' from the Lord, this one."

"We've both been blessed, broder." Gareth wrapped his arm around Haley and rested his hand on her shoulder. Just then, Annie and Benny Wagner dragged Bobby, unhappy and struggling, over to the table where the adults sat.

"What have we here?" Eoin said.

"He stinks, Uncle Wen," Annie said.

"I think he's poopy," Benny added.

"No, I not."

"Oh, that's yer ma and da's job." Eoin grimaced at the pungent smell.

"Annie wants you to take care of it, *Uncle Wen*," Haley laughed.

"*And* he spilled punch *all over* his clothes," Annie said to Eoin.

"No. No, I not."

"How'd he get the punch?" Gareth said, unhappy to see a big splotch of red on his brand-new clothes.

"Fiahd and Angie Brannen gave him some," Annie tattled diligently.

"No—they not."

Haley made a face. "Never a dull moment." Tonya and Eoin chuckled.

"Just you wait. You'll have this kind of fun soon," Gareth teased. "You got it, girl?"

"Yeah, I'll be back." Haley sighed. "C'mon, Bobby, let Momma clean you up. Thanks, kids, and tell Fiahd that Momma said to stay away from the punch table!"

When Bobby was cleaned and released to chase after the other kids, Haley returned. Carrie Wagner and Penny Brannen followed her and sat with the MacCauley clan.

"Where are your hubbies?" Tonya asked.

"Keith is showing Scott the church's new computer," Carrie answered in dismay.

"Those guys," Gareth said, "they should be out here enjoying the reception!"

"That's what I said!" Carrie whined.

"They've become computer nerds," Penny joked.

"I suppose it's necessary for their jobs, managing a grocery store and pastoring a church—either one calls for it," Gareth said.

"We've had ta learn how ta use it fer our boardin' business," Eoin said. "If it wasn't fer Tonnie, I'd be lost!"

"I just get weary of Keith always in front of a screen." Carrie frowned. "He keeps his schedule on a day planner and is always looking at it."

"I'm just as bad as Scott at times." Penny chuckled.

"I don't think you were ever as bad as Scott," Gareth joked.

"Gareth." Carrie shook her head.

"What? She knows I'm kidding."

Penny nodded. "If Gareth hadn't been there to talk to Scott about the Lord, I don't know where we'd both be."

"God has been gracious. And we're all still praying for his brother, Steve."

"Thanks. God's grace and mercy has been given to us—much more than we deserve," Penny said, somberly. "And you're right about the computer, Gareth. It's so helpful for keeping a business. We can be much more organized at Piggly Wiggly now."

"Do you and Scott see much of each other while trading off hours managing the store and managing home?" Tonya asked.

"Nope. It will help when Jonathan and Angie are both in school full time."

"I can't imagine," Haley said. "You've got so much on your plate—"

"Says the girl who wants at least three more babies!" Penny chuckled and the others laughed.

"I can handle babies. But managing babies *and* a job managing people? You're tougher than I am, Penny. Carrie, are you guys adjusted to the full-time pastorate yet?"

"Not quite. Going from associate pastor to full-time was like a big flip-flop in our lives. We lost our weekends. Keith is free on Mondays now, but then, Benny is in school. I think Keith will have to adjust his week if we're going to get in any quality family time."

"And with all that, you went and started a ministry for women in town who miscarried or lost their babies at birth."

"How's that going?" Tonya asked.

"We have nine in the group so far."

"Man, Carrie, you're too busy," Penny said.

"We meet once a month. It's been cathartic for me. I share my story and then let the others talk. Then, I share the comfort of Scriptures with them. I don't preach or anything, but I want them to know how God, in His love and His sovereignty, has carried me through all the heartache and questions of losing a baby."

"It's amazing to see how you and Keith have handled the loss of your first child," Gareth said. "You guys were meant to be where you are now,

Carrie. People love you here. Keith handled the wedding ceremony well and it was nice Pastor Sutton was invited back to be a part of the ceremony."

Everyone agreed.

Fred and Alma Wagner approached the group. Alma was grinning from ear to ear.

"Ed is coming back stateside," Fred said.

"When did you find this out?" Haley asked.

"Mah boy just called us." Alma smiled.

"Wait. He called you here? How'd he do that?" Haley asked. "Did he call you on the church phone?"

"He doesn't need to. They have one of those cellular phones," Carrie explained while Fred held the small black gadget out for everyone to see the number pad.

"Oh, wow. That's so weird," Haley said.

"We keep it on us at all times."

"That's so cool. Can I see it? My dad has one," Tonya said.

"And *she* wants ta get one." Eoin frowned as he watched Tonya examine the Wagners' phone.

"Now we can always be in touch with Ed and won't miss his calls," Alma explained.

"I love these!" Tonya handed the phone back to Alma. "So, when is he coming back?"

"Sometime in July," Fred said.

"And he's bringing a fine girl with him," Alma added.

"Who? That army nurse he met?" Carrie smiled.

"Yes! Her name is Cassandra." Alma saw a couple headed toward the exit. "Oh, Fred, we need to go talk to the Masons befoh they leave! Please excuse us!" She grabbed her husband's arm and they disappeared into the crowd.

"It will be interesting to see Ed's girlfriend!" Haley said. "Tell me how they met again? I know Mrs. Wagner told us once."

"She came to Ed because he's the army chaplain," Carrie explained. "She was having a tough time of it, caring for the wounded soldiers."

"That was convenient." Eoin smirked.

"Oh, Prince Edward, me dashin' soldier, I'm feelin' a wee bit faint and need someone ta hold me close!" Gareth joked, and Eoin guffawed.

"Be nice, guys," Haley reprimanded.

"Well, very soon we'll all get to see this new woman who has entered Eddy's life," Tonya said.

"And Eddy, too!" Haley added.

"Are ya goin' ta finish yer cake, Carrie?"

"Eoin!" Tonya nudged her husband.

CHAPTER 3

The night was late. If it wasn't for WVCY, the "Voice of Christian Radio," blaring loudly in the rental car, Ed would have had to pull over and sleep on the shoulder of I-94. The red-eye from Amsterdam to General Mitchell International Airport in Milwaukee was beginning to affect him.

If Cassandra had come along with him, she would've kept him alert with her endless chatter. Boy, could she carry on a good story! How did her brain retain so many details and the rabbit trails off the details, anyway? Sometimes it overwhelmed him, but he sure missed it now. His heart lurched. He may as well get used to missing her. He shook his head. He hadn't seen it coming. Right before they were supposed to travel home together, she decided to go to her own home in the West, indicating the relationship was finished. How did he miss the cues? What was wrong with him? This wasn't the first time he missed the signs from a girl that it was over!

There was Haley. Wow. That relationship was a major fail on his part. He should've seen it coming and should've seen her falling for Gareth a long time ago. Well, maybe he did see it, but wasn't willing to admit it. He should've moved on, but instead, he kept fueling the fire of love for her way too long. And even when Gareth left her behind for three years to find his folks in Northern Ireland, Ed hoped for a chance with her. He should've known better.

By the time he joined the army and became chaplain, he was at peace with being single. And then he was stationed out in the Persian Gulf while Saddam Hussein terrorized Kuwait. During his time there, Cassandra kept coming to him for counsel and comfort for all the horrors of war she witnessed in the infirmary. He enjoyed feeling like the rescuer and started to fall for her. She was a cute, petite girl who kept her blond hairstyle minimal but her makeup at the max—when it was allowed around the base, anyway. She reminded him of his mother and he took that as a sign. He thought she was falling for him by the way she clung to him and acted like she wanted to be with him. But did she like to be with him for who he was? Or was it just because he brought her a sense of security and companionship in a troubled place? Was she just using him to help her get through her own trauma of dealing with soldiers day in and day out?

Once again, he read a girl wrong and got hurt. It was time to get his eyes off of women. He didn't understand them and maybe he wasn't cut out to be with one. Maybe this was God's way of telling him to stay single.

Soon, he was at the Highway 26 exit, headed toward Watertown. He perked up. It was already feeling like home and it would be good to be in the comfort of his family. He wasn't sure what he'd do after this. He'd served his time in the military. Maybe he'd travel. Maybe he'd see the world. He was a free man, after all. No wife and kids to come home to. This could turn out to be a good thing, being single, he told himself. He had some money saved and his dad promised a job at the dairy farm so he could save up a bit more. He needed time to think about his future.

Gareth brought out two cups of coffee on the front porch of the small house built for Haley and himself on the back property of Beckett's farmstead. He handed one to Ed, who sat contentedly staring out at the stream with one hand on Rusty, an offspring of Lucy and Ricky's first litter. The sun was setting, leaving a red wash of clouds in the sky and a colorful reflection on the water. A nice breeze brushed across the porch intermittently.

"It's a beautiful night," Ed said. He sighed and took in a long breath of summer air. "I didn't know how much I'd miss home. Just being back to Wisconsin—going barefoot in the summer, eating watermelon and seeing who can spit their seeds the farthest—"

"You were the best—"

"I think you beat me a few times! Spitting seeds the farthest was truly something to brag about in our younger years!" They both laughed. "Haley's mom grew the best corn on the cob—and those large sweet tomatoes from her garden? Ah! I missed even the littlest things while in the Middle East."

"I know what it's like to miss foods from your homeland."

"I'm sure you do."

"But now you're making me hungry. My da and Momma—Haley's mom—already have a great garden going. I can't wait to bite into those tomatoes!"

"Is that odd to call Mrs. Mac, Momma?"

"Aye, but she insisted. She may be small, but when she says 'spit,' *I spit*."

Ed stopped petting Rusty and laughed. The dog pushed his nose at Ed's hand and Ed stroked his fur. "Rusty is one of the most beautiful golden retrievers I've ever seen."

"That he is. His coat was darker than the others in the litter and he's very laid back. Haley and I were glad he didn't get sold and now he's taken up residence at our place." Gareth patted the dog's head and leaned over so he could go nose to nose with him. "Haven't ya, boy? Yes, you have. Ya like it here with us, yes, you do." He looked up at Ed and smiled. "It's good to have you back, old friend."

"It's good to be back. I love your home, Gareth. You and Haley have made it nice and cozy."

"It's made better by the friends and family who visit."

"I've missed all that—the little community we have here out on County Road QQ."

"We've missed you out here on this little road out in the middle of farmers, cows and cornfields, ya know."

"Yeah, that's what everyone keeps telling me."

"You're like a broder to me and Haley."

"That goes both ways. Well, Haley is actually more like a *sister*." They both laughed. Then, as if on cue, they lifted their coffee cups simultaneously and took a sip, each taking a minute to enjoy the view of the creek, the trees, the cornfield, and the sunset beyond.

"How's the boarding business doing?"

"Good." Gareth nodded. "Yeah, good, but busy. I'm concerned about its future."

"Why?"

"Eoin keeps talking of returning to Northern Ireland, and Da isn't getting any younger."

"He's not yet sixty is he?"

"No, I guess he's not *that old* yet. But I think he'd rather be focusing on his woodworking craft."

"Well, I'll take any extra work I can get right now." Ed put his cup down. "Turns out my father is thinking of selling the dairy business so I won't be working there much longer."

"No lie?"

"No lie. My folks are older than your da, ya know."

"What about mission work, Ed? You used to talk about that."

"Well, for now, my plans have changed. Peggy has gone into mission work and travels around a lot. Keith is busy with the pastorate. I want to be there for my folks as they're growing older."

Gareth let out a sigh of relief. "Well, this might be the answer to my prayers. By the time your dad sells, Eoin might be gone and I'll need your help."

Haley stepped out onto the porch with a cup of tea. "Wow, it's nice out here."

"Hi, Haley." Ed nodded.

"It's so good to have you back, Eddy."

"Are they all down for the night, honey?"

"Bobby was a bit restless and kept *conveniently* sliding off his new bed." Haley looked at Ed and explained, "He's not in a crib anymore. It's always a trick to keep them in bed with no railings at this age!" She put her tea on a little wrought iron table and Rusty came over to check it out. "No, Rusty, this isn't for you, silly dog." She ran her hand over his soft head as she sat down. Rusty sat beside her and leaned against her legs.

"Sorry, I should've helped," Gareth said.

"No. I said I'd be fine and I wanted you to get Ed all to yourself for a few minutes. I know how much you've missed him."

"Supper was delicious, Haley. You've definitely taken after your momma."

"Thanks, yeah, I had a great coach in the kitchen. And I'm learning a lot from my new 'da,' too." Haley smiled at Gareth as she took a sip of her tea.

"That smells of spice," Ed said. "What is it?"

"Ginger."

"Wait. Are you nauseated?"

Haley looked up quickly. "What are you? A midwife?"

Ed grinned. "Baby number four?"

Haley shook her head. "I can't get anything past you."

"I am a farmer's son," Ed said.

"Just don't tell anyone she's expecting," Gareth said. "We're waiting till she's in her third month to tell people."

"Mum's the word. Now I see why you need the business to stay intact and flourish. Your family keeps growing!"

"That it does." Gareth reached over and took Haley's hand. Years ago that simple gesture of affection would have been awkward in front of Ed and his feelings would've been hurt. But the years had healed all that and it felt good to be so relaxed in each other's company again, just like old times.

"So, Eddy, tell me about Cassandra."

Ed pursed his lips. "Well, it started out as counseling sessions." He sighed. "She started to show up at my door often—really struggling with the trauma, the physical injuries, the mental and emotional anguish she witnessed helping the soldiers."

"I can't imagine," Haley said. "I could never be an army nurse—or any kind of nurse, for that matter."

"We enjoyed our talks together and she really leaned on me for support. I thought there was more to it. I mean, we ate our meals together, took walks together when it was safe, sat by each other on movie nights— and one night, why, she was pretty distraught and threw herself into my arms. That's when I thought that maybe she was the one, you know?"

"But she wasn't?"

"No."

"What happened?"

"When I was leaving to return to the States, I asked her to come with me. That's when she got all weird and basically confessed it was over between us."

"So, she was just using you?"

"I guess you could say that."

"I'm so sorry, Eddy."

"Yeah, man, me too," Gareth said. "That's not cool."

"I'm okay now, really. I'm just learning more about myself and how I'm not good at all at reading women."

"Oh, Eddy—"

"No, it's true, Hale. And it's fine."

"I'm sorry."

"Don't be. I'm good. Onward and forward."

"So what days can you help with the horses?"

Haley looked at her husband aghast. "Really, honey, just like that you're talking about the horses?"

"What? I thought we were done with the other subject. Were you done, Ed?"

"I'm done," Ed said.

"*Men.*" Haley let out a long sigh.

"Let me talk to my dad and I'll get back to you on that." Ed slapped both knees as he stood. "Welp! It's getting late for us farmers! I better get back home before Momma calls me on this cell phone. I'm not sure I like these things. I'm too accessible to my mother." He chuckled and looked over at Gareth. "Oh, man, I'm sorry, I shouldn't complain. I wasn't thinking—"

"No need to apologize. Just because we finally found my ma's body—"

"It's only been about four years, hasn't it? Near Annie's first birthday?"

"Yes. Still, I don't want you to think you can't talk about your own ma around me, ya know?"

CHAPTER 4

Phyllis, Ian, Tonya, and Eoin sat in front of the TV in the living room of the "big house," formally known as the Beckett home. The evening news announced that the IRA had called for a ceasefire in Northern Ireland. Ian looked at Eoin.

"I don' believe it, do ye?"

"There's a chance of it, Da."

"Ach, yer just antsy ta get back there, aren't ya, lad?"

"Ya know it."

Tonya slipped her hand into her husband's strong one and felt him grip hers.

"*Yer off yer heid*, as the Scohts folk would say!"

"Da, let's not get inta it again. We're not leavin' yet. We'll wait and see how it goes."

But Tonya knew better. A few years ago Eoin had talked to many people over in Northern Ireland who had lost loved ones, now aptly called the "Disappeared." He felt a strong connection to them, to his homeland, and was anxious to help them get some closure. Ever since then, Eoin talked about returning and staying there. And she knew that when he was ready to go, she'd be right there with him.

That night as they prepared for bed, the subject came up again.

"So, what are you really thinking of doing, Eoin? How long are we really going to wait to move?"

"I dinnae ken. I'm goin' ta watch the news and see what develops. Hope is in me."

"Same here."

"Truly?"

"Yes."

Eoin took his wife in his arms. "I love ya, lass. I dinna deserve ya, neither."

Tonya snuggled into his chest. "I love you, too. And I'm ready to go back when you say it's time."

By September, 1994, the news reporters came across the TV screens announcing that the border crossings between Northern Ireland and the Republic of Ireland— heavily guarded since the beginning of the Troubles— had reopened. As the news crossed the ocean and landed on Eoin's ears, he felt hopeful. The reporters continued to add that the patrolling and security measures were in the process of being lifted. The RUC were patrolling Belfast without wearing their flak jackets and the British soldiers were going home. Tonya watched her husband's spirits lift as news reports like these continued through autumn, past the holidays, and into the New Year.

When daytime army patrols ended in Belfast in January of 1995, Eoin decided it was time for Tonya and him to return and live in Ian's rental home south of Laurelvale, County Armagh. They would visit the families of the Disappeared, and Eoin would get a job working with horses. Eventually, he would rebuild his old home near Lurgan, also in County Armagh.

"But ya can't leave yet," Ian said. "Yer broder's about to have another wee bairn. Ya ought ta stay fer that, don' ya think?"

"Da, don't put that pressure on Eoin and Tonya. If they're ready to go back that's their business," Gareth said. Haley looked at Tonya and pushed out her lower lip in a pout.

"Eoin, let's just wait a month," Tonya said, winking at Haley. "It'll take us a while to get things packed up and make flight plans anyway."

Eoin reluctantly agreed. They waited for Haley to give birth to Gareth's and her fourth child and by February, a wee little lad was born into the MacCauley household. They named him William but would call him Liam.

Ian felt a mix of joy and sorrow, gaining a fourth grandchild, yet saying goodbye to his eldest son and his daughter-in-law. The ocean's distance between them was painful and no one knew when they'd be reunited again.

***

The McGilroy clan, on the other hand, was excited beyond words to have Eoin and Tonya back in Northern Ireland.

Back in 1974, father and son Dave and Johnny McGilroy found Eoin lying unconscious on Waterfoot Beach in County Antrim after his mother, Anna, was killed and buried there by a suspected IRA group. Eoin, wounded from a shot behind his knee, was cared for by the McGilroy wives, Mary and Aggie, in Ballantrae, Scotland. After almost fourteen years, when Eoin set foot back in Northern Ireland, he was taken in by Dave McGilroy's older brother, George, former member of the Royal Highland Regiment Black Watch, and his dear wife, Margaret. They resided between Lurgan and Laurelvale in Portadown, County Armagh.

They met Tonya a few years later and it was George and Margaret who encouraged the young couple to come together in marriage after an up-and-down relationship.

Margaret helped Tonya unpack things and get settled into Ian's cottage that he found in Laurelvale after escaping from prison. Meanwhile, George and Eoin surveyed the property.

"What air ye doin', lassie?" Margaret asked, when she saw Tonya standing at the open window.

"Just taking in the scenery and breathing in the air."

"Aye, the damp earth—"

"So many shades of green as far as the eye can see! And what birds do I hear singing?"

"Weel," Margaret paused and listened for a while. "I believe ye hare the hoose spahrroos—"

"The what?"

"Hoose spahrroos."

Tonya thought for a minute. "Oh, you mean house sparrows!" Margaret looked at her funny.

"I mean—" Tonya realized she made it sound as if the American way to say the bird's name was the right way. Embarrassed, she backpedaled. "Yes, sorry, right, hoose spahrroos."

Margaret burst out laughing. "Ye aer fayne, lass. Eht's normal tae feel the need tae say eht ehn yer oon tongue. The ear needs tae haer eht right."

George crossed his arms and put his chin in one hand. "Et's goht'en a wee beht run doon, eh?"

"Aye, yer right. Looks like it could use a bit o' patchin' up and paintin'. I should get the roof repaired," Eoin said, discouraged.

"Ach, I ken that look, lad. An' I ken ya really want tae be fehxin' yer auld burnt-oot home whar ya grew up, tae."

"Aye, right again. So many things I *need* ta do. So many things I *want* ta do!"

"A lehttle at a tayme." George sat down on an old garden bench, breathing heavily. Eoin noticed the elderly man's weary, aging face.

"Ye look knackered."

"I'm fayne."

"Let's go back inside. I think Tonnie is puttin' on the tea by now." Eoin helped George get up and the two walked back into the house. "Did I hear Margaret say the McGilroys from Scohtland are comin' over in a few days?"

"Aye. We'll have a grand reunion, lad!"

"I can' wait."

"The downstairs sitting room and kitchen are still in pretty good shape, Eoin," Tonya said as she poured the men their cups of tea. "But the two bedrooms upstairs will need some repairs."

"It was remodeled by renters, but I'm not too fond of their work." Eoin sighed.

"All ehn good tayme, lad," Margaret said.

"I know." Eoin drew in a deep breath.

"Nae bother. Ye'll be gettin' plenty o' help," George said. "Yer part o' the McGilroy clan, the two o' ye."

Within a few months Eoin was able to secure a job at an Equestrian Centre and work with the horses. Margaret and George enjoyed going for long drives with Tonya, showing her the most scenic places for her to photograph. After sending her work to several places, she was able to secure a job as a photojournalist for a significant magazine company. People were interested in seeing the beauty of Northern Ireland and weary of hearing about all the depressing news in the media concerning the Troubles.

Tonya transformed the second bedroom in the cottage into a darkroom when needed. All it took was one heavy blanket over the small window and one to block the cracks in the door frame. She had to admit, the smaller windows and lack of light in this traditional Irish cottage made it a lot easier!

In the spring of '95, Eoin and Tonya took a drive to the old property that had belonged to Ian and Anna. As they stepped out of the car, Tonya stood still and closed her eyes.

"What are ya doin', lass?"

"Listening to the different birds and the sheep bleating way off in the distance. It's a foreign sound to me, not like the sounds at the farms in Wisconsin—you know, the mooing of the cattle and the chickens clucking," she said as the breeze blew her curls about her face and the tree branches moved in harmony.

Eoin smiled. "Well, while yer takin' it all in, me bonny wife, I'm goin' ta work." He chuckled as he walked around with a clipboard in his hand, taking notes about the crumbling stone walls, high weeds that wrapped themselves around and into the stonework, and unwanted trees that had taken root and grown into the foundation of the home. Tonya caught up to him and snapped pictures when Eoin pointed to a place that he'd want to look at later in a photo for reference.

"We'll have ta chop down the overgrowth first." Eoin paused, starting to feel overwhelmed. "Ach, there's so much ta do here." He smacked his head with the clipboard in frustration. "I'm already feelin' wired ta the moon!"

Tonya rushed over to him and wrapped her hand around his arm to prevent the clipboard from doing any damage. "Honey, stop it. Just one step at a time, one weed at a time, one bush, one tree—one thing at a time, and then, eventually, we'll go to work on the structure itself!"

Eoin let out a long sigh. "I need ya so much. Thank ya fer preventin' a concussion."

They both laughed. Eoin took her in his arms, fingered her dark curls, and moved them away from her face. When he leaned in and kissed her, Tonya pushed away, giggling.

"And just out of nowhere, in the middle of your frustration, you needed a—what do you Irishmen call it?"

"A snog."

"Yes, out of nowhere, you needed a snog. Did that help you feel better?"

"Much better." Eoin grinned, satisfied. "It always helps when I kiss ya, me bonny lass." He pulled her in again.

"Eoin MacCauley, you need to focus on this mess or we'll never get any work done today."

When the McGilroy clan pulled up in their cars, the reunion was akin to Christmas as Eoin and Tonya watched the familiar faces step out merrily and greet the young couple. The seniors of the group, Dave and Mary, came with their eldest son Johnny, his wife Aggie, and their two sons, Duncan and Graham. Dave and Mary's daughter Josephine and her husband, Neil, brought their three children: Elsbeth, Emmet, and Georgie.

The younger children were given the job of cleaning, digging through years of accumulation and sweeping the inside of the old frame. The men and older boys removed heavy pieces of timber and stone while the women cut away at the overgrown vines and bushes.

"Things are lookin' better already!" Eoin felt relieved after an hour of hard work passed.

"Aye, yer lookehn' braw!" Dave chuckled.

"Ye was lookehn' a bit peely-wally when we fehrst goht here," Mary said.

Tonya guffawed. "He's been so overwhelmed! Thank you so much for taking the load off of him."

"I foon' somethin'," Emmet yelled. "Come see!" The others gathered round. "Eht were buried under the floor an' when I heht the floor board wehth a shovel, eht cracked through."

"What ehs eht, laddie?" Johnny asked.

"Eht's a metal box!" Emmet held up the rusty container proudly.

"A treasure box!" Georgie jumped up and down.

"Gehv eht tae Eoin, son," Neil said. "Eht belongs tae hehm."

Emmet didn't mask his sad face when he handed the box to Eoin.

"Ach, we'll have nae broodiness, Emmet!" his father chided and then turned to Eoin. "Have ye seen eht before?"

"Nay, it's not familiar ta me." Just as Eoin took the box a spider crawled around it from the side. Eoin smashed it. Suddenly the group grew quiet and the children gasped.

"What's wrong?" Tonya asked.

"Eht's bad luck tae kehl a spider," Elsbeth whispered.

"Ach, I ferget meself in the presence of the Scohts," Eoin said and turned to Tonya while he tried to get the box open. "It's a superstition that it's bad luck ta kill a spider because a spider is what saved Scohtland. Robert the Bruce, a Scoht, tried ta drive the English out of Scohtland. Robert had been driven out of his country, hidin' out in some hut or cave, and he saw this spider tryin' ta build its web. It tried over and over and over until it finally succeeded. That spider's ambition gave Robert the Bruce the encouragement he needed ta go back ta Scohtland and drive out the English!"

"We Scohts have many superstehtions." Aggie smiled.

"Aye, we do," Elsbeth said.

"Eht's bad luck tae put new shoes on a table." Josephine smiled.

"And, a behrd in the chehmney ehs a sign of death," Elsbeth added.

"A 'bared'?" Tonya scrunched her nose. "What's that?"

"A bird." Eoin laughed.

"Och, don' believe eht. Eht's all a bit doolally!" Dave laughed.

"Doolally?" Tonya asked.

"Crazy!" Eoin smiled at his wife. He held the box up in frustration. "Like this box! It's locked. Ah, well, let's get back ta work!" Eoin took the box and threw it in the trunk of the car along with other remnants that had been found: tarnished jewelry, silverware, pans, and tools.

After working for hours, they sat on quilts around a large bonfire consisting of old pieces of wood and branches. They ate cottage pie while talking and figuring out when the men could return to help with the build.

"Sae, Tonnie." Josephine smiled as her children gathered around the two women. "We have questions fer ye. Dae ye mind?"

"No, of course not." Tonya wiped her mouth with her napkin and smiled at the eyes of the children, so full of wonder.

"Why dae Americans seem more confident, more outgoin', and as ehf they don' care what they wear sae much as we dae?"

Tonya smiled. "I didn't realize there was that distinction. Did you notice that when you came to America, Eoin?"

"Aye, I did. And Americans can get quite loud, ya know?" Eoin said, and the others laughed.

"I layke the pop music from the US," Duncan chimed in.

"Och, tae loud!" Johnny said.

"Nae, Daddy, ye just tearn eht doon!" Graham laughed. Johnny rolled his eyes and turned to Eoin.

Dusk was settling in and the women picked up the dishes, folded the quilts, and put the food away. While the men and boys gathered tools, Johnny said, "We'll be comehn' again tae help ye, laddie."

"I cannae expect ya ta come over here on the ferry and drive so far, men," Eoin said as he retrieved one of Johnny's shovels and handed it to him.

"Ye are part o' our fam'ly, Eoin, lad, and thehs bonny wife o' yers, tae. Ye have tae get thehs place rebuilt and start a life taegehther. We're that glad ye chose tae retairn tae thehs side o' the ocean!" Johnny patted him on the back

Aggie nodded when she heard her husband talking. "Sae glad we are, Tonnie and Eoin, tae have ye here."

And the others said, "Hear, hear."

CHAPTER 5

Ed and Gareth stepped out of the barn and felt the burning rays of the Midwestern summer sun.

"Whew. It's gonna be a hot one today."

"Ach, the humidity in the air—"

"Yep."

They heard giggling coming from behind the big house and walked over to see what was going on. Ian, Anna, and Fiahd were in the garden where Ian had been showing them how to weed between rows of tomatoes and cucumbers. The closer Gareth and Ed got, the better they could see the random flowers nestled in Ian's curls.

"Your dad is so good with your kids. I don't know if my dad would let little girls put flowers in his hair." Ed laughed as he wiped sweat from his brow.

"I don't know if I would either!" Gareth chuckled. "They've definitely distracted my da from mourning Eoin's move."

"I'm sure he misses him tremendously."

"And Tonya, too." Gareth combed his hand through his hair, wet from sweat, and pushed it away from his face. "He got pretty close to her before they left."

"That's special. Your dad has been through a lot and continues to adjust."

"We have to adjust to whatever comes our way or we'll never make it through."

"The older I get, the more I see what you've known your whole life."

"You're so old, Ed, me lad."

"Ha-ha."

"How old are we getting to be, anyway?"

"I keep losing track." Ed grinned. "But I believe we've hit thirty-three."

"No way."

"Yes way."

"Daddy!" Annie came running, her long golden hair shimmering in the sunlight, and took Gareth's hand, pulling him toward the garden. "Come and see what we did to Granddad!" Gareth swung her around behind his back and carried her to the edge of the garden.

"Doesn't he look all bonny and nice?" Gareth smiled. Ian stood up from pulling weeds and took a bow. "You must be special, Annie. Grandad never let Uncle Wen or me do anything like that!"

"Ach, neither one of ya was me bonny granddaughters!" Ian waggled his eyebrows, grabbed up Fiahd around the waist, and ran with her down the long rows of the garden and toward the others, her legs kicking behind him. She giggled heartily.

"The garden looks great, Mr. Mac."

"Thanks." Ian put Fiahd down gently and brushed the flowers from his dark hair just showing signs of grey. "Me lovely wife, Phyllis, deserves much of the credit. I'm just the maintenance man, though I sure do love it out here."

"Da and I have plans to plant an apple orchard this fall and potatoes in the spring," Gareth told Ed.

"Grand memories we had back in the day!" Ian said.

"That's a great idea," Ed said.

"Have you heard anything from Eoin, Da?"

"Last I heard, things were goin' well and the old place is comin' along. They're stayin' away from trouble, stayin' out o' Belfast and anywhere they might be at risk. But I'm still concerned. Somethin' can happen anywhere and County Armagh has its dangerous spots."

"There's truth in that," Gareth said.

Phyllis waved from the porch. "I just pulled out some fresh loaves of banana bread. Anyone ready for a mid-morning snack?" Gareth slid Annie off his back and the girls ran to their grandma with delight.

"Ach, she can bake even in this terrible heat, that woman of mine!" Ian said admiringly.

"She doesn't look tough, but she is!" Gareth grinned.

"Don't anyone cross her when she's set her mind ta somethin'!" Ian laughed.

"Is she really as stubborn, though, as Ma was, Da?"

"Aye, in her own ways." Ian nodded and then winked. "But I wouldn't change a thing!"

The men started toward the house.

"Has there been much happening in the way of violence in Northern Ireland?" Ed asked.

"Not heard o' much."

"There you go, Da. See, it's settling down like they said it would."

"Ach, away off and feel yer head!" Ian said. "It ain't that easy, lad. I just don' see why they had ta go back there."

"I kinda do," Gareth said. "Eoin is finding redemption and a reason for what he went through at the beach with Ma. I think he also bears part of the responsibility for you going off to prison unjustly, the house being burned down, and our separation as a family. Going back, helping others who have suffered the same and rebuilding our old home, is what he needs to do. I kind of envy him."

"Not youse, too!"

"No worries. I know this is where I need to be. But I do miss my homeland, ya know?'

"I miss it too. But Eoin needs ta be with family!" Ian said, his eyes watering slightly.

"You're a stubborn old man, Da." Gareth put his arm around his father. "Now, let's go in and get some of your dear wife's banana bread before my hungry daughters eat it all up!"

"Annie will make sure ta save us some, but Fiahd—well, she could eat a whole loaf. She must have extra storage in her belly!"

"They're both as skinny as their ma," Ed noted.

"And they can eat like their ma used to!" Gareth said.

"Ta be sure!" Ian laughed and Gareth was glad to see it.

It was a muggy evening. Phyllis and Ian sat on the front porch with root beer floats in their hands and the dogs at their feet. The western horizon was awash in shades of pink with yellow streaks shooting into the sky from the dying sun.

"This hits the spot, dear," Ian said as he took another sip of his float and gave a contented sigh. "It's such a close night." He turned to Phyllis with foam on his upper lip.

She laughed. "Do you boys ever grow up?"

"Nay, an' why should we?" He smiled.

Phyllis rolled her eyes and shook her head in mock disgust. "The humidity level doesn't seem to want to go down even though the sun is setting. Even the dogs are having a time of it with this terrible heat." Phyllis took another sip and relished the cold fizz and cream together. "I haven't made one of these floats in years, but it sounded so good to me all day today."

"Well, I'm that glad ya couldn't stop thinkin' on it!"

They rocked in the porch swing for a while, enjoying their cold treats and waiting for the sun to disappear, hoping the heat would go with it. Suddenly, Ian sighed.

"I miss him."

"I know."

"I just got him back."

"I'm sorry, Ian."

"I'm tryin' ta be brave. I'm tryin' ta be positive. I'm weary o' bein' positive. And there's the missin'."

"It's okay to feel that way and I love you for it. You wouldn't be normal if you didn't feel sad and miss your son."

"And my new daughter-in-law. That one—she's a corker."

"She's perfect for him. And he's so good for her. Funny how we all thought—and she thought—she'd be the single one of the bunch. She said she'd be happy just being a rich aunt to her friends' children." Phyllis smiled. "Tonya's always been a good friend to Haley."

"I'm thankful they're together."

"And that she's such a great photographer. We'll be blessed with many pictures of them and their future family."

"Aye—the future family."

"And, maybe, we could put some money in a stash to save up to go over there in the future—when things settle down in the country."

Ian sat up straight. "Ya would do that? Go with me?"

"Yes, I would."

"That puts hope in me, dear one! I love ya, sweet Phyllis." Ian put his tall mug down and took her hand in his. Ricky's head popped up at the sound of the abandoned dish. "Nay, me furry friend. There's aught fer ya," he joked.

"I love you, too, my beloved Ian. And I'm glad to see you smile again. I know you need to show sadness and that's good, but I do like it better when you're trying to make me laugh."

Ian pulled Phyllis closer and she rested her head on his shoulder. "Ya bring me such comfort, cailin."

"I was just thinking the same. You bring it to me, dear."

Ian kissed the top of her head and said, "I couldn't have borne so much without ya."

CHAPTER 6

Maisie and Erin walked from the bus stop to the Glencairn Estates up beyond the Shankill and north of Belfast to visit her brother Callum, and his family. The rain had fallen more frequently now that fall was here. Maisie was glad she'd thought to insist on wearing jackets. Molly greeted them at the door and invited them in, taking their wraps. When Shannon saw her little cousin, she scooped her up in her arms and whisked her away to her bedroom to play with her old dolls until it was time for dinner. Tommy took their dripping jackets and hung them on the hooks by the door.

"Come on in." Tommy waved Maisie into the sitting room. "How are ya, Auntie?"

"Grand, and ya?"

"Grand. Uncle Brodie is here, too," Tommy said.

"Fantastic. I haven't seen 'em in a while."

Brodie came into the sitting room and gave his little sister a big hug.

"Stayin' out o' trouble, are ya, broder?"

"Aye, just the usual tomfoolery." Brodie gave her a mischievous smile.

"I don' believe it! Have ya left the UVF yet?"

"Ya know I can't do that."

"I worry about ya."

"I know ya do. I'll be fine, sis."

"Not if ya go 'round wearin' that Union Jack T-shirt in Belfast, so ya won't."

Brodie pulled at the hem of his shirt, stretching it outward. He looked at the red-and-white crosses on the blue background of the British flag as if he'd never seen them before and then grinned mischievously. Maisie smacked his arm.

"So, how's Belfast anyway?"

"Don'ask!" Maisie said.

"Did ya hear the explosion? Were ya near when Murphy's was bombed?" Brodie let go of his tee and looked up.

"We were down the town, but not near enough ta be hurt."

"When ya goin' ta move out here where it's safer?"

"When ya goin' ta leave the paras?"

"Ah, ya've popped yer clogs!"

"And yer as mad as a box of frogs, so ya are!"

After dinner was over and dishes were cleared, the brothers went out to the sitting room. Callum waited for the kids to disappear before speaking. "I went by our old place, so I did."

"Callum, don't say too much until Maisie and I get out there," Molly yelled from the kitchen as she wiped her hands on her apron.

"Why, in the name of the patron saints did ya do such a thing?"

"Brodie, we're not Catholic," Maisie rebuked her brother as she and Molly sat down. "Why *did* ya go there, Callum?"

"Curiosity, maybe?"

"And?" Maisie asked.

"Nothin' ta speak of. But—"

"But, what?"

"Someone is buildin' on our Uncle Ian's property, so they are."

"Did ya stop and inquire?" Brodie asked.

"No."

"Why not?" Brodie said. "Ya shoulda."

"Maybe I will next time, ya know?"

"I haven't been out there since I ran from the place as a wee girl and I don' wanna go back."

"But what if they're kin?" Callum said.

"Ach, no! Our kin were all Disappeared."

"No, not all vanished, sister," Callum said. "Only Auntie Anna and cousin Eoin, so they were."

"Sure and our uncle wouldna come back ta visit the house and be reminded of such a horrid thing!" Maisie said.

"And what of Gareth? He ran with us lads ta escape those IRA men but after he went ta the RUC, he vanished," Callum said. "Rumors were he got shipped off ta America where Auntie Anna's family lived."

"Lucky fer him, ya know?" Maisie said.

"Ta go ta America?" Molly asked.

"Aye." Maisie didn't hesitate.

"Ya'd go there, would ya, Maisie?" Molly said.

"Straightaway. I hate it here. I hate Belfast and it hates me."

"So, move away." Brodie smirked.

"I'm not such a kite-headed-carried -away bein' as ya are, broder." Brodie guffawed.

"Ya have a tongue as sharp as a knife, lass!" Callum laughed.

"Where would I go? And with what money? I don' see any of me broders handin' me thousands of punts!"

"Ach, no! that won't ever happen." Callum slapped his knee. "We're barely making it by on what I can earn ta pay rent and feed the family. Harland and Wolff don't pay enough."

"I see yer fayne penny loafers are wearin' thin," Brodie teased. "How ya goin' ta keep up yer stylin', broder? Shipbuilding isn't goin' ta be around much longer, I hear, but I'm stayin' at it as long as I can." He added, "I'd like ta go with ya ta see who's workin' on our uncle's place."

"Of course ya would!" Maisie smirked.

"Sure an' I'll be lettin' ya know next time I go," Callum said and Maisie just shook her head. Her brothers were a bunch of stooks.

Excited to have his brother on board with the mystery of the MacCauley property, Callum called Brodie the following weekend and the two traveled south of Lurgan and just off of Plantation Road.

"I know ya feel an obligation ta Joe Campbell, Brodie, but ya gotta look out fer yerself now. He ain't one ta stay connected with."

"Remember when we was homeless, lookin' fer a place ta stay? Remember how he took us in? Sure an' he gave us a bed and provisions."

"I do. I'll give him that. But that don' mean I have ta sacrifice me life and the life of me family ta him. I gave him me gratitude when I left."

"I s'pose I felt I owed him more. I was more trouble than ya. I had demons ta deal with."

"Sure and ya did. But ya were younger than me and had a temper. Ya always were Ma's wee lad and ya couldn't get past the anger at her killin'. Not that I wasn't angry with what happened, but ya couldn't move forward at all."

Brodie sighed. "I missed them, an' Joe helped me deal with the pain. Joinin' the paras was a distraction and helpin' me dole out the anger I had inside."

"I know. But ya don' need it anymore, Brodie—all this killin'. It ain't healthy, it ain't right, and it ain't solvin' anythin'."

Brodie grew quiet. He knew his brother was right, but he felt trapped.

Eoin, Tonya, Johnny McGilroy, and his sons had just finished an afternoon snack of cheese, soda bread layered with thick butter, and some hot tea while sitting around a bonfire. They all looked up when a bright yellow Ford Escort drove slowly past the MacCauley property. The driver peered out the window and a passenger leaned forward and stared.

"That was weird." Tonya watched the car as it picked up speed down the street.

"Aye, very strange." Johnny stood and walked down to the edge of the property to see if the car was gone.

"Perhaps eht's just some neighbors waitin' tae see ehf someone ehs goin' tae occupy the property," Duncan said.

"I think I saw that same car the other day," Eoin said.

"Aye, I dehd tae." Graham nodded.

With hands on his hips, Johnny said, "As long as they don' mean any trouble—"

"From now on, we'll all have ta keep alert." Eoin gathered his tools to work on the house again. Tonya followed him and went back to cleaning up. Graham and Duncan competed to see who could throw peat directly into the fire.

"Laddies, gae tae work!" Johnny said. Graham and Duncan laughed at their father as they tossed the last of the peat.

"Me lads!" Johnny shook his head. "Nae respect, an' nuthin' but bampots, the two of 'em!"

They all went back to work framing the house within what stonework remained. And all the while they took turns watching the road.

"See what I'm sayin'?" Callum continued down the road.

"Someone's fixin' it up and I don' know how I feel about it, ya know? It's our uncle's property. How did they acquire it? It ain't right!"

"Settle down, Brodie. Ya don' know nuthin' about it!"

"We should go back and find out who these people are."

"And what'll ya say, ya laloo? Hey, get off me uncle's property?" Callum smirked. "Besides, we don' know who we're dealin' with."

"Sure an' it wouldn't hurt ta find out, would it?"

"What if they're the Provos or the regular IRA who drove us all off the MacCauley homesteads in the first place?"

"I ain't ascared of no Provos or IRA."

"Yer all talk, broder. Besides, we're outnumbered."

"Ya have a good point."

"I know. Yer just like the rest of 'em. You paras, ya think yer gonna bring down the entire British empire with a few stones!"

"I'll think more on it."

"An' that's all ye'll do about it." Callum slowed the car. "Let's check out our old place and then go back home."

Tonya woke one fall morning and turned in the bed to look out the window. It was raining again and the cold drops hit the window like the ticking of a clock. She snuggled under the quilt and felt the warmth of Eoin next to her. She could just stay here all day and watch the rain. She felt weak and a bit nauseated and that didn't give her the energy to get up.

"Before you go to work this morning can you make your own breakfast, Eoin? And can you pack yourself a lunch? I'm going to stay in bed a bit longer."

Eoin put his hand on her shoulder. "Aye, I don' blame ya, lassie. It's a dreich day."

"Well, that and I just don't feel right."

"What's wrong, Tonnie?" He touched his wife's forehead gently and then ran his fingers through her curls.

"I don't know. I feel so worn out and even thinking of food this morning doesn't sound good. Maybe I overdid it at the homestead yesterday."

"Will ya be okay if I leave ya here and go ta work?"

"Yes, I'll be fine. I've had the flu dozens of times and that's probably all this is. I took care of myself in Wisconsin. I think I can manage myself in Northern Ireland!"

"Yer a trooper, Tonnie MacCauley, no doubt about it!"

"Are the McGilroys going to be there with you?"

"Nay, not today."

"What if those men come back?"

"I'll hit them with me hammer."

"Eoin—"

"Nae bother." He chuckled. "I'll keep one eye on the nail and one on the road."

Tonya groaned, rolled over, and went back to sleep. When she awoke, Eoin was gone. She rose slowly, and after visiting the toilet, she went into the little kitchen and put on the tea kettle. The rain had subsided so she decided to take her tea, a piece of toast, and go outside. She sat on a bench letting the cool moist air revive her as she sipped her hot breakfast tea. Everything felt so different here and she loved every bit of it. Even the air was different. Sure, in

Wisconsin there were wet, humid days, but here, the damp air often felt heavier, and because of it, the colors of the landscape were deeper hues of green and more varied than the green of the farmlands where she grew up. It made for some very beautiful shots and she loved the pictures she was able to produce for a good price. She felt herself falling in love with Northern Ireland more than that first time she came to surprise Eoin and be with him.

After munching on the toast she felt even better.

The following morning, the same thing occurred. And the next. And the next.

Tonya called Margaret and explained her symptoms.

"Lassie, yer carryin' a wee bairn!"

"What?"

"Yer with child!"

"I'm pregnant?"

"Aye!"

"What do I do now?"

"Ye gae tae the doctor and get a checkup! Or at least gae tae the store and get one of those tests." Margaret laughed. "The Lord be praised! We're goin' tae have a wee'un tae spoil and cuddle!"

A few days later, when Eoin came through the door after work, Tonya took his hand and led him to the kitchen. He found the table his father had built set with the white, fine bone china designed with Scottish thistle that the McGilroys had given them for a wedding gift. There were candles lit, and a finely seasoned roast chicken with colcannon that filled the room with a wonderful aroma.

"Sure and there's a special occasion," Eoin teased.

"Why, yes, my dear, we have reason to celebrate."

"What? Did we win the lottery?"

"No."

"Ya sold one o' yer fantastic photos ta the Louvre in Paris?"

"No."

"The Queen of England is comin' ta dinner?"

"No."

"The leader of Sinn Fein finally admitted he's connected ta the IRA? That'd be class."

They both laughed. "Wrong again. Are you done guessing now?"

"What a craic! I suppose I am."

"Sit down first."

Eoin sat in one of the old wooden chairs at the table. Tonya sat in his lap and held his face in her hands. "Well, my dear husband, here's what I'm excited to tell you. We're going to have a baby!"

Eoin's eyes widened, and then they watered. He cupped her belly with one hand. "There's a wee bairn in there?" His voice squeaked.

"Aww." Tonya ran her fingers through his sandy-blond hair. "Are you going to cry?"

"Me? Never." Eoin smiled and Tonya kissed his cheek.

"I still have to go to a doctor and have it verified, but all other signs say, yes."

"This is the flu ya couldna shake?"

"I'm so dumb to not even think of being pregnant."

"Ach! I want ta call me family!"

"Let's wait till I see the doctor and get more information and find out details. You know they'll all be asking!"

Eoin pulled Tonya closer and they sat together for a while, pondering the prospect of bringing a little baby into the world: a little person who would be part MacCauley and part Miller, a baby born with dual citizenship just like Eoin and Gareth and Gareth's children. They felt excited, blessed, and a bit nervous about it. And they wondered if this was how Anna and Ian felt so long ago.

CHAPTER 7

The MacCauley homestead was finally framed in. The sitting room and kitchen were larger than Ian's cottage and they added an upstairs with three bedrooms. It was important to get the roof up quickly, knowing the amount of rain would increase during the fall and winter seasons.

Eoin was up on a ladder at work on the homestead one Saturday morning when the same familiar yellow car passed by. Then, a few minutes later, it came again, only from the other direction. Eoin grew concerned, being the only one at the site. What if it was loyalist paramilitary, or worse yet, the Provisional IRA?

After passing the site of the MacCauley homestead and seeing only one person working, Brodie and Callum decided it would be safe to stop and investigate. Two against one, after all. They parked the car. Eoin stepped outside the framework, a hammer in one hand and a rough plank in the other.

"We're not comin' fer a fight!" Brodie yelled.

"What do ya want, then?" Eoin said. "I've seen ya pass by here before!"

As the men drew closer, they studied one another, eyes squinting, heads tipped. Callum and Brodie glanced at each other, puzzled. Why did this intruder on the MacCauley property look familiar to them? Eoin thought the same thing.

"This land belongs ta the MacCauley clan!" Callum stated.

"I am just that," Eoin said, feeling nervous.

"Yer a MacCauley?"

"What of it?" Eoin gripped the hammer tighter.

"Ah, catch yerself on and calm down. We're MacCauleys, too."

"I'm Callum and this is Brodie. We're sons of—"

"Uncle Sean MacCauley? I know who ye are! Me lost cousins from County Armagh!"

"Wait, yer too tall and blond ta be Gareth." Brodie paused. "Could ya be Eoin himself?"

Eoin laughed and nodded. There was a moment of silence and then Callum spoke up.

"But we thought *ye* were the lost cousin!"

"Nay, not lost. Here I am!"

Brodie studied Eoin, still trying to grasp who stood before him. "Like a ghost returnin' from the dead!"

"Ya don' know how close ya are ta that truth!" Eoin put his "weapons" down and his arms out. Callum and Brodie closed in for an embrace. Emotions were a mix of joy, laughter, and happy tears.

"So, tell us what happened ta ya, Eoin?"

Eoin sighed. "It's a long story. Back in '74 Ma and I were kidnapped outside the Divis Flats by men in balaclavas and a woman with a stockin' over her head. We were thrown in a van and taken up ta Waterfoot Beach. They took us out on the sand, kneecapped me, and murdered Ma. I was rescued by some fishermen from Scohtland who took me across the sea and nursed me back ta health. I returned ta Northern Ireland in '87, lived in Portadown, and found me da in Laurelvale. Eventually, he and I went ta the States ta be with Gareth and his new wife. It was there I met me lovely wife,

Tonnie. We moved back a few months ago and I've decided ta rebuild our home here."

The cousins shook their heads in amazement.

"We're that pleased ta see ya, cousin Eoin," Callum said, still a bit teary-eyed. "And we're that glad ya survived and are livin' a life here, so we are."

"I've told ya me story, but what about youse? Me da and broder didn' know what happened ta all of ya?"

"It's a bit of a story, too," Brodie said.

"Why don' ya come ta me home with yer wife and meet me family? Then we can all sit down at the table, eat, and have some tea and talk?" Callum said.

"That sounds grand, thank ya," Eoin said.

"Tomorrow eve, then?"

"We'll be there!"

It was raining hard the afternoon Eoin and Tonya drove north toward Callum and Molly's place.

"What are these mountains called again?" Tonya asked.

"Those are the Mourne mountains." Eoin pointed south. "And the Sperrin Mountains that way." He pointed to the north.

"I love them!"

"Sure an' they're just mountains!" Eoin laughed.

"Did you see any mountains where I grew up?" Tonya asked sardonically. "Did you notice any at all in Wisconsin?"

"Hmm, I guess not."

"Well then, husband, except for the bluffs around the Mississippi, there aren't mountains like these in Wisconsin so I'm impressed with these!"

"I guess I've been schooled, so I have."

Tonya grinned with satisfaction.

"I'll take ya by Lohrgan so ya can see the town I grew up in." They drove on Market Street through town and Eoin pointed out the shops where his ma took them to buy clothes and treats. He explained the invisible divide between the Catholic shops and the Protestant shops and laughed about how fearless his ma was shopping downtown. She was American and wasn't going to be intimidated by anything.

"I think I would have gotten along well with your mother, Eoin," Tonya remarked as she studied the buildings and the people in the town.

"Yer the same in many ways."

"Haley told me one time that Gareth said she reminded him of his mom. Isn't it interesting that you and Gareth both married American women—like how your dad married your mother? Do you think there's anything to that?"

Eoin reached over and took Tonya's hand. "I never thought of that before, but now that ya mentioned it, perhaps we found special things in ya lassies that we had seen in our ma. Y'are both confident with who ya are, and know what ya want."

Eoin drove around Belfast and up to Glencairn Estates to Callum's home. A dark mountain hovered on one side of the tenement housing and Tonya pointed in awe.

"What's that called?" she blurted.

"It's Divis Mountain." Eoin smiled, beginning to enjoy his wife's jubilant explosions about things in his country he had always taken for granted.

Tonya held Eoin's hand tightly and snuggled with him under their umbrella as they stepped up to the apartment door. He knocked and they waited for someone to come. What new world was she entering now? It was one thing to associate with Eoin's Scottish friends, but most of those friends were people older than she or much younger. Now, she was about to be immersed in her own peer group from another country and it kept her in a place of curious anticipation. The door opened to a bright, smiling face with which Tonya felt familiar. Brodie was shorter than Eoin and had dark curls about his face. One couldn't deny him to be a relative of Gareth and Ian's!

"Ach! Come in out of the rain! It's like water pourin' down from a fire hose, so it is!" Brodie said. As they stepped inside, Tonya looked around at the small sitting room. There was no fireplace here but electric heat and she felt a slight chill to the room. Callum stepped in and approached them.

"This is Tonnie," Eoin said and then pointed. "These are my cousins, Brodie and Callum."

Callum reached out to shake Tonya's hand. "It's grand ta meet ya." Tonya could see the likeness between Gareth and Brodie, but Callum had a different look altogether. He was taller like Eoin but with straight dark hair. It was combed downward and his paisley shirt reminded her of something out of a '70s movie. Maisie and Molly came down the stairs. Tonya guessed right away that Eoin's cousin was the one with the long flowing auburn hair and she was right.

"Maisie!" Eoin's voice boomed.

"Ya know it, dear cousin!" Maisie said as she went right into Eoin's arms. She stepped back and took a good look at him. "All tall and big and handsome, so ya are. I'm thinkin' yer the tallest of the cousins!"

"Nay, I hold that position!" Callum teased.

"Not anymore, dear broder." Maisie smirked.

"And this is my wife, Molly," Callum said. Molly nodded shyly, her short, smooth hair moving freely about her head. Tonya thought Callum and Molly could almost pass as siblings.

"It's grand ta meet ya, Molly. Everyone, this is my wife, Tonnie," Eoin smiled.

"Hi, it's really nice to meet you all," Tonya said.

"So yer from America, eh?" Brodie said.

"That's right—Wisconsin," Tonya said. There was a slight pause in the room as the cousins took in her Yankee accent. Molly, feeling the silence, called for the children to come and meet the guests.

"Children, this is me cousin Eoin and his wife, Tonnie. She's from America," Callum said and the children's eyes grew wide.

"And this is our Shannon and our Tommy," Molly said. "And this is Maisie's wee'un, Erin."

"It's nice to meet you." Tonya smiled. The children grinned and stared.

Shannon spoke up first. "Ya look like a fillimactor—"

"Do ya know any cowboys? Do ya know John Wayne?" Tommy asked. "Do ya live in the desert? What's it like?"

"I never saw a cowboy," Erin said.

"Children, enough," Molly scolded.

"What's a fillimactor?" Tonya asked.

"A movie star," Eoin translated. Tonya looked at him puzzled. "Film actor."

Tonya laughed. "Oh, well, Wisconsin is only a small part of the United States and it's a lot of farmland. I've never traveled out west to see cowboys or to New York to see movie stars. And I don't know John Wayne. Sorry."

"I've been upstaged, so I have," Eoin said and everyone laughed.

There was a continual hum of conversation in the small kitchen as they all sat around the table eating bangers and mash, an Irish sausage and mashed potato dish. Tonya listened carefully. She missed some of the things spoken, their accents so thick at times with words running together quickly. She didn't realize until now how soft Gareth's accent was all the years growing up with him. Even Eoin's accent was easier to understand than this part of the family. It made sense. Both of the cousin's parents were Irish, unlike Gareth and Eoin's folks. And they had lived their entire lives in Northern Ireland.

Brodie and Callum took time to explain what happened to them after their parents were murdered. When they finished, everyone looked to Maisie to tell her story. She explained, "I was put in a Catholic orphanage and taken out when me broders found me. End of story." Everyone paused.

"That's it, Maisie? That's all yer gonna share?" Brodie chuckled, finding humor in his sister's abruptness.

"So, Eoin," Callum said, breaking the awkward silence as he pushed his plate away, "do ya ever wonder who did this ta us? I mean, do ya wish ya knew who was behind it?"

"All the time."

"Lads, there are ears that shouldna be a part of this conversation."

"Ma! We're older now," Shannon argued.

"Away off ta yer rooms and take Erin with ya, me dears," Molly said.

"I have one more question fer Tonnie," Shannon said. "Me teacher says Americans don' use the metric system. Is that true? Why not? Are Americans that daft?"

Brodie guffawed.

"Shannon! Away off and feel yer head!" Callum shook his head.

"It's okay, Callum. Frankly, I don't have a good answer for that one, Shannon." Tonya laughed.

"She's just askin' ya ta get ya ta talk some more and hear yer accent," Tommy said.

"Am not!" Shannon punched her brother in the shoulder.

Callum stood and pulled his daughter's chair from the table. "Away with ya, all of ye!"

The others laughed.

After the children disappeared, Callum spoke. "So, Eoin here says he's been talkin' ta others like us who have lost loved ones and never knew what happened ta them."

"When ya talk ta them, do ya feel like y'are gettin' any closer ta answers about yer ma?" Molly asked.

"Well, not really," Eoin said. "For one thing, most avoid that topic."

"Why?" Brodie asked.

"Fear," Eoin answered. "Fear of rumors flyin' that they're informers themselves. Fear of the same people comin' back fer them. The McConnely family—ya know about that case—"

"Everyone in Ireland knows about that case!" Molly interrupted.

"That's who Ma and I were tryin' ta visit the day we were kidnapped."

The room grew quiet. The clock ticked loudly on the wall and the muffled voices of the children could be heard in a room upstairs. Everyone's thoughts were the same, including Tonya's. It was the event that changed all of their lives.

"I've talked ta some of the children from the McConnely family, too," Eoin continued. "One of them says he knows who kidnapped their ma. Even the neighbors knew who did it but they wouldn't say. Some of them were part of the Provos, the IRA, or Sinn Fein."

"An' that's how they knew of yer ma's visits?" Molly said, almost in a whisper.

"It is."

"That's awful—ta know who did it and ta stay silent," Callum said. He and Brodie looked at their sister, who remained quiet throughout the conversation. Maisie caught their glances.

"What? How many times have I told ya?" Maisie said. "Sure an' I don't remember a blessed thing."

"Not a thing?" Eoin asked.

"Nay."

"Apparently she was found afterwards runnin' along the road screamin', out o' her mind. She was in shock, so she was," Brodie said and Maisie shifted uncomfortably in her chair.

"We were all in shock, I think," Callum said. "We saw the men standin' o'er our parents and then Gareth went wild with anger, pulled Da's ol' gun off the rack and fired recklessly. One man fell."

"I'm surprised we got away when we did," Brodie said.

"So, ya saw Gareth shoot?" Eoin asked.

"We saw Gareth shoot the man and watched him fall!" Callum said. "An' then we took off for the fields!"

"Gareth told me how, years later, a man broke into the home he was livin' at in the US, accusin' him of killin' his broder," Eoin said.

"Oh, I remember that!" Tonya blurted. "Haley said Gareth was ready to kill the man and it frightened her so much to see the fire in Gareth's eyes. She'd never seen such a thing!"

"O' course she would be ascared. Yankees. Ya wouldn't get it!" Callum laughed sarcastically and the others chuckled. Tonya felt stupid for opening her mouth.

"The man went all the way ta 'merica?" Brodie said. "Cheeky monkey!"

"I'll have ta ask Gareth what the guy's name was," Eoin said. "Maybe it will stir a memory for ya, Maisie."

"What, are ya daft? I'd rather *not stir* any memory of that awful day, thank ya."

Tonya glanced at Eoin. He wasn't fazed by Maisie's abruptness. He, of all people, could sympathize with Maisie and what she went through. Tonya remembered how long it took her husband to rehearse what happened on the beach at Waterfoot.

"It's so wrong that these people are gettin' away with the things they did," Brodie said. "There has ta be a way ta get justice."

"Is that why you're part of a paramilitary group?" Eoin asked.

"Aye. I joined it as soon as I were old enough."

"An' we wish ya hadn'." Callum scowled.

"Aye," Molly and Maisie said in unison.

"Why is that?" Eoin said, feeling the stiffness in the air.

"They're a dangerous group ta be a part o'," Callum said, glancing at his sister, but her eyes were downcast.

"Are they on the Protestant side or the Catholic side?" Tonya asked.

"Both," Brodie said.

"So, there are paramilitary groups on both sides?" Tonya asked, with palms up and moving as she spoke. "And why? Who are they fighting? Each other? Or the IRA? Or is it the RUC? I'm so confused."

"Do all Americans talk with their hands?" Maisie said abruptly and the others chuckled. Tonya sat back quietly, feeling embarrassed again. Eoin took her hand and squeezed it. He was comfortable here, but she was like a duck out of water. He remembered how he felt when he first came to America and how she was the one to push him into being a part of the group of friends there. It was his turn to help her here.

"Tonnie doesn't represent all of America, Maisie, and she's one of a kind anyway," Eoin answered. The women "awwwed." Tonya smiled gratefully. "Both sides have paras, Tonnie," he explained gently.

"And they're all out of control," Callum said pointedly. He looked at his brother and shook his head.

"Leave it be, broder," Brodie said, low and quiet.

"There are several paramilitary groups on the Loyalist side," Eoin said. "There's the Ulster Defense Association better known as the UDA, the Ulster Volunteer Force, the UVF—"

"That's the gang Brodie's in," Callum said and by his tone, Tonya could tell he wasn't pleased. "And there's the Red Hand Commandos, RHC," Callum continued. "Then, there's the Republican side with the notorious IRA and its out-of-control branch, the Provisional Irish Republican Army, better known as the Provos."

"It's fantastic if ya don't remember it all, Tonnie," Molly said dryly. Maisie chuckled and Molly continued. "Just a bunch of boys fightin' fer no good reason." Tonya nodded gratefully. There certainly were a lot of initials for things and she was sure she wouldn't remember them all anyway.

"Well, it started out as a good reason ta fight fer the separation of Britain from our country and ta shut down the Provos' random acts of violence, but it's escalated inta innocents bein' killed," Brodie said.

"I'm that glad ta hear ya say so, broder," Callum said.

"A son of the McConnely woman told me that he's seen the people who kidnapped his ma on the street and they walk past him like nothin' ever happened," Eoin said. "Out of fear fer his own family he won't turn them in."

Maisie shivered. She couldn't speak it, but she knew that if she ever crossed paths with the men who murdered her parents and suddenly remembered things about it, she'd probably drop in some corner and be sick to her stomach.

"It's hard ta forgive, but somewhere in our lives the fergivin' has ta happen, so it does," Molly said.

"I can't," Brodie said. "Can ye do that, Eoin?"

Eoin looked at Tonya who sat back again, meekly soaking in the conversation. She rubbed his arm tenderly as he spoke. "I pray fer it—a fergivin' spirit—because an unfergivin' spirit will eat ya up inside and ruin yer relationship with the ones ya love."

Molly picked up on the sweet connection between Eoin and Tonya. "Tonnie has helped ya with that, then?"

"I was a mess comin' ta America. If it weren't fer Tonnie—" Eoin's voice caught and Tonya leaned her head on his shoulder.

"Thank ya fer helpin' me cousin," Brodie said to Tonya and she smiled fondly.

Callum couldn't handle the tender moment and feared he'd get a tear in his eye. "Brodie's had the hardest time fergivin'. He used ta have a big mouth on him whenever he faced the enemy—hard ta believe, I know." He succeeded in breaking the emotional moment. Everyone laughed.

"The truth is on me, broder, but one day, I learned about an old friend of mine who had no respect fer the IRA. One evening he was lured across the border inta the Republic and inta an abandoned barn where he was beaten ta death with an iron bar—"

"Brodie, no details with the women present, especially an American lass, ya know?"

Tonya glanced at Maisie and Molly and wondered what they had been exposed to growing up here.

"Ach! Don' be protectin' *meself,* broder," Maisie said forcefully. "I live closer ta the fightin' and dyin' more than ye rich broders who can afford ta live outside the city. I see it all the time— the bombin', the body parts—"

"Maisie, enough!" Callum said sternly. "And ya well know, we're nothin' of the rich."

"Our sister has had ta be a tough cailin," Brodie explained. "We suspect she was the only one who actually saw our folks close up after they were murdered. She weren't much older than Erin. And then—"

"I'm truly sorry, Maisie," Tonya said.

Maisie cocked her head. "It wasn't yer doin'—"

"*Cousin,*" Eoin reprimanded softly.

Maisie saw the confused look on Tonya's face and said in a sweeter tone, "But thank ya anyway."

"And then," Brodie continued, "she lost her husband in a scuffle—"

"Enough about me."

"We worry about ya," Callum said.

Maisie turned abruptly to Tonya. "When's yer wee baby due, Tonnie?"

"I'll find out at the doctor's tomorrow." Tonya smiled, happy to have the conversation turn amicable.

"Let us know. It's nice ta have pleasant news, so it is."

"I will," Tonya said, "and it's nice for me to get to know more MacCauleys, and, no offence, guys, but it's nice that there are some female MacCauleys here."

"We'll have tea together sometime," Molly said. Maisie nodded in agreement and Tonya felt a little more welcome.

CHAPTER 8

"I don't understand where this is all going," Gareth said, after Phyllis and Ian filled him in about President Clinton's visit to Belfast. "The president shook hands with the president of Sinn Fein? Isn't that guy suspected of being involved with the IRA and the Disappeared?"

"That he is."

"And the crowd in Belfast applauded their union," Phyllis said.

"Is our president taking sides or is he trying to make peace?" Gareth asked.

"Only the Lord knows." Ian poured himself another cup of coffee and sat at the table. "I couldn't believe it when Clinton invited Sinn Fein ta the St. Patrick's Day celebration at the White House last March!"

"I'll bet the Brits weren't too happy about that!" Gareth said.

"Well, one thing I've learned since I've been here," Ian said, "is that St. Patrick's Day is celebrated here more than in Ireland. Sure and the Chicago River is dyed green fer the day, ya know?"

"Yes, it's quite the feat. I've only seen it done on TV. But didn't you celebrate St. Patty's Day over there much?" Phyllis asked.

"It's St. Paddy, with a 'd,' me love. In Irish, Patrick is Pàdraig," Ian said. "All the years Gareth's been here and he never corrected you?"

"No, he didn't." Phyllis looked at Gareth.

"Ach, I thought it was funny, so I let it go. It sounded like we were celebrating a hamburger." Gareth laughed and Ian began to chuckle. Phyllis acted offended and embarrassed, but ended up laughing with them. "By the way," Gareth explained. "Did you know that the US holds the largest population of Irish ancestry than any other country—maybe that's why the US appears to have more huge celebrations on the day?"

"Interesting," Phyllis said.

Ian explained, "The problem over on the Island is that the Catholics and the Protestants each want ta claim St. Patrick as their hero—but they can't share a hero. So, it's been confusing who gets ta celebrate him! Here in America it doesn't matter if ye've got Catholic ancestors or Protestant, if yer Irish or German or Dutch or French, they all celebrate St. Paddy's Day like one big happy family." Ian laughed.

"So, is that the only thing you called us over here to tell us?" Gareth said.

"Nay, lad, we're just chattin' away the time while we're waitin' fer Haley ta get here before we tell ya the real news!"

As if her ears were ringing, Haley stepped into the house with the children.

"Okay. So, what is going on?" Gareth said, impatience showing itself the longer he waited.

"Let yer wife get settled a minute," Ian said as he happily watched the children run to the box of toys stored in the study and drag it out into the living room.

"Haley, do you want a cup of coffee?" Phyllis asked.

"Sure. Sounds good."

"You guys are killing me," Gareth put his head in his hands.

Ian smiled at Phyllis. Haley put Liam on the floor to crawl around with the kids and sat down. Phyllis poured her a cup of coffee.

"Okay." Haley leaned over and took in the pungent aroma wafting from her mug. "What's going on?"

"We have news will warm the cockles of yer hearts!" Ian said.

Gareth let out a long sigh of relief. "Finally! What is it?"

"Tonya is pregnant!" Phyllis said. An excited gasp escaped Haley's lips.

"Fantastic!" Gareth said.

"Our kids will have a cousin!" Haley said. "When is she due?"

"Late March or early April." Phyllis grinned.

"Oh, I'm just so happy to hear this! I need to tell the girlfriends!" Haley started to get up, but Ian caught her arm.

"Well, hold yer horses, lass, there's more news. This one is even more unexpected."

"What is it, Da?" Gareth asked.

"Well, speakin' of cousins, so ya were, Eoin was workin' on the homestead and met up with yer cousins, Gareth."

Gareth put his cup of coffee down and sat back in his chair, his jaw hanging open. "What? Our MacCauley cousins? We thought we'd lost them! How'd that come about?"

"They're all livin' in Belfast! Callum and Brodie happened ta drive by the property a few times when Eoin and the McGilroys were workin' on it. They were concerned about who was messin' with the MacCauley property. They finally stopped by ta see what was going on one time when it was only Eoin workin' there. Eoin picked up a hammer and piece of wood, ready ta fight. What a craic! And they all had a good laugh in the end!" Ian chuckled.

"That's incredible. I never thought I'd see them again! What about Maisie? Did he see little Maisie, my wee ginger bap?" Gareth said.

"Aye, Tonya and Eoin had dinner with them all. Maisie is a widow and has a child, Erin. Callum is married—her name's Molly. They have two children: Shannon and Tommy."

"Wow." Gareth slipped his hand over Haley's and grasped it.

"I'm so happy for you, honey," Haley said.

"I'm just so taken aback by this!"

"What's a ginger bap, Gareth?"

Gareth laughed. "That was one of my nicknames for my wee cousin. Maisie had a head full of strawberry-blond hair like our Annie. Bap means bread. I forgot about that. I'll have to use it on Annie."

"As in ginger*bread*? Oh, brother, Gareth." Haley smirked. "You're king of nicknames."

"It's what I do." Gareth gave his wife a loving glance. "Anyway, I'm jealous of Eoin. I wish I could see them all again. Last I saw them we were playing hide-and-seek in the barn. Callum, Brodie, and I scattered when we saw those men in balaclavas, but we didn't know where Maisie was at the time. I never saw my cousins again and I always wondered if Maisie was okay." Haley slipped her fingers between Gareth's. The feel of her hand in his was comforting. He would love to return to Northern Ireland someday and now there was an extra draw, to see his cousins. There was always this conflict of interest for him—going back to his homeland or staying here with the woman he loved.

And though Haley wanted him to stay here, she felt for him. Fortunately, he was a responsible man and would never leave his family. He would never go there if it meant he would be putting himself in imminent danger. She was pretty sure of it, anyway. She knew she shouldn't doubt him and continued to pray that she could leave it all in God's hands.

It was Christmas day. Ed, Bobby, and Gareth spent the latter part of the morning in what used to be Robert's study, setting up a Sauder computer desk and a Dell PC computer, five-and-a-quarter-inch floppy drive, dot matrix printer, monitor, and keyboard, all for the huge sum of $2,200. The boarding business needed an office and to get updated. Everyone agreed that the best place to set it up was in the big house.

"I hope ya know what yer doin', boys." Ian looked on from the doorway.

"You'll be happy to know, Da, that Uncle Bobby's the one in charge here." Gareth laughed. "I'm completely in the dark with these things."

"Keith and I helped our folks set one up and that's the extent of my expertise," Ed said.

"I still don' understand why we need it ta run a business. People have been runnin' businesses fer centuries without a computer!"

"Times are changing, Ian," Bobby said. "You got to learn how to keep up!"

"Bah." Ian waved his hand and went out to the living room to play with the grands.

"So, I'm depending on you to get this up and running, Uncle Bobby."

"Of course. We've been using these at the office for a while now. Remember Drew Carter?"

"Ach! How's he cuttin'?"

"He's doing well. Trying to lose all the weight he put on living in Northern Ireland eating all that Irish comfort food!"

Gareth laughed. "Tell him I said 'hi.'"

"You can tell him yourself sometime. He's back in the US now."

"He's back?"

"Yes, I don't need him over there anymore and he's been helpful getting these computers set up at the station. I'll help you do this part, but you'll need to learn how to use it yourself."

"I know. I'm just afraid I'll mess something up."

"Gareth MacCauley—afraid?" Ed said and Bobby laughed.

"Ah, you've found my Achilles' heel—modern technology."

"Honestly, it's going to get the business organized so much better," Ed said.

"Ed's right. You'll be able to keep better files with easy access to information on customers and payments made. You'll eventually grow to prefer it over pen and paper."

"We'll see about that." Gareth sighed.

Haley peeked in. "Hey guys—" She looked around the room. "What a mess you're making in here! Anyway, we're going outside now to put ornaments on the tree before lunch. Can you stop all the *fun* with all the wires and strange machinery and come outside with us?"

"Of course, Haley girl." Gareth smiled. "Wouldn't miss it!'

"Oh, is this that tree tradition Anna started?" Ed asked. "Tell everyone to wait while I call and get my folks to come over here. I know they've loved being a part of it in the past." Ed went to a quiet place in the house to call his mom on his cell phone.

"Actually, she didn't start it," Bobby said to Gareth. "Our mother did."

"Grandma Hanford started the tradition?" Gareth asked.

"Yes. We had a beautiful blue spruce out back that Mom insisted we decorate on Christmas day after all the presents were unwrapped. But we didn't sing. Mom, Dad, and I couldn't carry a tune! Your dad added the Wexford Carol to it and Anna loved it. There was something special to Anna about decorating the tree. When she was young she used to spend hours outside in the cold putting up more of her homemade decorations. Mom would eventually have to call her in. I remember one time when Anna got scolded for almost getting frostbite. When she was determined to do something she was focused and forgot about taking care of herself."

"Sounds like Ma," Gareth said as they piled all the extra wrappings and Styrofoam from the computer components back into the boxes.

"One time she stayed up all night writing a piece for literature class. Dad found her the next morning asleep, sitting at the kitchen table with her head on the keys of the old Royal typewriter," Bobby said. He and Gareth laughed. But then, the storytelling of his family brought the old feelings of grief and his expression changed. "I miss them. All of them."

"I'm sorry, Uncle Bobby."

"I'll be fine. It just hits me every once in a while—the loss of people I love. I know you understand that. I'm glad Anna passed on this tradition with you so that it can continue to the next generation."

Everyone waited for the Wagner couple to come over before bundling up and going out in the cold. Once they arrived, the tradition began. As they stood outside, Phyllis held a box of ornaments and Haley handed them out to everyone. Then they each took turns hanging ornaments on the tall pine tree out in front of the big house. Gareth helped baby Liam put an ornament on the tree. Ian held Bobby in his arms as they hung their ornaments together. Annie and Fiahd stood on tiptoes to hang their ornaments as high as they could. Alma was ecstatic to be a part of their tradition again as she placed her ornament on a branch and Fred's eyes glistened as he hung his. It was a beautiful thing then to hear many raise their voices in song: the mature, the young, and the sweet children's timbres, in a rendition of the Wexford Carol.

"Good people all, this Christmas time
Consider well and bear in mind
What our good God for us has done
In sending his beloved son..."

CHAPTER 9

It was a cold winter in Northern Ireland, the ground was covered in a white blanket of snow and everyone hoped they didn't get hit with the terrible storm like last winter's blizzard. The MacCauleys and the elderly McGilroys, layered in their warmest wool clothes, stood around the ancient fir on Ian's old homestead. Margaret and George were excited to finally meet more of Eoin's family. Eoin and Callum built a fire for warmth and extra light under the moonlit sky. The cousins were all excited to celebrate their aunt's tradition again. The branches hung low with the snow and the load of ornaments they all bountifully donated. It was a beautiful sight to behold. Eoin led them in the Wexford Carol and everyone joined in when a familiar phrase came to mind.

"Remember the fehrst tayme we dehd thehs wehth ye, Eoin?" Margaret asked as she pulled her wool scarf tighter around her throat.

"So I do," Eoin said, deep in thought.

"Eht were what brought ye and yer da together," George said.

"Yer right." Eoin turned to the others. "Collins brought me da here that same Christmas we came out here and he saw the ornaments George, Margaret, and I left on the tree! That made him curious. Then, he and Collins decided ta go check out me Uncle Sean's place and that's where they saw Gareth's old bike. Collins remembered how, when he met up with me at the

Enniskillin bombing, I had said somethin' about returnin' ta me old homestead and seein' me broder's bike!"

"And that's the begehnnehn' of all thehs!" George said.

"The Lord be praised!" Margaret said as her teeth chattered.

"Margaret, you're freezing," Tonya said. "Are you okay?"

"Och, we're two auld folk ehn need o' some heat!" George said.

"Eht's a braw evenin' but we'd better be goin' home," Margaret said. The older couple gave their Christmas greetings to everyone and said goodbye. Eoin and Tonya helped them walk carefully to their car and gave hugs. Everyone waved until the lights of their car disappeared down the road.

"I remember Auntie Anna. She was fun," Maisie said when Eoin and Tonya returned to the fire. "I think she paid extra attention ta me because I were the only lassie. I think she always wanted a daughter of her own."

"Ya were her favorite!" Callum said. Eoin and Brodie agreed.

"It's so sad, all that happened to your family," Tonya said.

"Thanks, Tonnie, lass." Brodie smiled. "Yer an okay Yank, so ya are." The others laughed.

"I try. So-I-do." Tonya smirked.

Maisie guffawed. "She's a corker, cousin."

"Don't I know it!" Eoin pulled Tonya in close.

"Just keep yer Yankee accent," Maisie teased.

"We like ta hear it, even if it does take a minute sometimes to understand," Callum said.

"But my accent sounds so plain," Tonya said. "You guys are the ones hard to understand!"

Brodie tried to mimic her accent, talking very nasal and clipped. "Buht. Mahee. Aksent. Sownds. Soh. Plaaain." Everyone laughed, including Tonya.

"Sure and yur accent is sing-songy, ya know?" Tonya unsuccessfully copied the brogue.

"Sorry, lass, stick with the Yank in ya, yer Irish accent is—"

Maisie smacked her brother. "Sure and we can be nice, Brodie." Eoin guffawed. "So, Eoin, yer da brought a Yank ta live on this land and yer doin' the same, are ya?"

"So I am." Eoin grinned at the thought.

"How much longer do ya expect it'll take ta finish and move in?" Brodie asked.

"By next fall, we hope."

The men wandered around the build, discussing the upcoming projects.

Molly looked at Tonya. "Sure and it woulda been nice ta have it done before yer wee babe was born."

"It would've been," Tonya said, "but that's life."

"We'll help where we can," Maisie offered and Molly nodded.

"Oh, thank you. It's good to have some women close by."

"It's our pleasure an' we love ta have somethin' ta celebrate around here!"

The women each took one of Tonya's arms and the threesome strolled around the property.

"So, you and Eoin," Molly said. "How'd ya meet? How'd ya end up tagether?"

"When Eoin and Ian came to America, they lived on the Becketts' farm—yes, the Haley Beckett who Gareth grew up and married. There were three of us girls who hung out at the farm with Haley—we've been best friends since kindergarten. And we hung out with the guys, too: Gareth, Eddy, and Keith Wagner. My folks were gone often, so I liked to come over to the Becketts' place. It was natural that I was at the farm a lot after Ian and Eoin got there. We tried to include Eoin, but he was a stick-in-the-mud at first and I gave him a hard time about it."

"What a craic! *A stick-in-the-mud.*" Molly laughed.

"I knew we'd get along, so we would!" Maisie said.

"In fairness, Eoin was struggling with a lot of baggage from his past and he didn't feel like part of our group. He had a lot to deal with."

"Don' we all?" Maisie said and the others nodded.

"He sulked around at first, and I didn't understand, so, I wasn't exactly the nicest. I gave him an earful a couple of times—"

Maisie guffawed.

"An' yet, ya ended up tagether?" Molly asked innocently.

"I think deep down Eoin knew he needed help and not pity. He just couldn't see it at the time. "

"When did ya know ya were in love with him?" Maisie asked.

"I think I was falling for him from the start. I just didn't realize it. I didn't understand why his long scraggly hair and beard bothered me so much. I think I knew that underneath it all he was a very handsome man—and I was right!" The women giggled.

"I see how much ya love each other," Molly said.

"I'm glad he found someone like ya," Maisie added.

"Thanks, girls." Tonya warmed at the connection she was making with her new family. "And, Maisie, can I ask, what's the story with your husband?"

Molly side-glanced Maisie. "She doesn't like ta talk about it."

"Oh, I'm sorry."

"No bother. Michael died and I had ta move on and keep up a good face fer me wee lass."

"How did you survive all that?"

Maisie looked at Tonya squarely. "I didn't have a choice, Tonnie. We learn very young ta survive here, so we do."

"I just can't imagine."

"I s'pose not. Yer world in America must be such a haven," Molly said.

"Compared to what's been going on here, yes. It's pretty safe. Especially in the country. The big cities in the US aren't always the safest. But still, no bombs are going off, *usually*."

"So, how could ya leave America and come here?" Maisie asked. "This is the last place on earth I'd come ta right now with all the violence at any corner—at any given moment."

"Well, at first it was because I was just a hungry photographer who wanted to photograph another part of the world than the one I grew up in! And then, it was because Eoin was here and I realized I was in love with him. And when he showed me his country, I fell in love with that, too. I want to help him visit the families of the Disappeared."

"It's a noble thing ya care ta do," Molly said.

"I wouldn't want ta see this part of the world if I didn't have ta."

Tonya put her arm around Maisie. "No, I suppose you wouldn't. But I still see so much beauty here."

Before parting ways, Maisie came up to Tonya and, patting her growing tummy, said, "I want ta help ya as much as I'm able when the babe comes. Yer gettin' big fast. Maybe this wee one will come early!"

"I will certainly take any help I can get. Thanks, Maisie, that means a lot to me."

"Ya need some best friends here, so ya do."

It was "auld year's night," the 31st of December, 1995, that Tonya and Eoin sat with George and Margaret McGilroy to celebrate Hogmanay—a Scottish celebration that occurred the last days of the old year and the first days of the new year. They ate a feast of steak pie with skirlie—oatmeal, fat, onions, and seasonings fried, making a "skirl" noise—and roast tatties with parsnips and green beans. After eating they gave each other gifts and enjoyed each other's company. Then, because it was believed to be bad luck to start the New Year with a dirty house, Eoin helped George clean out the fireplace while Tonya and Margaret swept the floors. When the clock struck midnight Margaret had them stand around in a circle, cross their arms, and hold hands while they sang "Auld Lang Syne." They had nearly finished singing when there was a knock at the front door. Eoin opened it and there stood Callum with a gift of fruitcake. As he stepped into the house, George and Margaret shouted out together, "Och, fehrst footehn'!"

"Oh, I remember you telling me about first footing!" Tonya said to Eoin, who was grinning widely.

"Ya brehng the year good luck tae us bein' the fehrst tae step ehnta our home wehth yer tall dark features!" George laughed as Callum, his family, Maisie, and Erin came into their house smiling and wishing all a "Happy New Year!"

"How dehd ye ken aboot fehrst footehn and that eht aught tae be Callum who dehd eht?" Margaret asked.

"How did we know? Why, Eoin told us, so he did!" Callum said, smiling widely and satisfied that their late-night trip down from Belfast was not wasted at all. In fact, it was completely worth it by the looks on the faces of these old Scottish folks.

It was the end of February. The constant rain had let up for the day and so the city folk were out and about. Brodie and Paul sat down behind a partially crumbled wall in an alley next to an abandoned old building. Others in the gang moved behind cars and went up by the windows of the building with their assault rifles, homemade submachine guns, and pistols in hand. They were quiet, waiting for another transport of weapons from the British on the Crumlin Road. There were women out shopping together, mothers pushing strollers, and children playing football on the street, but when they saw the men pan out in their black uniforms, they cleared the area, ducking into stores and running down the street toward safety.

The last attempt to steal weapons had failed and Joe was determined to win this battle. Brodie's heart had sunk when he learned of the new scheme. Suddenly, they were up and firing on the soldiers' vehicles. The men under attack stopped, stepped out behind the open doors of their vehicles, and started shooting back. Joe's men advanced in the attack, but then, out of nowhere, a group of the UDA showed up to the west of them and the fighting grew crazier than before. The battle lasted all afternoon until a few old black taxis approached from the south. Everyone knew what that meant. The IRA had shown up.

"Everyone beat it!" Joe yelled.

The IRA was known for these taxis that had been formerly used for service in London but were replaced. Now, the IRA had acquired them and it made their presence even more intimidating. The paras started to scatter as the British soldiers were overcome by the IRA. Shots rang out through the street. A helicopter appeared overhead and when the IRA saw it they bolted.

After the battle ended, Paul told Brodie he couldn't find his brother, William. As soon as the IRA, the UDA, and the British soldiers disappeared, Paul and Brodie searched throughout the abandoned building, went down the alley, and came around to the tattered wall where they had originally fought.

When they heard his cries they looked behind the broken hood of a car that had flown off during the battle. They found him lying on the ground, holding a bloodied leg and moaning.

"Grab yer broder's other arm," Brodie said as he started to lift William. Paul obeyed.

"Here." They heard a voice from the tenement housing across the street. A Protestant man in his mid-fifties motioned for them to bring William into his apartment. The man's wife rushed to get rags and a bowl of warm water to tend to William's wounds.

"Sure and he's the same age as our Steven," the woman said. "He died last year in a brawl, God bless his soul. Such young boys fightin' fer what?"

Someone pounded at the door of the home.

"It's the police!" the wife said.

"What are we goin' ta do?" Paul panicked.

"Youse boys get on with ya," the man said. "We'll care fer 'im."

"We can't leave me broder," Paul said.

"Yer no help ta him here! Leave him with us."

"We gotta leave 'im and make a run for it!" Brodie said.

"I agree," the woman said. "Go now, and return ta yer mothers. I'll take good care of 'em."

"I ain't got a mum," Brodie said under his breath as he and Paul rushed out the back door into the alleyway.

Brodie arrived safely at his old apartment and slumped in his stuffed chair, feeling miserable. He was weary of all the fighting and killing. Was he truly bringing justice to his parents? Or was he just a part of more people dying and suffering in a useless fight? Poor William. He wondered what happened to him. Did the police take him? Did he survive? Exhausted, he closed his eyes and fell asleep in his dusty, sweaty clothes. He overslept and missed a day of work. When he returned to the docks the following day his boss was irate and almost fired him, but Brodie begged him for another chance. He was fortunate, the boss said, but if it happened again, he'd be out of a job. All the more reason to get out of this mess with the paras.

A week later the men and boys sat around once again waiting for Joe Campbell to show up.

"Hey, Brodie, we hear ya got some American relations who come ta Norn Iron?" Redhead asked.

"I do." Brodie felt uncomfortable. He sighed. Everyone knew everything in Ireland.

"I'll bet she's a bonny lass," Cigarette-lad said. Whistles echoed throughout the room.

"Cut it out, guys."

"What's this American woman like?" Paul asked.

"She's nice," Brodie answered succinctly.

"What foot does she dig with?"

"She's a Christian, Paul."

"So, Protestant?"

"More Protestant than Catholic, I guess, but not really like the Protestants here." The young men clapped.

"Is she like the Protestant girls here who are so perfect?" Paul asked.

"Does her mummy choose her clothes and comb her hair?" Redhead said. The others laughed.

"Is she a prude?" Paul asked. More laughter.

Brodie gave Paul a dirty look. "Stop actin' the goat, guys. She's just a normal lass, only with a Yankee accent and a bit more moxie than our lassies here."

"Is there violence on the streets in America?" Cigarette-lad asked.

"I don't know."

"Do they celebrate St. Paddy's Day over there?" A voice from across the room broke into the conversation and a tall, skinny fellow stood up.

"I don't know."

"Do the Protestants and Catholics get along over there?" the tall, skinny one said.

"Better than here. Now knock it off guys."

"Did ya hear about William gettin' lifted?" Redhead said.

"What?"

"Yeah, he got wounded in that last skirmish," Cigarette-lad said. "He was dragged inta a civilian home and the gardai came and took him. They've detained him fer questionin'."

Paul and Brodie looked at each other.

"I hope he doesn't spill the beans on our place."

"He won't," Paul said.

"He'll keep his mouth shut," Brodie said.

"How do ya know?" a voice from the corner of the room asked.

"He's me broder," Paul said firmly. "That's how I know."

"Joe is takin' long," Brodie said. "Where is he?"

Just then someone stepped into the room and announced, "Joe's likely on the run. Did ya hear about the Fenian he shot last night?"

"What?" A few of the younger men's heads popped up in surprise.

Some of the men nodded.

"The lass were sleepin' with a Protestant friend of Joe's. Joe was half langered, spent the evenin' at the pub, he did, and couldn't accept that his friend was with a Catholic girl. He walked right inta his friend's house and shot her dead in her sleep."

There was a rumble amidst the men and boys. Cold-blooded murder wasn't in the makeup of most of them. Sure, they'd fired at the enemy with the intention to kill but that was different. That was war. But killing a young woman in her sleep was on a totally different level of murder. It was against their code and it created fear and disdain for the man whom they served. If Joe could shoot a lass in her sleep, he'd surely not hesitate to put a bullet in one of them. Of course, some of them already knew that. They remembered their friend Michael and how Joe shot him for trying to leave the paras. The newer lads had heard the story from Joe himself but, well, actually witnessing it was another thing entirely.

This latest murder was the last straw and Brodie had had enough. Joe was getting out of control. Brodie needed to get out of this gang and he would do whatever it took before he was implicated or associated with the likes of Joe Campbell anymore. He didn't know how he'd make the separation but he decided he'd figure it out as he went. That was his usual mode of operation anyway. He stood up and started to walk out.

"Hey, Brodie, where ya goin'?" Paul followed him.

"Home. I'm not waitin' any longer fer Joe. He's a stook."

"But ya can't go!" Paul grabbed his arm. "This is what we do!"

Brodie pulled away. "Yer wrong. It's not what *we* do anymore, ya know? We don't go murderin' lassies in their sleep! I'm out!"

"Yer jokin' me! What else is there?" Paul jumped in front of him and tried to stop him.

"Are ya daft?" Brodie pushed his friend out of his way. "Have ya nothin' else fer doin'?"

"Brodie, just stop and listen ta me. We joined up ta fight fer what everyone in this country wants—freedom from British oppression, ta have our own country and not be manipulated by a government outside of us! We're in this fer a noble cause and if it takes a few innocents ta suffer fer the cause, then so be it!"

"Do ya hear yerself there, Paul? Me da and ma were some of those innocents who suffered in this war and I ain't gonna be part of other innocents who suffer in this fightin' fer the cause. So don't go around wastin' me time and shoe leather with that nonsense!" Brodie turned on his friend and walked off in a huff.

CHAPTER 10

"Da, I know it's not safe, but I cannae give up on this project," Eoin said over the phone. "We're almost done with the house. If I leave it now, others might break in and ruin all our work, not ta mention all the spring rain that will come and soak the interior. I have ta get a roof up."

"But ya got ta think about yer wee bairn comin' soon, lad. And won't he have ta be born in hospital where danger is imminent. Ferget the house!"

"I cannae."

"Then send Tonya back ta the States. Let her have the babe here in Wisconsin. She can return when the country calms down."

"Let her go by herself? Nay! What are ya, short two planks? She can't travel alone, it's not safe. She'd be too vulnerable alone. Do ya not remember the Heathrow Airport bombin' a few years ago?"

"We'll figure somethin' out, surely," Ian said.

"Aye, Da. I do understand yer concerns."

Ian hung up the phone and slumped down on the couch. Phyllis sat down by his side.

"What's going on, dear? Why are you so troubled? Have you heard more bad news?"

"The last two months the violence has escalated in Norn Iron and now there's a vigilante group called D-A-A-D."

"What does that stand for?"

"Direct Action Against Drugs. It's a front name used by the Provisional IRA ta justify killin' loyalists."

"Heavenly days." Phyllis sighed. "I'm so sorry." She put her hand on Ian's arm. He wrapped it around her and pulled her closer.

"The ceasefire has already ended. A bomb exploded at London's Canary Wharf district. Two men were killed and there were a lot of damages reported." He rested his chin on Phyllis's head and they cuddled together as they watched the flames dance in the fireplace.

They both knew that Tonya and Eoin were in a precariously dangerous place. But they were adults and it wasn't Ian or Phyllis's place to *make* them return to the US.

"'Even in darkness light dawns for the upright, for the gracious and compassionate and righteous man...'" Phyllis began the 112th Psalm and Ian continued where she left off.

"'He will have no fear of bad news; his heart is steadfast trusting in the Lord. His heart is secure, he will have no fear; in the end he will look in triumph on his foes...'"

***

The cousins came down to Laurelvale, County Armagh, to eat dinner at Eoin and Tonya's home. Margaret and George came over to help feed the group. Eoin explained their dilemma.

"Tonnie, do ya want ta go back ta yer home ta have this child?" Callum asked as he put a Scottish pie on his plate.

"I don't know. I'm so torn," Tonya said. "I'd like to be nearer my folks and my old friends and be where it's safer, yes, but I don't want to leave Eoin, either. I want him to be by my side when the baby is born, but I understand that he needs to stay here and finish the house."

"Poor lass." Margaret clicked her tongue as she scooped Cullen skink into Tonya's bowl. "I wehsh ya could be wehth yer folks back home."

"Me too," Tonya said. "What's in this soup? It smells delicious."

"Tatties, onions, and smoked haddock," Margaret said.

"What's stoppin' ya from goin'?" Maisie said as she lifted her spoon to her mouth, eager to taste the soup.

"She can't travel by herself like this, eejit," Brodie said. "Even I know that."

"I'd go with ya if I could," Maisie said. "Mmmm. Margaret, this soup is brilliant!"

"Would you, Maisie?" Tonya lit up. She sipped the soup from her spoon. "Oh, my word, Margaret. Maisie's right. This is excellent." Margaret nodded at the young women and smiled with satisfaction as she continued round the table filling bowls.

"I'd go in a heartbeat, Tonnie. But I can't afford such a trip. And there's Erin. I couldna leave her."

George looked at Margaret. Margaret nodded.

"Sae." George's voice rose above everyone else's. "I'd layke tae say somethehn." Everyone stopped talking and looked at George. "Me Margaret and I were talkehn aboot thehs very thehng. We saved a beht fer the wee bairn's provisions but thehs ehs more important."

"What do you mean?" Tonya asked.

"What are ya sayin'?" Eoin put his pie down.

"We want tae help pay for the lassies tae gae tae America. Ehf others can contribute, I thehnk we'd have enough."

"The lassies, plural?"

"Aye, Tonya, Maisie, *and* Erin."

"I can contribute a wee bit," Brodie said.

"Nay, cousin, we couldn't ask ya ta help."

"It's just me I'm supportin'."

"We can, too," Callum said after getting a nod from Molly.

"Callum, we can' let ya do that. Ye got a family ta support."

"Molly has been gettin' a bit o' spondolicks fer some extra work she did fer the neighbors."

"Spondolicks? What's that?" Tonya looked puzzled.

"Cash," Eoin said as he reached for Tonya's hand. "We might be able ta afford it with all the help."

"Do ya mean—" Maisie's eyes widened. "I'd be goin' ta America? Erin and meself?"

"We can't let you all do this," Tonya said. "Maybe my folks would pay for us."

"Let yer famehly help from both saydes." George smiled.

"I just can't believe it." Tonya's throat tightened. "This would be an answer to my prayers!"

"Maisie, ya'd better be gettin' started quickly on yer passport and visa!" Callum said.

Eoin shook his head. "I think that would be fantastic. Thank ya, me dear, sweet, and generous family and friends! I'll get Collins and me uncle, Detective Bobby Hanford, ta pull some strings!"

Later that evening, after everyone said their goodbyes and left, Tonya and Eoin sat by the cozy fire. The smell of burning peat permeated the air while a singly lit lamp sent an orange glow across the room.

"It was good ta have everyone here."

"Yes, and to have Margaret's good cooking! Maisie is so excited to travel." Tonya leaned into her husband. "I have so many mixed emotions right now."

"Aye. Me as well." Eoin put his arm around her.

"I don't want to leave you here." Tonya sighed. "I wish you could come with me, too."

"I wish I could go, but if we're goin' ta make this our home, I need ta stay, ya know?"

"I do know."

"And yer okay with it, are ye?"

"Yes. As long as I can come back as soon as possible. As it is, the baby won't see his daddy—you'll miss the birth—"

"But my wife and child will be in a safe place and that's more important ta me right now. We'll have plenty of years tagether ta bond."

Tonya snuggled in closer. "I love you—more now than ever. You're such a part of me and I hate to be away from you, Eoin."

"I know how ya feel, lass. I'll miss ya like crazy." Eoin leaned down and kissed the top of her head. "I love you, too."

By the first week of March of '96, Tonya, Maisie, and Erin were boarding a direct flight from Dublin to O'Hare Airport in Chicago.

Erin was happy to take the window seat of the plane. Maisie sat beside her and Tonya took the aisle seat to have easy access to the tiny airplane bathroom. Even then, she wondered how her pregnant self would fit in the closet-like bathroom space, but she would certainly make do when the urge was there!

All passengers were seated, the stewardesses gave their safety instructions, the rumble of the engines vibrated the cabin, and then the plane began to move down the tarmac.

"Ooo," Erin said as she looked wide-eyed at her ma. Maisie and Tonya smiled.

"Are we goin' ta fly o'er the ocean soon?" Erin asked.

"We are that," Maisie answered, her eyes as wide as her daughter's. The plane began to move faster and then tilted upwards slightly. "Here we go, lassie! Up, up in the air on a new adventure, so we are!"

"Your maiden voyage!" Tonya said. "You two are brave souls!"

Erin looked through the window. "Ma, I can see the ocean! Tonnie, sure and I can see the ocean!"

"That's the Atlantic, my sweet lassie." Maisie turned to Tonya. "What a craic she is, that one!" The new travelers' heads stayed turned toward the window until the view of the ocean became obscured by clouds.

Tonya laughed. "Not everyone adjusts to flying as well as you two."

"Am I pullin' the wool over yer eyes that brilliantly?" Maisie said.

"Ah," Tonya said, "you're being brave for your daughter's sake, is that it?"

"Aye."

After an hour passed, Erin drifted off to sleep.

"So, I can talk more now that the wee'un's asleep."

"About?"

"About bein' brave. This flyin' thing has had me up at nights."

"Oh, no! I'm sorry. I couldn't tell."

"I've learned how ta hide me fears."

"I suppose."

"I was put in a Catholic orphanage as a wee lass. I had a friend there, her name was Bernice, who helped me learn ta be brave, so she did. She was very kind ta me even though she knew I was Protestant. She understood it was goin' ta be hard on me amongst so many Catholic girls and the nuns. Of course, everyone—Catholic or Protestant—suffered from the wrath of the nuns. Some of the crueler nuns carried a cane and if ya weren't gettin' yer spellin' right, or if ya were daydreamin', they might come up behind ya and whack yer ear or yer knuckles. Sure an' I got caned a few times. There was one nun who thought that, because me hair was red, I was possessed! She'd grab me arm and twist it around me back and say, 'Ya got the devil in ya, so ya do!'"

"Oh, my goodness." Tonya clicked her tongue.

"I tried ta hide me religion, but some of the girls—especially the older ones—could tell I was Protestant and didn't they give me a hard time of it."

"How did they know? Did you tell them?"

"Are ya daft? Of course not! In our country we learned early ta say nothin' about our religion ta protect ourselves. But there were some minor differences between me and the others. Typically, Protestant girls are a bit more pampered by their mums with what they wear, how their hair is done, and so on. I was used ta me ma helpin' me dress and helpin' me with me hair, so I was. My first few weeks at the orphanage I fumbled with me hair. I made the mistake o' askin' a nun ta help me pick out me clothes. The nun just laughed at me and walked away. The girls that heard the exchange pointed and giggled. See, most Catholic girls took care of themselves, albeit a bit sloppy, but they did it themselves and didn't care."

Suddenly, Tonya pushed up from her seat. "Hold that thought. I'll be right back. Gotta go to the bathroom!"

"There is no *bath* room on this plane! There's only a toilet." Maisie laughed.

Tonya had no time for teasing about an American euphemism so she ignored Maisie and lumbered down the aisle, excusing herself along the way for bumping clumsily into people in the aisle seats. When she returned she urged Maisie to continue telling her story. She was excited to have Maisie, who was usually very quiet about her past, suddenly open up about it. She found it all interesting and strange.

"So, several of the girls knew I wasn't from a Catholic home," Maisie started.

"Were they mean to you?"

"Some were. They'd call me Proddy. That's slang fer Protestant. They'd trip me as I walked past them, pull me hair, steal the clothes and things given me by the charities. There was a wee stuffed rabbit in the package o' things I got one time and I latched onta it. It was—" Maisie's voice caught. "It was just like a rabbit that I had back home that most likely got burnt up in the fire. His name was Jack. Like Jack rabbit, ya know?" Tonya smiled.

"One day, Jack—I named the new rabbit Jack—he went missin'. I panicked. Then I saw him in the hands of one of the bigger girls. I asked her ta give it back, but she refused and started ta swing it by its ears. I grabbed at Jack and that's when the head ripped off. The girl threw his head on the ground while the others laughed. Sure and I fell ta the ground weepin', holdin' the body and the head ta my chest."

Tonya put her hand on her heart. "Aw, I can't bear it, Maisie."

"Well, Bernice sat me in a chair, pulled out a little sewin' box and sat in the chair next ta mine."

"Oh, is this going to have a happy ending? I hope so!"

"Bernice pried Jack's head and body out of me clutches, pushed in his stuffin', and pinned his pieces tagether with straight pins. Then, she began ta talk ta me about how brave I was ta rescue Jack. I said I didn't think I was bein' very brave, but she said I showed courage even if I didn't feel like it. She said I were a good protector. She continued talkin' as I watched her carefully stitch up Jack. I think I grew stronger that day."

"You were brave to approach that girl to get your rabbit back, knowing you were outnumbered."

"Bernice encouraged me ta be even braver from that day on. God knew I'd need it in the days ta come. She taught me ta not fear others."

"Did she know you'd been through horrible things already?"

"Tonnie, every girl there had been through horrible things. We were all orphans and children of the Troubles."

Tonya put her hand on Maisie's. "I just can't imagine."

"Don't try ta. I don' want yer sympathy. What I want is ta see yer country fer meself."

"Aww, Maisie, you're going to see it pretty soon!"

"Speakin' of yer homeland. All yer friends ended up married and livin' happily ever after, did they?"

"Well, not completely, Maisie. Carrie and Keith Wagner lost their first baby—almost full term. That was so sad. Penny and Scott Brannen had a very rough start in life. Penny's dad fought in the Vietnam War and was never the same after that. Scott came from a rough home where the parents were drunk most of the time. And then, there's Eddy Wagner. Well, I told you about his heartbreak with Haley. Then, he met someone in the army—but apparently, that didn't work out either."

"Why? Is he some kind of eejit?"

"No!" Tonya reacted so quickly she startled Maisie and Erin stirred. "Sorry. Eddy is anything but an idiot. He's a great guy—"

"Just can't get a lass!" Maisie smirked.

"The funny thing is, we all had crushes on him growing up. He's always been so handsome—kind of a pretty-boy face, you know, and with blond hair—he had bangs in the '70s that used to fall in his eyes and with a shake of his head he'd make it all bounce back. We used to watch him—" Tonya sighed dreamily for effect and Maisie chuckled. "We girls would just watch him with starry eyes. But most of all, he was so kind. I just don't get why he doesn't have a girlfriend. But now, he's pretty dedicated and content to be a bachelor."

"Yeah, I get that. People can change yer ideas of wedded bliss."

"Michael?" Tonya knew she was taking a chance saying his name.

"Aye." Something in Maisie's expression showed a minute of hurt and then a quick recovery. "I'm happy where I'm at takin' care of this bonny lassie." Maisie caressed the head of her sleeping daughter. Tonya wished Maisie would talk more of her husband but she caught on quickly that there were things Maisie avoided. Two things in particular: her life with Michael and the murders of her parents and husband. And who could blame her?

Tonya didn't ask anymore questions, but talked on and on about her friends back home.

Several hours later they landed in Chicago.

CHAPTER 11

Gareth couldn't get to the airport soon enough. Haley kept reminding him to slow down on the seemingly endless trip on I-94 East and then on to I-294 South. When they finally arrived, it took forever to find a parking place and get into the airport. Soon he and Haley found the gate where the travelers would be deboarding.

Gareth was beyond excited to reunite with his cousin. The last time he saw Maisie was right before he closed his eyes to count while she and her brothers hid in the barn. He had just made up another nickname to bother her—what was it?—seems it was the name of some bird that made funny noises. She had stuck her tongue out at him and it made him laugh. He had needed some laughs back then. She was so feisty for such a wee girl and it delighted him. Getting to know Haley and her feisty spirit when he came to Wisconsin had brought him a slice of comfort. Here was another girl to taunt. He just couldn't help himself.

"Gareth!" He heard a shout over the heads of the people carting their luggage, trying to move through the crowds. A head of reddish-brown, wavy hair popped up and then disappeared. Then he saw it again.

"Maisie?" he yelled back in disbelief.

"Gareth?" Maisie saw a head of dark curls just like her da's and Brodie's! Could it be? As she drew closer she saw him smile and she knew right away it was him. "Gareth!" She forgot herself, abandoned the luggage with Tonya, and came running, dragging her little girl along with her. Gareth wrapped his cousin up in his arms and wept. Haley hurried over to Tonya, where they had their own sweet reunion and helped collect the luggage.

"I thought I'd never see you again!" Maisie cried.

"I didn't think I'd ever see you again either," Gareth said.

Maisie pulled back, tears streaming down her cheeks. "Ya sound like a Yank, so ya do."

"That's old news." Gareth laughed and then squatted down to connect with the little eyes that looked up at him, watching him curiously. "And you must be Erin."

"So I am." Erin smiled. "Are ya me 'merican cousin?"

"So I am! Can I have a hug?" he asked and she went into his arms willingly. Haley came up beside Gareth and he introduced her to Maisie.

"I already know all about ya." Maisie smiled. "Yer good friend, Tonnie, here has told me all about ya on that very long flight we took!"

"I'm pleased to finally meet you! And I hope Tonya told you all the good stuff! We did some pretty crazy things in our younger days!"

There was an abundance of chatter on the trip home and when they pulled into the homestead Maisie's eyes grew big. It was just as she had imagined. The very traditional Americana, white-sided, two-story farmhouse with a big front porch that had a white railing, an enormous red barn to the left, a chicken coop just past the barn, big oak trees and a large pine in front, vast wide-open fields behind the property, and groups of trees in the distance. Then she saw a middle-aged man step off the porch. There was something about his gait that reminded her of her own father. It had to be her uncle! The closer he got the more the likeness was unmistakable. Maisie's breath caught. She stepped out of the car. "Uncle Ian?"

"Maisie, lass!" Ian's eyes were brimming with tears as he hurried to meet everyone out on the driveway, his focus on his lost niece.

"Ya remind me of Da—so much—I wasn't expectin' it," she said, fighting back tears.

Phyllis came out with three grandchildren running around her and one in her arms.

"An' who is this wee one lookin' like her nana with her pa's hair?" Ian said.

"Erin. I named her after Ma," Maisie said, her words strained.

"Erin? Such a beautiful lassie. 'The new generation is always an improvement on the old stock!'" Ian knelt down to greet her.

"Sure an' there's a lot of folk here," Erin said boldly and everyone laughed. She pulled back and stood behind her mother.

Ian stood up to look at Tonya. "Ah, there she is, me bonny daughter, home again! How we missed ya here!" He hugged her carefully.

"I missed you all, too. This whole reunion thing is getting me quite emotional!" Tonya said, hugging Ian back. He had become like a second father to her and she had missed him as much as her own dad.

"Erin, how old are you?" Gareth asked, noticing how his girls were eyeing her.

"Almost seven, so I am."

"Well," Haley said to her, "you'll have fun playing with our girls who are around your age!"

"These are your second cousins," Gareth said. "This is Annie—"

"Ya named her after Auntie Anna?" Maisie asked.

"Aye, but we just got in the habit of calling her Annie."

"Sure and we have our ma's namesakes meetin' each other! How old is Annie?"

"She's seven. And this is Fiahd who's five, Bobby, three—"

"And this is Liam, the baby," Phyllis said, as she held the wiggly child forward. Erin looked from child to child, examining them all.

"Yer me Auntie Phyllis, so ya are." Maisie came forward and gave her and the baby a hug. "It's grand ta meet ya."

"I'm so happy to meet you, too, Maisie," Phyllis said as Liam tried to go to Maisie. Everyone chuckled as Maisie took him in her arms.

"Would you like to see our doggies and horsies in the barn?" Annie held her hand out to Erin. The Irish cousin looked up at her ma. Maisie nodded. Erin carefully put her hand in Annie's. Fiahd boldly took her other hand and the three girls skipped off to the barn with Bobby trailing after them.

"Well," Phyllis said, "you girls must be exhausted after such a long flight. I've got the two bedrooms upstairs made up just for you."

"Oh, thank you! I think jet lag is settling in early—and this baby is kicking me all over inside. He must have four arms and four legs!"

"You look like you're ready to go, honey. Are you sure you're not due sooner?" Phyllis said.

"Pretty sure. But I'd be more than happy to deliver now. Then maybe I could get some rest." Phyllis, Haley, and Maisie all looked at each other and laughed. "What's so funny, ladies?" Tonya said.

"That you think you're going to get more rest *after* the baby is born!" Haley said as they walked up to the big house. "By the way, I'll take you to your old doctor tomorrow. It'll be nice to catch up on news during the drive there. Maisie, you should come along, too."

"I best stay here with Erin, so I should."

"Oh, she'll be fine," Phyllis said. "She'll be off playing with her cousins and I'll keep an eye on them all."

"Are ya sure ya can handle her?"

"Of course! What's one more?" Phyllis smiled.

The following morning Haley, Maisie, and Tonya piled into the car. As they started to pull out, Gareth ran out of the barn to stop them. Ed followed, combing hay out of his hair.

"Haley!" Gareth yelled.

Haley stopped and put the car back in park. "What's going on?"

Gareth ran around to the driver's side and pulled cash out of his pocket. "I forgot to give you this. Take the ladies out for lunch."

"Oh, thank you, honey, you're so thoughtful."

Tonya waved out the window. "Hi, Eddy!"

"Tonya! Good to see you again! Wow! You've gotten big!"

"Gee, thanks."

"You know what I mean."

"Ed," Gareth said, "this is my long-lost cousin, Maisie. Maisie, this is our good friend, Ed Wagner."

Maisie leaned forward, looked out the window, and waved politely. Ed was caught off guard by the auburn sheen of her hair that fell in waves around her petite shoulders and the color of her eyes, like the green fields of summer. He smiled back and waved. "Nice to meet you, Maisie."

"Same ta ya," Maisie said, lifting her hand in a quick wave.

"We'll talk more later, Eddy," Haley said. "We've got an appointment to get to!"

The girls pulled out of the driveway and the men turned back toward the barn. "That's so awesome you're meeting up with your long-lost cousin," Ed said.

"It's a miracle. I never dreamed I'd see any of them again!"

"Except for the long auburn hair, Maisie looks like she belongs to your MacCauley clan."

"Good-looking, you mean."

"Much better looking than *you,* my friend."

"Well, I'll have to agree with that."

Maisie looked out the car window at the scenery outside. Houses grew closer together as they approached town. Before they came into town they passed by the Christian college that the Wagners and Carrie had attended in a beautiful setting up on a hill. Tonya explained the history—once a monastery to train Catholic monks, it was sold off to a Baptist pastor and became a Baptist college and high school.

"The Catholic priest sold it ta Baptists?" Maisie asked. "I have a hard time believin' that!"

"Yes, I know," Haley said. "Gareth couldn't comprehend it when he first came here either. It's a lot different here, Maisie, than what you have seen in Northern Ireland."

"I knew that it were different before I came, but seeing it fer meself, well, it's somethin' ta get used ta, so it is."

When they drove into downtown Watertown, Maisie was amazed to see there were no graffiti, charred cars or smouldering buildings, no blockades, and no soldiers at checkpoints with guns. It was a charming old town with ancient brick facades as storefronts, and people walked along the street contentedly—their only worries concerning what shoes they might buy, or what present they might find for a friend. Just like a storybook town. As they passed Mullen's Dairy, Tonya yelled out.

"Oooh! We need to go there after my appointment! I can taste their chocolate milkshake already!"

"Already in the plans!" Haley said. "Eddy said you'd be craving Mullen's!"

"He was so right!" Tonya said. "Dear, sweet Eddy."

"Everyone seems ta think the world of 'im!" Maisie said.

"Who, Eddy?"

"Aye."

"Well, was I right? Didn't you think he was handsome?"

"Of course. I'm not blind. Sure and he's like that American fashion doll everybody goes crazy over, what's his name? Ya know—the Barbie doll friend?"

Haley guffawed. "Barbie's boyfriend, Ken?"

Tonya laughed with her "I think she means *Malibu* Ken! Yeah, that's our Eddy, tanned and bleach-blond, especially after he's been working out in the fields all summer."

"We've never heard that comparison before, but it fits!" Haley said.

"And me cousin's grown inta quite the good-lookin' Irishman."

"I'll agree with you on that! And, along with all that handsomeness, he's such a good man and a warrior for any good cause. He's my hero, a wonderful daddy and a great example to our—"

"Okay, now it's my turn," Tonya interrupted. "Eoin is—"

The three young women burst out laughing.

It was nice, this frivolity and innocent talk about nothing too important, nothing serious, and nothing about politics, bombings—just pleasantries and men. Maisie felt her breathing slow and grow deeper as the beautiful expanse of farmland, dotted here and there with a pop of a red barn and a farm house or a silo beside it, passed quickly before her, putting her in a wonderful, calm trance.

A few days later, Maisie and Erin sat with Phyllis and Ian eating an interesting breakfast of toast covered with egg and a cheese sauce that Alma had sent over with Ed.

"It's called 'rarebit,'" Phyllis explained. "Ed's mother likes to send over some of her Southern dishes on occasion. She appreciates how much I've fed her boys over the years."

"So, the Wagner family is from the South? Eddy doesn't sound like it," Maisie said.

"No, just Alma. Fred was born and raised in Wisconsin and so were the children," Phyllis explained.

"Between Alma and Phyllis here, I'm puttin' on the pounds!" Ian sat as he patted his gut.

"Uncle Ian, sure an' yer not a wee bit fat," Erin said and the others laughed.

"Yer nana was a great cook, too," Ian said. "She could do up an Ulster fry like nobody."

Maisie's eyes grew wide and she put her fork down. "I forgot about that!"

"What's an Ulster fry?" Phyllis asked.

"It's sausages, bacon, eggs, tomatoes, black pudding—you call it blood sausage here—griddle-baked soda farls—that's soda bread cut in quarters— and potato bread that's fried until crispy on the outside and fluffy on the inside," Ian said.

"Why haven't you ever made it here?" Phyllis said.

"It's too much work fer a man," Ian said and the ladies laughed.

Later, Maisie took a stroll about the yard. She stopped at the chicken coop and watched the hens scratch at the ground. A rooster came up close to her and looked like he was challenging her so she backed away, smirking at the proud bird. Ricky and Lucy came bounding up to her and she reached down to pet each one before they bounded off, playing together as they ran. It made her smile. She walked down to the fields and stopped to breathe in the wide-open space, pausing to watch the trees in the distance, their branches swaying together as white clouds passed along a baby-blue sky. Maisie was falling in love with the place quickly. As she walked toward the house she heard boisterous laughing in the barn so she headed in that direction to see what was going on. She asked the men, still doubled over and red-faced, what they were laughing about. Gareth said, "Ya had to be here to see it!"

"Buck kept stealing Gareth's cap while he was getting brushed!" Ed smiled.

"Gareth kept scoldin' him," Ian explained, "and when Ed and I started laughin', Buck lifted his muzzle and made a sound like he was laughin' too." The men burst into hysterics again at the memory. Maisie smiled. Just seeing her uncle and her cousin so happy in this place warmed her heart.

She wandered around and read the plaques on the walls of the barn that gave tribute to Phyllis's deceased husband, Robert, with his quotes and his favorite verses. Ian came up behind her.

"'Tis a grand memorial ta Haley's da, isn't it?"

"Very much so. He seems like he were a fantastic man."

"From what I've heard, he was."

"I love this one that says, 'Happy is the man…'"

"He was a content and grateful fellow." Ian watched Maisie as she looked around some more. "Ya seem a bit melancholy, lass."

"I wish I had more memories of me ma and da. I loved yer comment about ma and her Ulster fry this mornin' but it made me realize I don't have that many memories of them."

"Ya were a wee lass when ya lost 'em."

"That I was."

"Sure an' I'll do some thinkin' on the past and maybe tonight we can sit together fer a bit and I'll give ya some memories."

"Thanks, Uncle Ian. That would be fantastic." Maisie kissed him on the cheek and went out of the barn.

After she left, Gareth and Ed asked him what their conversation was about.

"The poor lassie hasn't much of a memory of her folks and it pains her."

"That's really sad," Ed said and Gareth agreed.

"I told her I'd sit with her tonight and give her some memories."

"I'd like to be a part of that, Da."

"I think we all would, if that would be okay?" Ed said. Ian looked touched. He nodded and walked away, deep in thought about the years he spent growing up with his brother Sean. He thought about how both got married and had children. It felt good to think about passing family memories on and grand to have the next generation care about them.

CHAPTER 12

Friday evening turned cool for late spring so Ian started a fire in the fireplace of the big house. After dinner, the family sat around ready to hear Ian tell stories of his past with his brother in Northern Ireland. Bobby Hanford found himself fortunate to have dropped in on this very night that Ian would be telling stories that would include his sister.

Ed felt special to be with this brood of MacCauleys. As Ian began to talk, Ed looked around at everyone and realized these people had become a second family to him. Haley and Gareth were like siblings, of course. That had been established a long time ago. And their children were as comfortable with him as his own nephew. Mrs. B., now Mrs. Mac, had been a second mom to him ever since he could remember. He was just as sad as the family when Mr. B. passed away and just as excited as everyone when Mrs. B. and Mr. Mac came together in marriage. What a story!

And now, he looked over at Maisie and Erin. He wanted to get to know them better, but Maisie seemed a bit standoffish. He'd give it time. She put on a good front with her pleasing smile, but her resting face had a look of sadness and intensity. He wasn't too surprised. She grew up in and had been living in Northern Ireland a lot longer than Gareth and Eoin, so perhaps this was the look of a person who'd spent their whole life watching the horrible things of the Troubles. And what about her cute little child? Every time Erin talked in her high-pitched Irish accent Ed's ears perked up.

"Me broder and I were married about the same time," Ian said. "Me folks needed us ta get out on our own and start our own lives, ya know? Our ma and da had lived through the Easter Risin', albeit they were far away from the fight, it bein' in Dublin. That was the beginning of our country's separation from the Republic of Ireland. Me broder Sean went ta school with Erin—they were childhood sweethearts."

"Ach! I didn't know that!" Maisie said, smiling.

"How romantic!" Haley said to Maisie and she nodded.

"I met Anna in London. She was a nosy and determined journalist," Ian said as he glanced at Bobby, who nodded immediately. Everyone laughed.

"Sean and I found these old cottages together. We loved that we'd each own several acres, close by but separatin' our homes with the vast property between with trees and rollin' hills. Erin and Sean were married first and moved inta their home. Then, when Anna came back from America we were married and moved in. And didn't Anna and Erin get along fantastic! Those two became close like sisters." Ian stopped to take a sip of coffee from his mug while staring into the fire. "They were there for each other with every baby—first Eoin, then Callum, Gareth, Brodie, and then our sweet little Maisie." He turned to Maisie. "Ya know that quote that is in the barn from Robert? Well, yer da felt the same fer such a bonny wee'un as yerself." Maisie's eyes teared up. Ian couldn't leave the story hanging in sadness. "We used ta have brilliant picnics and loved to drive over to Craigavon Lough or Lough Neagh and take long walks while you kids ran around playin'."

"I remember that!" Gareth said.

"I do, too!" Maisie said.

"Isn't that where Brodie fell in horse manure one time?" Gareth asked.

"Didn't he fall in the lake, too?" Maisie asked.

"Both. Yer ma, Erin, wasn't a wee bit happy with him. He seemed to find the biggest messes wherever he went," Ian said, and everyone laughed.

The storytelling and revival of memories continued and no one grew tired of them. Maisie had not felt so connected to her folks like this since before they died. She shed many tears as Ian talked on, but they were all cathartic, and in the end, his memories left her with joy in her heart.

Ed noticed and it made him smile.

The following night, the friends gathered at Pizza Hut. The talk was never ending until it was time to order and figure out how many pizzas to get and with what ingredients. After the waitress patiently got their big order, the talking recommenced. At one point the subject of what kind of schooling is best came up when the talk centered around the new generation.

"Remember when we were in grade school and Keith and Haley used to fight about their schools?" Penny said and the others, except for Maisie, nodded and laughed.

"I thought yer families were both Protestant," Maisie said.

"We were. We are," Ed answered.

"Then why the different schools?" Maisie asked.

"You see, we had the public schools here that were paid for by the government. There were private schools around back then—"

"Back then, Eddy? Like we're all so old!" Penny teased.

"Right, well, you know what I mean," Ed said. "There were private schools that were Catholic but, being Baptists, we didn't go to those. So, eventually, Protestant—and, in our case, Baptist—schools started up. But it cost money to go there and not everyone could afford them. My family went to the private schools, but Haley and all her friends didn't—that is, until Carrie and Keith got together. Carrie went to our school in ninth grade. But that's another story. Back in grade school, so many times we saw skinny little Haley, nose to nose with my stocky brother out by the Becketts' old barn, or standing in the foyer at church, or out on Farmer's Market Day, yelling at each other, arguing about their schools."

"And now, there's homeschooling to add to the argument about what is best. Momma says, in the end, it's the children and the parents working together that matters," Haley said.

"I was quite the private school snob at the time," Keith said. "I'm embarrassed to admit it now. I needed to be better than Haley at something."

"Why did you, Keith?" Gareth asked.

"I'm not sure, except that I wanted her attention. She was our only neighbor around our age but she only wanted to be with Ed."

The girls all broke out with "awws."

"I'm sorry, Keith," Haley said. "It's just that, well, it was Eddy."

"You weren't the only one vying for her attention, Keith. Ed was like royalty in the girls' eyes," Gareth teased. *"Prince Edward!"*

"Oh, man." Haley laughed. "Gareth had all kinds of names for Eddy."

"Edward the Great!" Gareth said. Ed stood up and took a kingly bow. Everyone clapped and cheered. The other patrons at the restaurant looked over at their table. Maisie smiled widely. She looked up and saw Ed smiling down at her. She grinned shyly and looked down at the table.

And Carrie was the only one who noticed it and thought about it later.

CHAPTER 13

It was a surprise to everyone when Tonya went into labor a few weeks after arriving in Wisconsin. She was anxious to talk to Eoin on the phone after the delivery, and, when she finally gained permission from the hospital to make the long distance call, she was ecstatic.

"Eoin?"

"Tonnie, is thatchyou?"

"Yes, yes—" Her throat closed up. It was so good to hear his voice.

"Tonnie, what's wrong, me love? Are ya okay? Is the pregnancy goin' well fer ya?"

Tonya swallowed and gained her composure. "Everything's fine, really fine."

"Then what's wrong?"

"Nothing—just overwhelmed and emotional, and then, hearing your voice—I wish you were here to be with me and your sweet boys."

"Hold yer hour!" There was a long pause at the other end. "What do ya mean—boys?! Did ya say boys? What boys are ya talkin' about?"

"*Our* boys, Eoin." Tonya chuckled slightly. "We have twin boys, honey."

Another long pause.

"Did you hear me, Eoin?"

"Aye." He paused. "Ya said we have two wee laddies—but—how do ya know that?"

"Well, they're right here in my room in the hospital and I'm lookin' at them as we speak."

"Ya had the baby—I mean ya had two babies? An' they're already born? Two of them? Twins?"

"Yes. I went into labor early."

"Oh, wow. I need ta sit down." Eoin pulled up a chair, feeling a bit woozy. He looked around at the small cottage and tried to imagine two little boys running around in this place with two high chairs, two cribs, and lots of toys. The urgency to get their home built suddenly grew greater.

"And, honey, well, I'm not going to name them by myself. We—you and I need to come up with two boy names. They won't let me leave the hospital without naming them."

It grew quiet over the phone for a while as they both thought it through, talking here and there.

"We had some ideas but now we need two boy's names—maybe from each side? And I'd like them to sound good together."

"What was the name of yer grandda that ya always talk about?" Eoin said.

"Samuel."

"I like that name. We could call one of them Samuel—Sammy."

"I'd love that. What about a name from your side, Eoin?"

Eoin thought for a minute. "Ach, me grandda's name was Seamus."

"I love that. Seamus and Sammy. That was easy. Oh good. I'll tell the nurse."

"Tonnie, who do they look like?"

"It's hard to tell right now, but they both have a head of fuzzy, curly hair. It's dark right now, but I guess some babies are born with dark hair that falls out and turns blond. So, who's to know?"

"Are they identical?"

"Yes. I've already taken pictures of them and sent the film off with your brother to develop. He said he'd send them to you. It might take a few weeks."

"I can' wait."

***

Eoin had to remain busy in order to keep his mind off of what he was missing in Wisconsin. He rode with Collins to the home of the O'Donals. The clouds overhead were ominous and threatened rain.

"Sure and yer a proud da with two lads, are ya?" Collins said as he turned onto a small road bordered by dry stone walls.

"That I am." Eoin grinned broadly.

"An' I'll bet my life yer anxious ta see them."

"Tonnie says she'll send photos as soon as she can," Eoin said as they pulled onto the street of the cottage where the O'Donals lived. Collins put the car in park. Suddenly the rain poured down on the car, tap-tapping on the windshield as the wipers swished their hypnotic rhythm.

"Mary O'Donal is now involved in a support group called WAVE: Widows Against Violence Empower," Collins explained, watching the downpour. "It was put together by widows whose husbands were murdered during the Troubles."

"How sad there's a need fer that, eh? But grand they can come tagether."

Eoin and Collins opened their car doors and made a run for the front door of the house.

Mary greeted them.

"Ach, come on in, it would founder ya out there, so it would!" She laughed as she stepped aside to let the men in.

"Sure an' yer face is as bright as the mornin' sun!" Collins said.

"It's a fayne day ta see ya, so it is!" she said, looking much happier than the last time Eoin had been there to visit.

"And same to ya. How're ya cuttin'?" Eoin said.

"Well, just grand since we just finished talkin' ta a constable who came ta our door earlier taday. He had some information on a possibility of where me dear husband Hugh might be buried, so he did."

"Ach! Sure and that's grand!" Collins said as Mary escaped into the kitchen to put the kettle on for tea. Her daughter, Siobhan, greeted the men and pointed at the stuffed chairs for them to sit.

"They're goin' ta let us know when they'll start the search and then they invited us ta come along when it happens!" Siobhan said.

Mary poked her head out from the kitchen door. "We're hopin' ya come wi'!"

"Tabesure, tabesure," Collins said and Eoin agreed.

Three weeks later, Collins and Eoin joined the O'Donal family for the search. They drove in a caravan and crossed the borders down to County Monaghan, Republic of Ireland. There was a bog in Colgagh, Iniskeen, where it had been revealed, through unknown sources, that Hugh O'Donal had been taken by the IRA, murdered, and buried. Collins brought Detective Sean McCain over to Eoin and the family.

"Sure and ya remember Detective McCain, Eoin?"

"Aye," Eoin said, excited to see McCain again. "I'll ne'er forget those days in Waterfoot when ya found me ma!"

"None of us will, lad!" McCain shook his hand. "And youse must be the O'Donal family."

Mary nodded and Siobhan smiled politely.

"Is there a good chance, this lead?" Collins asked.

"As good as any," McCain said. "We got the HRD dogs ready—"

"What does HRD stand for?" Siobhan asked, looking at her ma for assurance that it was okay to ask questions.

"They're human remains detection dogs," Collins explained. "Sometimes we call them cadaver dogs."

"Can they really find a body?"

"Aye, although sometimes it's the body of an animal. But it narrows down the search," McCain said. "We also have ground-penetratin' radar. We'll use both."

"It's a slow process," Eoin said. "It can take days and even weeks."

The onlookers stayed for the first day and then returned home. Mary said she'd keep Eoin posted about the progress whenever she heard anything. It was quiet for weeks and Eoin began to wonder what was going on. Finally, Mary called. The search party had one more place to dig and after that a decision would be made. Collins and Eoin joined the family again at the site.

But the last dig was for naught. After several weeks, McCain called off the search. The information was determined to be bogus and on the last day the O'Donals were sent to their car deeply disappointed. Eoin watched as Siobhan helped her mother to the vehicle, weakened by the excitement and devastation. He looked back at McCain. He looked just as lost. How much more could these people take? How could these murderers get away with so much violence? How could they just live and breathe, and walk the streets like normal citizens in the cities and counties of Northern Ireland? Eoin wanted to do more for this family and for the others who suffered. And he wanted justice for his mother and for his own family.

The following weekend Eoin met his cousins at Fa' Joe's pub in Lurgan. It was one of the only places to eat on the streets of Lurgan that both Catholics and Protestants could come and feel welcome. After ordering fish and chips sprinkled with malt vinegar and salt, the men rehearsed all the details they each remembered from those horrific days back in '74. They hoped to come up with some more clues about the people who attacked their families and burned their homes, but there wasn't much to go on.

"Maisie probably heard or saw more than any of us, but she's erased it from her mind," Callum said.

"I noticed she wouldn't have anythin' ta do with our conversation about it. I can't say that I blame her. It took me a long time ta recount the details of my ordeal at the beach. I only remembered that there was a woman with the men that took Ma and me in a van. All their faces were covered and it was dark."

The waitress brought out their food and they fell silent as she put their plates down on the table.

Brodie waited for her to leave and then said, "I heard from one of the paras about this woman who was assigned a lot of jobs ta *disappear* people. She belonged to a group called the 'Unknowns.' They said she was pretty ruthless—came from a family of tough characters—and she was fierce. What if that were the same woman who kidnapped ya? *And*, a Volkswagen van was used by this same band of people. Maybe we could find out who they were, knowin' these details."

"Are ya daft? They were called *unknown* fer a reason!" Callum said. "Sure and it's because no one really knew who they were?"

"I asked Gareth about the broder who came after him in the US," Eoin said as he put a chunk of batter-fried haddock in his mouth. He took a minute to enjoy the crunchy coating and the tender white fish. "His last name was O'Grady. And, I learned, a cousin of his was in the H-Blocks with me da."

"That's good ta know!" Callum said while he sprinkled a bit more malt vinegar and salt on his chips. "It's a start, at least."

"I've asked the people in my paramilitary group ta keep an ear and an eye out, but nothin' has turned up yet," Brodie said, hungrily waiting on his brother for the vinegar and salt.

"The people who did this may not even be alive anymore," Eoin said.

Callum eyed his brother. "The gangs are dangerous. Sure and those people have met up with their own deaths in some skirmish."

"But others who sanctioned the killin's might be around." Brodie took a bite of a chip and nearly burned his tongue.

"The higher-ups?" Eoin asked.

Brodie nodded as he took a cold drink quickly.

"But there's no messin' with them."

"Not yet, anyway." Brodie set his drink down. "I could ask me friends in the gang."

Callum sat back, crossed his arms, and shook his head. "I'd rather they weren't involved in this."

"Callum, while I feel the same as ya, these lads might give us somethin' ta go on, ya know?" Eoin said. Brodie looked at his brother smugly.

"Ach, it's biscuits ta a bear!" Callum said. "Waste o' time!"

"Nay, broder, let me give it a go," Brodie begged, and Eoin nodded in agreement.

"Gerronwiddit, then!" Callum gave up. "If ya both think it will help."

The men grew quiet, putting the conversation out of their heads temporarily so that they could relish every last bite of their meal.

CHAPTER 14

The girls were playing nicely with Annie's dollhouse. They spent quite a while with the setting up of the beds, dressers, tables, and chairs in the rooms and then deciding where miniature dishes, little clocks, blankets, rugs, and such should go. It was a tedious process, but it was something little girls loved to do. Finally, after the dollhouse was arranged, each girl took one doll in her hand to move and live in the house. They enabled them to discuss what to make for dinner in sweet, high-pitched voices. Fiahd's doll suggested they fry some fish and Annie's suggested that they fry some potatoes to go with it. Suddenly, in a random outburst, Erin went into a frenzy and made explosive noises as she threw her doll up in the air. She destroyed the nicely set-up kitchen and proceeded to do similar damage to the living room but Annie yanked her away from the house.

"What'd you do that for?" Annie yelled as Erin wiggled and fussed to get out of her grasp. Fiahd wailed.

"It was a bomb! They shoulda been watchin' and been more careful, so they should!" Erin said, her eyes wild.

"No! No bomb! That's not nice! You shouldn't have done that. I don't want you to play with my dollhouse anymore!" Annie pushed Erin toward the bedroom door. Now all three were crying. Upon hearing pathetic sobs coming from the girls' bedroom, Haley appeared at the door.

"What's going on? Please quiet down, girls. You're gonna wake up the boys from their naps."

"Erin bombed the dollhouse!"

"What? What do you mean she *bombed* the dollhouse?" Haley instinctively surveyed the dollhouse for damages but all she found was furniture, dishes, and dolls strewn all over it and the floor around it.

Erin backed into the hall, watching Haley with frightened eyes.

"She did this." Annie demonstrated, making noises and throwing her hands in the air. "And she was being mean and ruined everything we just made!"

Erin ran down the hall toward the front door. Haley's heart sank. She was concerned about how this little one—coming from the same place Gareth had come from as a child—was going to behave with her girls. Haley called for Erin but there was no answer. Liam started to cry from his crib. She rushed into the boys' room, picked him up quickly so that he didn't wake Bobby, carried him on her hip, and went outside. "Erin!" she yelled, over and over, but there was no answer. She headed toward the big house.

"Did Erin come over here?" Haley asked, trying to stay calm.

"We didn't see her come in," Phyllis said. "What's going on?"

"She and the girls had a fight. I'll explain later. She ran off and I can't find her!"

Ian and Phyllis looked for Erin, calling out her name, but she was nowhere to be found in the house or outside around it. Haley went to the barn where Gareth and Ed were cleaning stalls and asked if they'd seen her. They hadn't.

"We need to find her before her momma gets back with Tonya and the babies!" Haley was frantic and Liam started to cry. Meanwhile, Annie came running up the driveway from the little house.

"Did you find Erin, Annie?"

"No, but Fiahd is scared, she's crying her eyes out and Bobby woke up because Fiahd won't stop bawling so loudly." Annie gestured dramatically. "And now, Momma, *Bobby's* crying! It's too noisy and hurts my ears. Do I have to go back there?"

"Oh, honey—"

"Haley, why don't you go back to the house and take care of the kids," Gareth said. "Ed and I will look for her. She can't be too far."

Haley returned to the little house and quieted her children while the two men searched for Erin. When Ed peered into the chicken coop he heard some whimpering noises that certainly didn't belong to hens.

"Erin?" he asked.

"Nay," the chickens answered, "there's no Erin about."

"Well, that's too bad, because I'm looking for a special little girl with that name."

"Ya won't find her in here, so ya won't!"

"Can you tell me where I might find her?"

"Ya can look in the barn," the voice offered, "ya can look in the garden—"

"I did. No Erin in either place. I'm just so sad."

"Look in the big house."

"Nope, not there."

"Well, sure and she's in the little house then."

"Not there either." Ed paused. "Maybe she went riding off on a big horse!"

"That she did!" Suddenly the voice sounded very pleased with the idea.

"And then the horse flew over the barn," Ed said, animated.

"Ach, no. Horses can't fly, ya big laloo!"

"How do you know? I heard them talking the other day and one of them was bragging about how they could fly."

Erin peered around the corner, her face streaked with tears. "Who was braggin'?"

"I believe it was Prince, but I can't remember."

"It mighta been Mabel, she's such a bonny white color and she looks like she could fly, so she does."

"Let's go see, shall we?" Ed held out his hand and Erin reached slowly to take it. The feel of her little hand in his made his heart lurch and the look in her teary eyes was endearing. He smiled and she smiled back weakly. They walked hand in hand to the barn, passing Gareth on the way. Ed winked at him, and glanced at Erin. Gareth took a turn toward the houses and made sure Haley, Ian, and Phyllis knew all was well.

Tonya and Maisie returned shortly and when Maisie was told what happened and that Erin was in the barn with Ed, she went to find them. As Maisie entered the barn, she saw her daughter with Ed sitting on the floor, leaning against a stall with Mabel's nose hovering above them. Maisie moved quickly out of sight and listened.

"I give up. I don't think she's goin' ta tell us anythin'," Erin said.

"I think she's too embarrassed to tell us humans."

"Why?"

"Well, most humans would laugh at a horse claiming she had wings and could fly, don't you think?"

"I s'pose."

"So, she's going to keep quiet about it."

Erin stood up and rubbed Mabel's nose. "I promise I won't tell anyone that ya fly, Mabel. An' ya can tell me anythin'." She kissed the horse's nose, sat down again, and snuggled up next to Ed.

"So, do you want to go back and play with your cousins now?"

"Nay. I just like it here with ya, so I do. They don't like me anymore anyways."

"Well, I'm sure they still like you. Just don't go blowing up their dollhouse anymore, okay?"

Maisie felt her stomach turn. She was dismayed to hear all over again what her daughter had done. Erin pretended to blow up the dollhouse? Maybe she should interfere with this conversation and stop Erin before she talked too much about what she'd seen in Belfast. For some reason it embarrassed Maisie now, to think this American man would know what kind of a place she lived in and worse yet, what she'd exposed her daughter to. Ed spoke again and she waited.

"I didn't do it, my dolly did it—I named her Fiona like my best friend back home."

"So, why did you, I mean, why did Fiona do it—blow up the dollhouse?" Ed asked.

"It were the fish and chippies they wanted ta make."

Maisie's heart sank. She thought Erin had forgotten about all that.

"Who was making fish and chips—I mean *chippies*?"

"The other dollies. See, first, Fiahd's doll—the one with the long black hair and no pants—because Fiahd took them off—well, she said she wanted some fish and then Annie's doll—the one with a ponytail and a pretty pink dress—sure and she wanted chippies—well, she called it something else—ta go with that."

"And Fiona didn't want fish and chippies?"

Erin's eyes began to water. "She did." Her voice caught. "She always did, but Mr. Murphy, he can't—he can't make them anymore fer her! Tomorrow I—she wanted some." She started to cry and when Maisie heard her daughter weep she covered her own mouth to suppress a sob.

At this point Maisie didn't dare reveal that she'd been listening in. Erin continued, "It was on Saturnday—Saturrrday—and Ma and I almost had some—we were almost there—but his fish and chippies went 'boom! boom!' up in the air." Erin's hands went up over her head. "And, now, I will never see him again! His family will never see him again! An' I will never have his fish and chippies ever, *ever* again," Erin cried. "Sadness is on us all!"

Maisie moved away from the barn quickly before she cried aloud.

Ed put his arm around Erin and she leaned into his chest and wept. The name sounded familiar to Ed and then he remembered what he'd heard about the Shankill Road bombing. He was pretty sure it was a fish and chips shop that was bombed and that the owner had died in the explosion. Did this little innocent child witness that horrible scene? His heart went out to her and he wished he could make her feel better.

All the men in the military. All the times he sat with Gareth. He'd always had words to say to these men and his friend who had seen horrible things. But now, with this little girl, he couldn't find the right words to say, or the right thing to do. He knew his emotions were getting in the way but he couldn't help it. How does one erase a terrible memory from a child? How does one make her feel better? *Oh God, help me. This girl has taken my heart down a path I've never been down before.*

And then, he had an idea. It was worth a try. "Erin, how about we have fish and chips for dinner tonight in memory of Mr. Murphy? And we could pray for you and for his family to not be sad. Would you like that?"

Erin lifted her head and, between hiccupping sobs, she said, "I think it—I think it a fine—a fine idea. And may we have malt vinegar and salt on it?"

"Of course," Ed said, "whatever you want." *I'd give you anything in the world to make you happy again and heal your little broken heart.*

Maisie walked quickly into the pasture and behind the barn where no one could see her so she could cry alone. Eventually, Erin surfaced and skipped to the big house. When Ed came out of the barn Maisie watched him take long strides out to the field. He seemed so perfect to her in so many ways. He was the typical American hero that Hollywood lifted up and that she'd seen on the telly. His looks, his physique, his clothes—they were all part of the picture of the ideal film actor, and it was embarrassing to her that he had just witnessed how pathetic Erin's life had already been for such a young child. Maisie felt like a bad mother living in a pathetic city, living paycheck to paycheck, barely making ends meet. How could she face him again? And yet, he was so kind and sweet to Erin. She ought to thank him. Why did he have to be so good when she wanted to snub him?!

She wiped away her tears, put on a good face, and went back to the big house and up to the bedroom to the left of the stairs—Haley's old room. She needed some time before she saw Ed, lest she react terribly. She sat on the bed and realized how silly was the direction her thoughts had gone. She went over to the window and saw Ed return from the field and lean against the barn, hands in his pockets, deep in thought. Her heart skipped a beat. She could see why the other girls had worshipped him when they were just teenagers and why Gareth mocked him and called him princely names.

Ach! But what did it matter anyway? Who cared what Eddy knew about her daughter's life in Northern Ireland? Eddy Wagner wasn't anyone significant in her life and soon she'd return to her homeland. She'd been up against people who were a lot harder to rub shoulders with than him. She stood up, smoothed out her blouse, ran her fingers through her hair, and went downstairs.

It was a fine dinner of fish and chips enjoyed at the big house by everyone, but especially by Erin. After all the children were put to bed, Maisie stepped out onto the porch in the cool of the evening. She took in several deep breaths. The contrast between her daughter and Gareth's girls was obvious. How lucky Gareth was to escape from the Troubles in Northern Ireland at a young age. And how fortunate for his children to live such innocent lives out here on this farm! She leaned on the rail of the porch and heard the door open behind her. Ed walked up to the rail where she stood.

"You all right, Maisie?"

"I am."

"You haven't looked all right since you came back today from the doctors. Was that because of Erin's little mishap?"

"*Little mishap*? Sure and she fairly blew up the dollhouse! Tell me, what little girls around here do that?" she snapped.

Ed didn't know what to say. Frankly, he knew little girls weren't prone to do that under normal circumstances, but he couldn't say that to Maisie. "She's a tough little girl with a big heart."

"She's had ta be tough. Maybe too tough."

"But she's sweet, too."

"She sure took a likin' ta ya, she did."

"I just happened to be the one to find her and rescue her out of the chicken coop. Those chickens…"

"I'm not a fit ma."

"Why do you say that?"

"Bringing her up in Belfast, seein' all the violence. She's too young fer all that, so she is."

"While I agree with you, you're doing the best you can. Anyway, weren't you brought up seeing it too, and you survived?"

Maisie looked at him. "Are ya tryin' ta help me feel better? Or worse?"

Ed was taken aback. "I'm sorry. Usually I'm better at making people deal with their problems."

"Well, yer muckin' it up. Yer a bit of a failure tonight, lad!"

Ed looked at her puzzled. He'd never been talked to quite like that.

Ed's expression pricked Maisie's conscience. What was behind the sarcasm that flowed from her mouth and why did it come so easily in front of him? He looked hurt and she needed to rescue the situation quickly.

Ed watched in amazement as Maisie's eyes widened. Her freckled nose wrinkled and her delicate mouth drew up in a smile.

"Ach, I'm just givin' ya a hard time, so I am."

Ed put his hand to his heart. "My goodness! You really had me worried!" he said. Maisie smirked, turned, and went inside. Ed shook his head. He thought he had the Northern Irish people figured out after being with Gareth for so many years and then with Eoin and Ian. But Maisie was harder to read. Maybe it was the Irish *women* who were harder to understand. But, on the other hand, so were the American women. Maybe it was all women of any nationality. That thought reaffirmed his determination to stay single! It was extremely exhausting. He'd rather think about the horses.

Alma and Fred invited everyone over for a barbeque at their place. It was a beautiful spring day so the MacCauley family agreed to take a walk over to the Wagners just a half mile down the road. When they arrived at the Wagner home, the grandeur of their property caused Maisie to stop at the edge of the driveway and stare in disbelief.

"We're goin' here? This is where Eddy lives?"

"Aye, cousin." Gareth motioned with his hand. "Come on."

"What are they? Lords of the land? Sure and he *is* Prince Edward!"

"We're livin' in the twentieth century in America, Maisie." Gareth laughed. "They own a dairy farm that's been very successful for many years and Mrs. Wagner, Alma, came from a rich family down in Georgia. She inherited quite a good sum from her family, not to mention a lot of antiques. Wait till you see inside."

"I can' wait. It's a fantastic home on the outside," she said.

"It's one of the oldest homes in this area—probably built at the turn of the century," Phyllis said.

"That's about when our newer homes in Ireland were built!" Maisie joked and Gareth guffawed.

They walked up to the house as Alma and Fred stepped out on the porch waving and welcoming them all to come in. Maisie felt slightly intimidated by the richness of the property. The wraparound porch held more furniture than any home Maisie had ever lived in and nicer furniture at that! Alma's clothes were colorful and fashionable. Her hair was perfect and her jewelry expensive. Sure and this was Malibu Ken's ma, Maisie thought to herself.

When Ed stepped out to greet everyone, he was cleaned up and wearing a green-and-blue-plaid button-down shirt tucked into crisp new blue jeans. His hair was combed and his tapered bangs were pushed to one side. Once again, perfect in every way. Were these people film actors? Were they really just regular Americans? Whatever they were, Maisie didn't think she measured up to them and her first urge was to turn around and walk quickly back to her uncle's homestead. The dress she chose to wear tonight was ten years old and outdated. She felt as if she belonged to a lower class. It quieted her through most of the evening. She had to admit, the food was amazing and in abundance, and she enjoyed that. Alma and Fred were great hostesses and Ed was right there beside them.

The rich American family.

There it was.

Maisie was witnessing it firsthand and when she returned home to Northern Ireland, she would tell the story to her broders and Molly. Maybe Tonnie would take pictures so she could prove it to them. The only time she ever had seen anything similar to this was amongst the rich Protestant families in Northern Ireland who owned the castle-like properties that she'd had a chance to pass by on the busses and perhaps catch a glimpse of those who lived there. How did the Wagners come together so easily with the Becketts and MacCauleys?

All of Maisie's spunk and all her feistiness went out the window and dissipated into the cornfields. She sat back and listened to the different conversations going on and watched all the interactions of these people. There was no class distinction here and it baffled her.

CHAPTER 15

Tonya didn't lack for help with the twins, what with Phyllis, Maisie, and Ian right there ready to share responsibilities with cuddling, bathing, feeding, and bedtime rituals. Even Erin was quick to run upstairs and fetch fresh diapers or clean clothes when needed. The Millers came up from Florida where they had made a new home for themselves after Tonya had moved out.

They came with shopping bags from expensive stores filled with matching baby boy outfits, stuffed animals, and diapers. Tonya was thrilled to show off her sons to her parents and they were delighted to have two beautiful grandsons added to the family.

It was on a Saturday, after the Millers left, that Maisie and Tonya sat on the porch swing, pushing it with their feet, cuddling Seamus and Sammy who were alert, cooing, and enjoying the movement. Two robins hopped about the yard flirting, and a pair of rabbits jumped around at each other. It was spring, after all. The girls laughed.

"What kind of bird is that?" Maisie asked.

"A robin."

"A robin?"

"You don't have those in Ireland, do you? I never saw any."

"We have robins all over the place. But they don't look like that at all. They're smaller and lighter in color."

A cardinal landed on a branch in the tree and Maisie watched as the bright-colored bird bounced slightly on the end of the branch. "That bird is brilliant! What is that?"

"A cardinal."

"What did ya say?"

"A cardinal."

Maisie guffawed.

"What's so funny?"

"Ireland has a 'Cardinal.'"

"Only one?"

"Only one, and he's higher in rank than the priests in the Catholic church."

Tonya laughed. "Oh, I think I've heard that word used like that before."

"That's a grand bird, though. I love it," Maisie said, as the bird started to warble. "So many different creatures here. Animals look so different—even the rabbits. People are different here, too."

"I thought those same things when I went to Northern Ireland."

"So, are yer folks as rich as the Wagners?" Maisie asked.

Tonya laughed again. "Well, they do okay but no, they don't have as much money or property as the Wagners. I never really thought of my folks as rich. I think they'd be considered middle class, only maybe a bit higher up on the pay grade than the MacCauleys."

"They sure bought a lot of grand things fer yer wee bairns."

"Yes, they did and I'm sure they ran up their charge cards to do it!"

"Do ya miss them? Yer folks?"

"I do, but not terribly. I grew up with them gone a lot so I'm used to it. It's Eoin whom I miss so much. I wish he could be here to see the boys."

"I know the feelin'."

"Oh, I'm sorry, I shouldn't whine after what you've been through."

"No bother, really. It's been over eight years now, so it has. I've moved on." Maisie put her finger in Sammy's chubby hand and his fingers tightened around hers.

"But, I mean, well, do you miss Michael?"

"In some ways, I do. But in some ways, life is easier, ya know?"

"You don't talk about him."

"I don't keep him fresh in me memory."

"I'm sorry. I don't mean to pry." Tonya smoothed down Seamus's wispy curls. "So, you can just forget him?"

"When I think of something sad in my past, I put it in a boat and let it sail off far away inta the sea."

"I like that. I'm going to use that."

The women sat quietly for a while, snuggling two soft little bodies smelling of fresh baby shampoo. Finally, Tonya sighed.

"I hope we can go back soon."

"Do ya? I'm not in any hurry."

"Don't you miss home?"

"Ach, the city with its dirty streets and foul smells? And then, there's always the potential danger out there. I hate that Erin has ta see it all. There's peace on this farm that I had a hard time getting' used ta at first, so I did." Maisie laughed.

"You need to get out of Belfast and move out to the country where Eoin and I live."

"That would be grand. Still, I could stay here a wee bit longer."

"Well, I think you're going to get your way for a while yet."

Maisie smiled. She knew this couldn't last forever—this heaven on earth. The widespread fields and farms were green like her homeland in the country, but when they went into downtown Watertown she felt out of her element, and even more so when they went into a bigger city like Milwaukee to the doctor's office for Tonya. She wasn't as shocked to see Watertown undamaged by violence, but Milwaukee? No buildings were destroyed, there were no burnt-out cars, and no soldiers armed with rifles standing at their posts! When they had first arrived and traveled up to Watertown from O'Hare, Erin had asked along the way, "Is it safe here, Ma? There aren't any soldiers on any streets ta protect us."

Ed was right. Maisie grew up in the violence and mayhem of the Troubles and now her daughter was growing up thinking soldiers and blown-up buildings were part of city life.

Her thoughts were interrupted when a car pulled into the driveway. The Brannen family stepped out of the car.

"Who are they again? I think I met them but I can't remember everyone's names," Maisie said.

"Penny and Scott Brannen and their two kids, Jonathan and Angie," Tonya said. "Hi, Penny. Hey kids, go inside and find Erin. She'll be happy to see you." Jonathan and Angie ran up the steps and into the house.

Penny stepped onto the porch and peered over each baby. "Aw, the boys are growing so fast!" She sat in a lawn chair and turned to Maisie. "Hello again. I'm Penny. I'm just telling you once more because I don't expect you to remember me. I wouldn't remember me either."

Maisie guffawed and Seamus startled in her lap. The girls laughed. "Yer a corker, so ya are."

"Yeah, people say that about me here in Yankee-land a lot." Penny smirked. "*Not.*"

Maisie laughed again, albeit quietly this time so as not to disturb Seamus.

"What brings you guys out here today?" Tonya asked.

"Scott is going to help Ed and Gareth with some troubleshooting on the computer and then show them how to format things better for their business."

The conversation led into Penny's past. She shared a bit about her father serving in Vietnam and how this seemingly useless war affected her family. Maisie felt connected with this friend of Haley's and Tonya's. The men came out shortly and sat on the steps.

"Did you guys get everything squared away?" Penny asked.

"I think so. I think I get it better than Gareth," Ed said.

"I'm surprised ya got it at all, Malibu Ken," Maisie said, with a deadpan expression. Penny covered her mouth, suppressing a laugh. Ed looked at Maisie, confused. "Because yer *blond?*" She smirked. The others laughed, but Ed wasn't sure how to read her. Then Maisie broke into a smile and chuckled.

"Sheesh. I can never tell when you're joking or serious," Ed said.

"I got it right away," Penny said.

"*Of course you did,*" Ed joked. "You two should go on the road together as a comedy team."

"Ach, ya *do* have a sense of humor," Maisie said.

"I am capable, yes. But your Irish humor—"

"I thought ya hung with Gareth growin' up. Ye should understand our humor!"

"I did grow up with Gareth and I got *him.*" Ed looked to Gareth for help.

"Hey, you're on your own with my cousin," Gareth said. "She always was a feisty girl." Maisie gave him a smug look.

"I like her," Penny said.

"Why am I not surprised?" Ed said.

The Brannens headed back into town, Tonya grabbed up Seamus from Maisie's arms, carried both boys, and went inside to feed them and put them down for a nap.

"I'd like ta get ta know Penny better," Maisie said to Gareth.

"You two seemed to be hitting it off quite well. Penny's been through a lot of stuff—"

"She talked about some of it."

"Did she tell you about her years in high school and getting mixed up with the wrong crowd, doing drugs, etc.?" Ed asked.

"No. She seems fine now."

"That's all because of Christ's work in her life and in Scott's, too," Ed said. "We're thankful to see them both doing so well."

"So, not all Americans have an easy, rich life, eh?" Maisie glanced at Ed and he pursed his lips.

"No. Not at all." Gareth looked at Ed and he nodded. "You can't believe everything you see on TV about the US."

"Definitely," Ed said.

"That goes both ways, lads."

"It does. The media and Hollywood color things the way they want them to look," Gareth said. "There are beautiful places in Northern Ireland, but they don't show that in the news, only the violence in the cities. That was hard on me growing up here and just seeing the bad things happening over in my homeland. Now, it just makes my da worry more."

Erin came outside and sat down beside Ed. "Me friends are gone, so they are," she sighed.

"What about your cousins?" Ed said. Erin looked at her mother for an answer. Maisie shrugged.

"Hey, Maisie, why don't you take Erin down to play with the kids and then you can chat with Haley. She feels like she misses out on so many conversations when she's busy in the house with the children," Gareth said.

"Are ya sure? I won't be botherin' her at all?"

"Of course not!"

Maisie walked down with Erin to the little house. Both were reluctant after the fiasco with the dollhouse and Maisie wondered if Haley was reticent about having Erin around her children again. She knocked softly on the door. No one answered. Maybe Haley was taking a nap. She didn't want to disturb her. She turned and took Erin's hand, ready to leave, but the door opened and Haley was standing there with a big smile on her face.

"Oh! I'm so glad to see you! I've been talking to little ones all day." She laughed. "Come in! Can you sit for a while? Erin, would you like to play with the girls? I'll make some tea." Maisie relaxed at the invitation. Erin started to run to the girls' bedroom, but turned to her ma for a minute and wagged her finger in the air as she mouthed the words, "no bombs." After Maisie nodded approval, Erin disappeared into the hall.

Maisie sat down on the couch and looked around at the furniture. It looked like it was all second hand but it was still nice and made her feel at home. The worn grey-blue couch was covered with handmade mauve pillows and a homemade quilt with a blue, maize and off-white log cabin quilt design. The coffee table and end tables were laminate and bore chips on the corners, but the doilies and the artificial flower arrangements drew the eye away from the flaws. There were pictures on the walls of the children, a portrait of the entire family, and a big painting of a countryside with a little cottage nestled amongst some trees. She thought it looked a bit like a place in Ireland. What a cozy, pleasant home to bring up children, she thought. Gareth had done well. She envied him. Haley brought out some tea and cookies and set them on the coffee table. Maisie thanked her politely and picked up her mug. Haley sat down and did the same.

"So, I guess we're related." Haley smiled. "Cousins by marriage?"

Maisie grinned back. "Aye. I s'pose so. Ya have a grand place here."

"Thanks. We're very thankful for it," Haley said.

"So ya grew up together, did ya?"

"I was nine and he was twelve when he came here."

"When did ya know ya'd marry?"

"Oh, it took several years to come to that conclusion! But we grew to like each other—then hate each other—then like each other's company, and then, somewhere in there—somewhere in our late teens or early twenties, we fell in love. He proposed to me after he returned from being away in Northern Ireland for three long years."

"It all sounds romantic."

"It wasn't at times. Gareth had a lot of issues to work through and struggled for years."

"Sure and us MacCauleys saw some bad things as wee'uns."

"But *you* never got away from it, did you?"

"Nay."

"I'm sorry."

"It is what it is. Sure and we'll not dwell on that ugliness. Did Gareth give ya grief? Did he tease ya? He loved to tease, yet I loved me cousin. He was still nicer ta me than me broders."

"Oh, man, yes, he was so annoying and loved to tease. But there was a sweetness about him and I began to see that he really cared for me. He was even overly protective. Yet, he would take my stuffed animals and dolls and hide them, or he'd put them in random places like the bathtub or the chicken coop."

"The same! And he always called me names—"

"Yes! Me too!"

"You heard the one, 'ginger bap,' because of me strawberry-blond hair at the time. Now it's just a borin' auburn color."

"I love your hair. It's so full and beautiful."

"Thanks, but I envy yer silky-straight dark hair, I do."

"I guess women are never really happy with their hair."

"Aye." Maisie took a sip of her tea and then asked, "So come on, what did my cousin call ya? I want ta hear it!"

"He called me 'Stringbean' and 'Pipsqueak' because I was so skinny—I *hated* it."

"Ach! But here's a worse one that he called me: 'Corncrake.'"

"Ugh. What a horrible name! What is that?"

"It's a bird in Ireland that makes a rattlin' sound. When I was little I often got a raspy throat from the dampness and he thought me voice sounded like a corncrake."

"What a pain in the neck!"

"Aye, but I gave it back ta him!"

"So did I!"

The girls had a good laugh and when their laughter subsided, they each picked up their mugs. Gareth came through the house and the girls looked at each other and nearly spit out their tea.

"Ah, I know when I'm bein' talked about," Gareth said smartly.

"It's not all about ya, cousin," Maisie said. "But truth be told, we *were* just talkin' about ya!" More laughter. Gareth just shook his head and walked out.

Maisie took another sip of her tea and looked over her cup at Haley. She could see the admiration in Haley's face as she watched her husband disappear outside. Maisie furrowed her brow.

"What?" Haley said.

"You and Gareth. You were meant fer each other, so ya were. It's funny, that."

"What do you mean, 'funny'?"

"That he had ta come here ta find ya."

Haley nodded. "God works in mysterious ways."

"He surely worked in a grand way fer ya."

"What about you, Maisie? Sometimes you look like you're in turmoil or something."

"Do I, then?"

"Yes."

"Ya've got a good sense about ya, Haley. Tonnie as well."

"Maybe we've seen the same turmoil in our husbands' eyes."

"Maybe."

"Can I ask you something?"

"Aye."

"Do you think you'll ever find love again and remarry? Do you want that?"

"Nay. I gave me heart ta one man. I did what was expected of me. Where I come from, the wife is supposed ta be passive. I shoulda—ach! No regrets. Bletherin' won't get the baby a new coat!" Haley laughed at the expression. "Just the same, I don't see meself marryin' another man over there. Sure and they're all caught up in the fight fer justice."

"Such a different world."

"I see how Gareth is a part of this world. He's more at peace than me broders or even cousin Eoin."

"But he still has that yearning in him to fight and make peace in his homeland. I do have to hold him down at times. Sometimes I wonder if I'm right doing that."

"Doin' what? Holdin' him back from returnin' ta Norn Iron?"

"Yes. I think deep down he'd love to go if it weren't for me and the kids. If I'm being honest, I fear it!"

"Ya have a family, Haley. I don't blame ya at all."

"Having children here keeps his feet on the ground. But as I mentioned before, he did go back years ago and was there three long years. I thought our relationship was over."

"I'd heard he'd gone back in search of his family."

"Yes. When he learned that his dad had escaped from prison and had been possibly sighted, he went over there, found Ian, and then he wore himself thin looking for Anna and Eoin. He hung around Divis Flats—"

"Divis Flats? Ach, the eejit! What is he? As thick as two short planks?"

"I'll have to use that expression on him!" Haley said and Maisie laughed. "Perhaps when it comes to family, Gareth's emotions override any real logical thinking."

"That's Brodie—crazy as a box of frogs, that one. But Gareth was always a bit more level headed—a bit more like Callum."

"I'd love to meet your brothers."

"I'd like ya to. They're fine lads, so they are."

"I bet you miss them, huh?"

"I do. But, I surely love it here. I love bein' with me family that I haven' seen fer years. I love that ya've accepted Erin inta yer home so she can play with cousins her age and that yer all bein' patient with her. I love bein' with all of ye and feelin' so safe. This is so good for Erin—and fer me. I love it here, so I do."

CHAPTER 16

Alma invited the women and girls over for a tea party while the men and boys went horseback riding and the twins slept in an upstairs room of the Wagner house. It was a dressy affair and the females in attendance were adorned in Sunday dress, nice jewelry, and well-groomed hair styles. Haley lent Maisie and Tonya some of her dresses and Annie lent Erin one of her prettiest dresses since they had packed light for their flight and were not prepared for such an event. Mrs. Wagner was ecstatic when Phyllis—smiling widely—led the beautiful parade of girls and women into her parlor. They all sat delicately on two Victorian couches facing each other with a French provincial cocktail table between them. One of the couches was upholstered in blue satin with rolled arms and the other was upholstered in a soft blue damask. A blue-and-white wingback chair sat at each end of the table and smaller end tables held colorful Tiffany lamps. A large framed painting of a French field of poppies hung over the antique square piano, the china cabinets were full of colorful china and glassware, the pure white statue of a woman draped in flowing clothes carried a vessel, and all the while a record of Debussy's piano works played on the old Victrola.

While getting ready for this special party, the little girls had been instructed to sit quietly, not touch anything, and be very ladylike. Now, after seeing the marvelous room they were seated in, the museum-like ambience left the girls quiet. They craned their heads from side to side with looks of awe. It was a good thing that wide eyes and jaws agape had not been in the instructions of what not to do while at Mrs. Wagner's.

In the past, when attending a gathering with the Wagners, everyone filed past this particular room, but now, having the pleasure of being seated here left all of them spellbound, as if they had just traveled back in the past. And when Alma and Phyllis brought out trays of scones—blueberry and cranberry-orange—miniature muffins, butter cookies, and a platter of fruit, the oohs and ahs in the room were a pleasure to Alma's ears. Phyllis helped her pour tea into the china tea cups for each one and then poured some for herself and sat down.

"Mrs. Wagner, this is absolutely lovely," Tonya said and the others agreed.

"Yes, thank you for inviting us over," Haley said.

Maisie sat quietly, enjoying the feel of Haley's home-sewn cotton dress and the tiny patterns of flowers against a dark background in the skirt as it fanned out from the bodice. It had been a good fit for her. She watched everyone talking, sipping tea, and taking little treats to put on their delicate china plates. Alma took notice. She was aware that her home and her personality could be quite overbearing and intimidating to some. She had hoped that having everyone over would help Maisie and Erin get to know her more, but realized the formality of the invite was perhaps a bit crippling. Still, the tea party was a success and when it was over all the women offered to remain and help. Alma refused any assistance except from that of Maisie and Erin. She asked if the two might stay after and said that she would see them home later. Maisie, unsure how to respond, looked at the others but Tonya and Haley just smiled, waved at her, and went up to retrieve the twins just beginning to stir together in the large antique crib.

Maisie and Erin helped clear the dishes from the parlor and brought them into the kitchen.

"Ya have a grand house, ma'am," Erin said to Alma as she helped her wash the dishes.

"Why, thank ya, Erin. Ah noticed that y'all kept looking at the china cabinets. Yoh ma and I can finish up the dishes. Would y'all like to go and take a look at the dishes more closely while yoh wait?"

"I would." Erin looked at her ma and Maisie nodded.

"Y'all were awfully quiet at the party," Alma said to Maisie.

"It was—it was fantastic. I'm not used ta such nice things."

"Ah thought perhaps y'all felt a smidge out of place. Ah'm sorry if Ah magnafied that for ya."

"Oh, please, don't put me feelin's on yerself! I'd be an eejit if I didn' be so grateful fer the party ya gave."

Alma started laughing. "Ah've heard that word from the other MacCauleys. Down south we'd say about someone who was an idiot—or an eejit, 'Even a blind hog can find an acorn every now and then.'"

"What a craic!" Maisie started to chuckle and Alma was glad to hear her sweet laugh. "Sometimes, I say ta me broder, 'yer is as thick as two short planks.'"

Alma laughed. "Ah used to tell mah brother, 'Somewhere there's a village missing its idiot.' Or Ah'd say, 'y'all are not the quickest bunny in the forest.'"

"What a craic!" Maisie's eyes lit up. "I might steal those when I go back home." The two women laughed together. The back door opened just then and in walked Ed and Fred.

"What's going on here?" Fred said, smiling. Ed glanced at Maisie, surprised to see her laughing and so at ease with his mother. He recognized the dress as one of Haley's and thought it looked just as nice on Maisie. Her hair was pulled back on the sides with combs and loose wavy strands framed her face. She was pleasing to look at and he tried not to stare.

"Just getting the kitchen cleaned up!" Alma winked at Maisie.

"I should be gettin' Erin back ta the farm." Maisie withdrew to the parlor and Ed went upstairs to change out of his clothes smelling of horse and stable.

Alma followed Maisie. "Ah told her Ah'd show her the dishes. Please don't go yet, dear," she begged. They stepped out into the parlor where they found Erin, settled into one of the wingback chairs, asleep. Maisie felt uncomfortable with Ed in the house and wanted to get back to the farm. The awkwardness created butterflies in her stomach.

She knelt down by her daughter and tried to rouse her. "Wake up, agra, sure and it's too late in the afternoon ta nap!" Erin moaned and mumbled back to her mother.

"Why don't you let me carry her?" Ed suggested as he came down the stairs. "It's nice out. We can walk back to the farm if you're up to it. It might help Erin to wake up in the fresh air."

"She'll be all right and I don't want ta trouble anyone."

"Oh, it's no trouble at all." Ed ignored Maisie, picked up Erin, and cradled her in his arms. "It's not far down the road. Are you good for walking?" Ed asked.

"I like ta walk," Maisie said. She gave Alma a quick word of thanks and followed Ed out the door. The daffodils and tulips had come and gone and now only the stalks with their dry brown flowers were left, but the bright orange tiger lilies were out in full bloom along the ditches of the road where they walked. The heat of the sun felt good as it started to drop toward the west.

"You and my momma were having a good old time in the kitchen," Ed said.

"She's nice." Maisie watched as Ed carried her daughter and a tinge of melancholy sparked in her heart. If Michael had lived...

"You say that like you're surprised." Ed caught her looking at him and she turned away quickly.

"Well, I didn't mean that I thought she was unkind—"

"But you didn't know what to think of her, did you?"

Maisie felt embarrassed. "No, sure and I didn't."

"You're not the first one." He laughed and Maisie relaxed. "Her Southern ways stick out like a sore thumb here in the Midwest."

"Is she that different from people livin' around here?"

"Yes, she is. You see, people in the South talk different, have different ways about them, different expressions and different opinions—even amongst the Christian folk. Almost as different as you are, being from Northern Ireland."

"But yer all Americans here."

"America is a big place. If you go out west, over to the east, up north or down in the Bayou, you'll find differences there, too."

"Has that helped ya get along with me cousin's family?"

"I suppose so. I never thought of that before, but, yeah, I think you're right."

They walked on in silence. It was good to have a normal conversation with Maisie without all the sarcasm and there was something in Ed that made him feel good about carrying this weary little girl, resting so sweetly in his arms.

"Maisie, I hear you call Erin 'agra.' Is that a nickname?"

"It's like sayin' 'dear one.'"

"I like that," Ed said as he looked down at Erin. "She sure is a dear one."

How Maisie wished it were Michael looking down at this little girl and speaking so kindly. But it wasn't. It was this rich boy from America. Life could be so strange at times, so it could.

Sunday, after church, the family stopped by the cemetery just off Highway 16 to put some new flowers in the ground by the gravesites of Anna MacCauley and Robert Beckett. Haley and Phyllis worked around Robert's grave while Ian, Gareth, and Maisie took care of Anna's. The children were instructed to walk and not run as they wandered through the small country cemetery.

"Are ya able ta visit the gravesites of me broder and his wife?" Ian asked Maisie.

"No. Fer one thing, sure and they didn't have big stones, but small markers, and that made it hard ta find them. And then, after all the riotin' and destruction that has gone on, the cemeteries have been ravaged, each by the other side, so they have."

"I'm sorry ta hear that," Ian said.

"Me as well," Gareth said.

"Ach, looks like we got company!" Ian said as he stood up and wiped the dirt off his hands. Wagners pulled up alongside their cars and Fred, Alma, Carrie, Keith, and Benny got out of the car. Benny immediately joined his friends on the paths of the cemetery while the others went to the grave of little Katie. The MacCauley clan joined them in looking over it. Haley gave Carrie a hug. Maisie found herself looking for another member of the Wagner clan and she wondered why she even cared. Pushing her thoughts on to things that really mattered, she went over to Carrie.

"I'm sorry ya lost a wee'un," she said.

"Thank you, Maisie. She was a beautiful little girl," Carrie said somberly. "We still grieve her loss."

"Sure and the grievin' never leaves ya," Maisie said.

"I guess you're one to understand that!"

"Aye."

"You look tired, Carrie," Phyllis said when she came over to Katie's gravestone.

"I am, Mrs. B.—I mean, Mrs. Mac! I'm still trying to change that!" Carrie said. "Sundays just wear me out now that Keith is the pastor. When we get home today I'll be taking a nap with Benny!"

"Are you trying to do too much on Sunday mornings at church? I mean, you have the family to feed and get Benny and yourself ready while Keith gets over to the church early before everybody. Isn't that enough to do in one morning?"

"That's what I keep telling her." Keith came up behind Carrie and put his arm around her.

"But if I'm not teaching a class, people will wonder what I'm doing to serve."

"That doesn't matter. You serve just by being the 'pastor's wife' the whole morning and greeting people and chatting with them," Keith said and turned to Phyllis. "I know it wears her out, Mrs. Mac."

"So." Phyllis took her hands. "Your husband is the only one in the church you should feel any need to please. If he is happy with you just being by his side, being his wife and the mother of his son, on Sundays, then you shouldn't worry about everyone else."

"Thank you, Phyllis!" Alma said firmly, while she knelt in the grass planting geraniums. Carrie's eyes filled with tears. She felt a weight being lifted, and Keith hugged her.

"I guess the elder women have spoken!" Gareth said, breaking the tension. Haley smacked his arm. Keith laughed.

"Watch it, laddie," Ian joked.

Just then another car pulled up and Ed got out. He took long strides up the slope of the cemetery and joined the group gathered around baby Katie's resting place.

"Late to the party as usual," Gareth said.

"Yeah, yeah—wait, I'm not usually late to parties." Ed looked around at everyone and rested his eyes on Maisie. Why did he look for her now whenever there was a group of MacCauleys present? She caught his gaze, their eyes locked for only a moment, and then she looked away.

CHAPTER 17

Eoin walked with his cousins around their old property. They stepped into the ruins of the old cottage with gloves and shovels and dug through burned-out timber. After finding some of their ma's jewelry, their da's old razor, and pots and pans from the kitchen, Callum stopped searching for a minute, stretched his back, and sighed.

"Is there really any chance of discoverin' clues that would help us find who did this?"

"Who knows?" Eoin said. "But it's worth a try. It's obvious that no one has tampered with things here. Just the fact that I found Gareth's old bike tells me that. Someone woulda taken it fer parts, ya know?"

Callum pulled up a chain with a pendant hanging precariously on it. "Ma's."

Brodie stopped to look at it with him. His eyes misted over. "Let's save it fer Maisie. Sure and she'd want it."

"Ah, that's grand," Eoin said, thinking of his ma's locket. "We have the locket of me ma's that was found on the beach where she died. Me da is savin' it ta give ta Annie when she's old enough ta appreciate it."

"Perhaps Erin can have this, so."

"A fine idea that, broder," Callum said as he put the necklace in his pocket.

"There wasn't much of our belongin's left ta gather up and we thought Maisie was kidnapped," Brodie said. "We felt so terrible that we left her."

"What could ye have done?" Eoin stopped and looked at Brodie. "Ya couldn't stay there ta look fer her when the men were pursuin' ya! If anythin', ya led them away from her."

"Thank ya, cousin, fer that thought. I always felt guilty fer us runnin' and leavin' her," Callum said, and Brodie nodded. "It was a grand day when we found her with the nuns."

"I know the feelin' of a grand reunion with yer sibling, so I do! But, how is it that Gareth still ended up with Ma's journals if youse had ta run from the burnin' house?" Eoin asked as he pulled out some old cooking utensils where the fireplace had been.

"Gareth hadn't unpacked yet and his suitcases were in the barn. When we came back, he retrieved them." Callum pushed a big board out of the way. "We lads had planned on sleepin' there the first night until our parents figured out where Gareth would sleep in the house. Gareth was leery o' unpackin' yet anyway. He wanted ta be ready ta run again if he had ta."

"I guess he had ta run sooner than he thought, eh?"

"And the police didn't take much time here ta investigate the fire or the murders. Everyone figured it was IRA. There were too many signs— balaclavas, Armalites, and the connection ta yer family, Eoin. So we none of us stayed there very long."

"And then Gareth was whisked off by an RUC named Collins," Brodie added disdainfully.

"Aye! Collins. I know him well," Eoin said. "Ya don' seem ta like—"

"Some people here aren't too fond of the RUC." Callum looked at his brother.

"That's putting it mildly," Brodie said. "They don't have a great reputation among us lads. They'll stop ya on the street, make ya put yer hands against a wall of a buildin' and spread yer legs out ta do a search. They like ta humiliate the lads. They don't trust anyone."

"Well, Collins is a good man, no matter the reputation of other RUCs. He stayed connected ta the family all these years." Eoin stopped and kicked at something. "He's helped in so many ways."

"Has he, then? An' he's the one who shipped Gareth off ta America, was he?" Brodie asked.

"Aye." Eoin knelt and dug at the mysterious hard object at his feet but, finding it just another piece of burnt timber, he moved on with the search.

"And why did he get whisked away like that?" Callum asked.

"Da was being held in connection with Ma's activity at the Divis Flats. The IRD, the Information Research Department working for the British, thought she was connected ta the IRA."

"That's ironic since the IRA thought Auntie Anna was fer the other side," Callum said.

"Right? The IRD thought Da could give them valuable information but they were wrong. Meanwhile, ta get the information they wanted they threatened him with sayin' things like, 'we know what school yer sons go ta.' Of course, Da figured they couldn't hurt me because I was missin' and, sadly, thought I was possibly dead. But he feared fer Gareth left at home and Collins knew that."

"We heard rumors that those things happened—threatenin' political prisoners with their own families' safety," Callum said, "but we didn't know fer sure if it really were takin' place."

"Me ma's broder, Bobby Hanford, met Gareth in America. He works out of Milwaukee, Wisconsin, and he met him at the airport there. Gareth was a poor frightened kid. Imagine all that had just taken place and now he's transported out o' his own country, inta a new country and a new life. Uncle Bobby connected Gareth with a fantastic couple, Robert and Phyllis Beckett. He figured it would be a grand place ta hide me broder on a farm in the south of Wisconsin. Everybody over this side o' the ocean says, if they had the chance ta go ta America, they'd go ta California or New York or even Florida—but no one talks about goin' ta Wisconsin, ya know? He was right ta do what he did back then."

"And then the love story between Gareth and Haley began!" Brodie announced.

"God willed it," Eoin said.

"Are ya sayin' all this death was God's will—our folks and yer ma?" Callum said.

"I've come ta believe it."

"That's a bunch o' codswallop!" Brodie said.

"I know it's hard wrappin' our heads around it all, cousins, and I don' know what God has planned fer us all, but I have ta trust."

"I don' know if I can believe that and trust God!" Callum said, watching his brother on his knees, poking around in the dirt. "What are ya doin' there, broder?"

"I think—wait—look!" Brodie said, holding up a small bone. "Part of a human hand?!"

"It could just be from an animal, ya know," Eoin said.

Callum and Eoin got down and hovered around the area where Brodie knelt, pushing dirt away carefully.

"It's hard ta say what it's from," Callum said as he pulled up another bone.

"Yeah, we're not paleontologists," Brodie said.

"Uh, I don' think this is a dinosaur bone. Maybe yer talkin' *forensic scientists*?" Eoin said and Callum guffawed.

"No matter." Brodie laughed at himself and then grew serious. "I do know one thing, this couldn't be our folks. We saw them take their bodies away. An' our church gave 'em a proper burial."

"So they did," Callum agreed. "So, d'ya think these are the bones o' Billy O'Grady's broder?"

"The police didn't take the body of the guy me broder shot?" Eoin asked.

"Sure and his body was gone when we came back," Brodie said as he raked through the dirt. "The police figured the perps must've taken him."

"Then who else would it be but the broder?" Brodie said.

"If it's not an animal," Eoin said and then added, "or a *dinosaur*." Callum laughed.

"Ach, cousin, now what good would an animal skeleton do us?" Brodie teased.

"Not a whole lot, I'm afraid!" Eoin sighed. "Sure and we need ta stop diggin', call the police, and then let *real* forensic scientists do their work."

Brodie laughed. "What a craic! But can ya call yer buddy, Collins, instead?"

"I'm surprised ta hear that comin' from ye, broder," Callum said.

"I trust me cousin," Brodie said.

"I'd rather call Collins anyway," Eoin said. "I trust him more than the police."

After sharing recent snapshots of the twins with everyone, Eoin discussed the cousins' findings with Collins at the McGilroys'. Margaret served tea while the men talked.

"I'm that sorry yer family has never gotten any answers fer these murders, Eoin," Collins said.

"I never really wanted ta pursue it as much as Gareth did, but suddenly bein' with me cousins and seein' the widespread effect the IRA and paramilitary have had on innocent civilians—even their own people from each side, I'm motivated."

"Sure and it could be dangerous fer ye young men ta get in too deep," Collins said.

"That's why I'm talkin' ta ya! Thing is, we found bones on me uncle's property that might put the O'Gradys at the scene of the crime."

"Ya did what?" Collins eyes grew large.

"We found bones that possibly belonged ta a human bein'."

"What are ya lads up ta?"

"Wasn't it an O'Grady who broke into the Becketts' home lookin' fer Gareth years ago?" Eoin asked.

"Aye."

"And he's in prison now?"

"Aye, after he served in the US fer breakin' and enterin', he went back ta Northern Ireland and got caught stealin' weapons from the gardai. What would be the purpose of stirrin' up *that* troublemaker?"

"Didn't he give an account of his broder bein' kilt by Gareth right there on me uncle's property? Was the body ever found?"

"He did and nay, the body wasn't there when the police came. But they figured that his body was taken by O'Grady and whoever was with him. Sure and they wouldn't leave a body behind. The Catholics especially have ta have a body ta pray over and bury."

"Maybe they didn't take it. Maybe they had ta hurry out o' there."

"It's possible."

"So, if we find out that this is O' Grady's brother, wouldn't that implicate O'Grady fer bein' there at the fire? And then, maybe, we could find out what was behind it and who ordered it?"

George couldn't stay silent any longer. "Lad, are ya sure ya want ta step ehnta the lion's lair? Ye got these two sweet bairns ta think o'." Margaret remained quiet, doing her needlework, though her head nodded.

"Sure and I'll see what I can learn in the office, but Eoin, ye and yer cousins need ta lay low on this."

"Brodie has already been askin' around in his paramilitary group."

Collins shook his head and clicked his tongue. "Those groups are just tickin' time bombs waitin' ta explode. Sure and yer not thinkin' o' joinin,' are ya, lad?"

"No sir, I'm not. I have two wee babes and a beautiful wife ta think o'." Eoin looked over at Margaret. She didn't look up at him, but he saw the grin spread on her face while Collins and George gave loud sighs of relief.

After the scientists went to Sean MacCauley's property and carefully dug up the bones, they determined immediately that they were indeed human remains. They were taken to forensics and after studying the DNA they were able to identify them. Collins met with Callum, Brodie, and Eoin in Laurelvale at a pub. It would've been more convenient and closer for Collins to meet at the Glencairn Estates since he was stationed in Belfast, but rumors would circulate about an RUC meeting at a place where the paramilitary were welcome and the RUC was not. That wouldn't bode well for the brothers or for Collins.

Collins walked into the pub wearing his dark-green trench coat and forage cap, carrying himself well, complete in his role as part of the Royal

Ulster Constabulary. Some men looked up from their Guiness and grimaced, but Sean Fergus Collins didn't care. He was used to it.

Brodie's initial instinct was to run, but he refrained and decided to trust Eoin on this one. Eoin introduced the men to each other and they sat down at an old wooden table and chairs that looked and creaked as if they had seen a lot of history. The men joked that the place was as old as the rocks of Ireland themselves! Eoin was a bit worried about Brodie's lack of tact and what he might say that would offend Collins, but Brodie was congenial. After they ordered some cottage pies and coffee they got right down to business.

"What'd ya find out about the body?" Eoin asked.

"Sure an' the bones ya found were of Bobby O'Grady, Billy's younger broder. The family was contacted. Turns out Billy is out of prison now, too."

"But he's a murderer workin' fer the IRA, so he is!" Brodie said through clenched teeth.

"We're not sure if it was the original IRA or Provisional IRA. And all they had on Billy was breakin' and enterin'."

"It ain't right!" Brodie stood suddenly with fists clenched as he knocked his chair over. Everyone in the pub stopped for a quick minute to see what the commotion was, but each went back promptly to his own ale and troubles.

"He's a hothead, that one." Collins smirked.

"Pick up yer chair and sit down, broder," Callum ordered.

"What does it take ta put these guys away fer good?" Eoin asked.

"Well, the real question is, how do we get O'Grady and his accomplice ta tell us who the orders came down from and why? Sure and it has ta all be tied together," Collins said.

"Surely," Eoin said and the cousins agreed.

"So, can ya still bring in O'Grady fer questionin'?" Callum asked.

"I can, but I doubt he'll give us any information. We need more evidence. I wish yer sister could give us more facts."

"She can't," Callum said.

"Can't, or won't?"

Callum and Brodie looked at each other and shrugged.

"Can ya ask her?"

"*We have*," Callum said.

"And?"

"She won't say nothin'," Brodie said, "an' we ain't pushin' her."

"Seriously?"

"She's a feisty cailin, an' well, sometimes, well, me broder an' I, well, we don' like ta set her off."

"Brodie, I know ya originally thought it might be helpful if ya stayed with yer paras but at this point it might start ta get pretty heated and ya could be involved in serious questionin' by a lawyer or judge." Collins picked up his coffee cup. "It won't look good fer any of the family if yer connected ta these renegades. If ya seriously want ta gain justice fer the family, I suggest ya try ta get out."

"I've already been thinkin' on that. The leader, Joe Campbell, has created a bigger source of fear amongst the men because he's gone a bit crazy in some off-books killin'."

Callum looked at his brother with dismay. "Ya didn't tell me that, broder."

"I didn't want ta worry ya. I'm ready ta pull out and so are some others, but it's dangerous ta do it."

"Collins," Eoin said, "can we get this guy, Campbell, fer his crimes and put him away so that Brodie can get out safely?"

"I'll check into it." Collins took a long sip of the last of his tepid coffee. "Brodie, would ya be willin' ta write up a witness statement against Joe?"

"Won't that incriminate me?"

"Nay. We can make yer statement anonymous fer yer protection."

When Brodie didn't show up to the next two UVF meetings, Joe grew suspicious and sent his men looking for him. Paul got to his door before the others and warned him. Brodie left home quickly and went into hiding with Collins' assistance. His apartment was ransacked and when the paras realized he had taken a lot of his belongings with him, they went to his brother's place. Callum was at work and Molly was just giving the children an after-school snack when four men pushed their way into the house. The children screamed as Molly gathered them together in a corner of the kitchen. "Away off and get ye from me home!"

"Where is he?" one of the men demanded while another walked across the main floor and the other two went upstairs. She heard them rumbling around and wondered what destruction was coming to her house. And would they hurt her and the children? She felt the adrenalin rise in her chest.

"What are you doin' here? And who are ye lookin' fer?" Molly was irate.

The ugliest and biggest of the group stepped up close to her. "Ah, sit yer ground, me bonny lass! Where is the lad, Brodie MacCauley?" Molly backed away from him.

"I don't know! He's not here! Now get out!"

"Ach, she's a feisty one she is. I like 'em that way," the ugly one said as he took Molly's wrist and pulled her to him. The children huddled in a corner, crying. Molly felt a surge of panic. Shannon was turning into a pretty teenage girl. Would these men hurt her? *Lord, protect us!*

The men came downstairs shaking their heads.

"He ain't here," one of them said.

"If youse know where Brodie is hidin' youse'd better come clean or yer lives are in danger!" the ugly one said as he released Molly. The men turned and left the apartment. Molly sat on the floor with her children and wept. When Callum came home he found the place in shambles and a note from Molly that said she and the kids went to her parents' home and wouldn't come back until things had settled down for Brodie. He sat on a kitchen chair, slammed his fist on the table, and put his head in his hands. "If Joe doesn't find ya first and kill ya, dear broder, I might just do it meself!"

Collins sat with Brodie as he wrote up a testimonial of all that Joseph had been part of and gave in detail the recent random shooting of the Catholic girl. That, Collins said, would be the final straw that would put him in prison.

Meanwhile, Joe Campbell disappeared from the scene, but Collins' men kept on the lookout for him.

CHAPTER 18

"Tonnie, yer safer at the farm."

"But I thought it would just be for six weeks after the boys were born and then we'd get to return."

"I thought so, too, but the violence is pickin' up again and now this thing with Brodie hidin' out from the paras—we're all bein' careful here. Callum's place was ransacked and the family ascared out of their wits. Molly and the kids are stayin' with her folks. I'm sorry. I feel bad. I want ta see me wee lads and me wife!"

"Oh, no! Are they okay? I hate to hear that! Poor Molly and the kids!"

"I feel sorry fer Brodie when Callum finds him!"

"Well, this is disappointing news. I miss you so much."

"I miss ya, too. I do have some good news. Remember when I told ya about Mary O'Donal and her daughter Siobhan, and how they searched unsuccessfully fer Hugh's body?"

"Yes. That was sad."

"Well, they found his body in a bog that was close ta where they originally suspected!"

"Aw, that's awesome. I'm so happy for the family."

"It was all well and good until the IRA interrupted the funeral. They planted a bomb under the hearse. Fortunately, no one was in it when the bomb went off. I think they just wanted ta make a statement that they were still around."

"Oh, Eoin, that's terrible."

"I've talked ta the family. They want justice. Justice from the IRA for the death of Hugh and justice for the death threat."

"I don't blame them."

"Things are still unpredictable here."

"Isn't it safe out in the country where we live? Can't we come home?"

"It's more the travelin' that scares me. In Dublin and London the IRA are reachin' out and attackin'. Heathrow Airport had that scare a few years ago and I know we flew ya out since then, but things had settled down a bit. Now it's all heated up again. I just can't imagine two women and three children travelin' alone. Ya'd be so vulnerable."

"I wish there was some way—"

"Me as well, but, how are two of ya goin' ta maneuver two babes and a child on flights across the Atlantic anyway? And if ya had to run ta safety? Ach, I just can't think on it!"

"We'd manage. What if we flew in through Edinburgh?"

"And what? Drove yourselves down ta McGilroy's?"

"And then came over to Northern Ireland on a ferry. We'd be avoiding the big cities that are being attacked."

"Once again, by yourselves with three children. I mean, I could come over ta Scohtland. Ach! It's just so complicated."

"Maybe it doesn't need to be, Eoin."

"I'll think it o'er. We need ta wait till Joe Campbell is behind bars."

The troubleshooting between Eoin and Tonya continued until, exhausted and concerned about the cost of the long phone call, they said their final sweet words of love to one another and hung up.

Tonya stepped out of the big house and walked to where Maisie, Erin, Annie, and Fiahd sat on the rail fence while Gareth and Ed led horses out toward them.

Maisie watched Tonya as she leaned against the railing and put her chin in her hands. "Ya have a long face like a Lohrgan spade."

"I just talked to Eoin."

"How's he cuttin'?"

"Oh, fine. Joe Campbell is causing trouble with the family—Brodie left the paras."

"He did?" Maisie's eyes lit up and she clapped her hands. "Praise be and God protect him now!"

"But that's the problem; the whole family isn't safe until they find Joe. His thugs burst into Callum's home while Molly and the kids were home alone. They were searching for Brodie and they threatened Molly."

"Ach, poor Molly." Maisie's expression changed to sympathy. "Sure and the children will never ferget that."

"Molly and the children are with her folks now. She won't bring the family home until things settle down. And Eoin doesn't want us coming home until Joe's behind bars. And then, we'll have to figure out a safe way to get home."

"Ah." Maisie dropped her gaze to the ground.

Gareth and Ed brought three horses over to where the women and girls sat.

"Ready to go for a ride, ladies?" Gareth said. "Oh, hi, Tonya, we didn't know you'd be out here or we would've saddled up another horse. Do you want to ride?"

"That's okay. I just came out for some fresh air, but I really need to check in on the boys anyway. They'll be waking up soon."

"You're a full-fledged momma now!" Ed smiled.

"Yup!"

"Never thought I'd see the day!"

"Ya have a right brass neck, so ya have, rich lad," Maisie scoffed. Ed's head snapped up from getting Mabel ready to ride. Why would she call him that? None of his friends ever said anything about his parents' status that he could ever remember.

"It's okay, Maisie. Our *rich lad* here has every right to what he said." Tonya winked at Ed. "I vowed I would never have children, never marry, and just be the *rich aunt* to all my girlfriends' children." She laughed and then added as she walked away, "I was so wrong—but I'm glad I was wrong."

Maisie and Erin mounted Mabel while Gareth pulled Annie up with him on his horse. Ed took Fiahd.

Spring was in full swing. The fields showed signs of fresh growth, bordered by clusters of trees with yellow-green leaves. Maisie grew quiet, breathing in the country air, visually soaking in the vast stretch of land around her. She felt her lungs expand freely. Every part of her body felt calm. Everything was okay. There was no need to keep looking over her shoulder, no need to be prepared to run, and it was refreshing. The people here were growing on her. Uncle Ian reminded her of her da. Aunt Phyllis treated her like her own daughter. At first it was awkward, but she was learning to love it. Gareth was a good mix of Callum and Brodie. Tonya and Haley felt like the sisters she never had. If she stayed long enough to hang out with Penny, she thought they'd be the best of friends.

And then there was Ed. Well, she didn't know what to make of him— he seemed so perfect and so rich. She never acted quite right around him and he brought out the orneriness in her that her brothers often rebuked. Why did she feel the need to speak smartly around him and mock him with a nickname like Malibu Ken and now, "rich lad"? What a craic! Where did that come from? She had to admit, she found some kind of satisfaction in how her remarks drew fantastic expressions from him. The girls never stopped saying he was handsome, and while she agreed with them, it was his eyes—deep and soulful—that caught her attention. Were they blue? She thought so, but she never had the courage to stare too long. Okay, and maybe there was something about the way he sauntered about the farm, his long, sinewy arms swinging carelessly like everything in the world was righted. She'd seen him often from the view of her bedroom window.

All that being said, she didn't have any real need for him to notice her.

Ed watched Maisie. She was relaxed—more than when she first came. He was happy to see it. He was intrigued by her. Something about her drew his attention. Not in a romantic way, he told himself, though her looks were stunning, and he had to admit he loved the freckles that spread across her nose and pooled beneath her eyes. Those eyes—such a true green. More than Gareth's. He tried not to admit how he loved stealing glances at her face. It was probably her bold, clever remarks directed his way that attracted his attention most, though the "rich lad" comment hurt a bit. Why did she do that? Did it bother her that his folks did well for themselves? He thought she'd gotten past being intimidated by his mom. Anyway, he told himself, one could be intrigued by someone without being interested in them on a more personal level. He was positively done with the business of romance.

Maisie knew it was safer to be here until Joe Campbell was in jail and for that reason she was glad to have the trip back to Northern Ireland delayed. But when that was settled, well, there was the real possibility that Eoin and Tonya would figure out a way to get back to Northern Ireland way before she was ready to return. She felt sad. Ed noticed how her expression changed. He pulled his horse up next to her.

"Something wrong, Maisie?"

"No need ta concern yerself—"

"Oh, right, why would a *rich boy* like me care?" he said sardonically.

"I don't think that." It was as close to an apology as she could get and Ed was willing to let it go.

"So, what's up, anyway?"

"Tonya and Eoin are trying ta figure out how ta get us back ta Norn Iron when it's safe ta go back, so they are."

"Ah, still no answers?"

"No. An' it's not safe fer us women ta go back alone with three wee'uns."

"I'm sorry. I bet you miss home."

"Tonnie needs ta go back."

"Sure. And you do too, right?"

Did he want her to go back? She didn't blame him if he did. She certainly hadn't made herself endearing to him. She felt her throat constrict and couldn't talk. Embarrassed, she pulled ahead of Ed and put distance between them. Gareth caught up to him.

"What was that all about?"

"I'm not sure. That girl. She seems upset about not being able to go home. I wish I could help. It's not safe for them to go back right now and when they can go back, it won't be very safe to go alone."

"Someone else needs to accompany them."

"Are you thinking of going back, Gareth?"

"Not right now. I'm dying to go back, but Haley needs me, with four children. What about you, Ed?"

"What do you mean? What are you saying?"

"Are ya daft, man? Go with them! You always wanted to go see Northern Ireland and you have the funds for it, not to mention military status. Here's your chance to help the ladies return and see the land while you're at it!"

Eddy sat back in the saddle and slowed down.

"C'mon, Unca Eddy! Faster!" Fiahd said. Ed and Gareth picked up speed and caught up to Maisie. She made polite conversation with them, but it was obvious something was wrong.

***

The police found Joe Campbell hiding out in West Belfast in an abandoned warehouse and brought him in. He was put in jail until trial. There was no rush. Because Joe had been wanted for a very long time, the authorities were happy to see him behind bars and were in no hurry to take him to trial. So he sat, waiting. And when Collins told the MacCauleys the news, there was a great feeling of relief. Brodie, however, still remained in hiding until he could testify against Joe. This news traveled to America and now the plans for Tonya, Maisie, and the children were once again on the table. But there wasn't a good solution. Until the Wagners put their heads and their money together.

***

"Ah'll be sad to see you go again, son," Alma said as she laid a hand on Ed's arm.

"I will too, Ed, but I know even your momma agrees it would be a noble thing to escort the ladies and children back to Northern Ireland. You're the one to take them since you're the only one of us besides Hanford who has a permit to carry a gun," Fred said.

Alma shivered. "The ah-deah of mah son needen' to use a gun frahtens me like a rabbit in a fox hole!"

"Momma, I was in more danger in the Persian Gulf."

"I know, but that doesn't really make me feel much bettah."

Ed put his hand on his mother's shoulder. "We'll be fine, Momma. I'm sure I won't even need to use it. I'll talk to the MacCauleys and see if they can figure out the safest way to go."

"And y'all tell them, whatever way is best—even if it's a roundabout way, we'll pay for it. We want to get them back safely—" Alma's voice broke. "I think I've formed an attachment to those sweet Irish girls. Land sakes, I'll hate to see them go!"

"You know it could be a bit dangerous for all of us," Ed said. "But I'm willing to do this trip and take them back. Poor Eoin, he wants to see his new sons so badly."

"God protected you in the Middle East, son, and He can protect you all in Northern Ireland," Fred said.

The following day, when Ed peered out of the barn and saw the women sitting on the front porch with the babies, he walked over to them and announced to Tonya and Maisie that he would accompany them back to Northern Ireland. A wide smile spread across Tonya's face. She lifted her son in her arms until he was face to face with her. He smiled and cooed. "Did you hear that, Seamus? We're going home to see your daddy!"

But Maisie grew quiet, nodded politely, stood up with Sammy, and said, "Sure an' he needs a diaper change." Then, without another word, she disappeared into the house.

"Whatever is wrong with her?" Ed said. "I thought she'd be excited to go back."

"I suspect she was glad we were having trouble figuring out how to travel safely," Tonya said.

"You mean she doesn't want to return?"

"I don't think so. Not yet, anyway."

Ed smacked his forehead. "Here I thought I'd make her happy. Just the opposite. I can't figure her out, Tonya."

"Don't worry, Eddy. You don't need to figure her out. She'll be okay. Northern Ireland is her reality and she knows it. She's tough."

"Is there any way she could stay in America?"

"You mean for good? How could she afford it? She wouldn't feel right mooching off the farm here. And besides, her brothers want her back home."

"I suppose so," Ed said. But why did the thought of her staying in America feel like a good thing to him? It was obvious she didn't care for him and his *rich family,* but she still had family here with Ian and Gareth.

Ed went back to work, taking the horses out to the pasture. After Maisie put Sammy, nearly asleep now, in his crib, she went back to her room and sat on the bed. The prospect of going home didn't excite her at all. She was enjoying living on the farm, being with all these Wisconsin people and continually meeting others. Erin loved playing with her cousins and Maisie knew that brought a sense of delight to both sides to see the next generation getting to know each other. But what could she do? She stood up, went to the window, and looked out on the barn and the fencing that ran along the driveway and stopped at the chicken coop. She saw the tall, lanky movements of one of the men out with the horses and knew immediately that it was Eddy. She watched him for a while. His stride spoke of that easygoing nature again and his gentleness with the horse reminded her of his gentleness with Erin. That appealed to her significantly. He stopped and looked out at the sky as if pondering the weather and she found herself staring. Suddenly, Tonya appeared from behind her.

"We girls used to stare out this window and watch Gareth and Eddy working on the farm all the time." Tonya smiled as she bounced Seamus in her arms. "I used to pretend I was married here and was raising my family on this farm."

"Who did ya dream about marryin'?" Maisie said, stepping away from the window, hoping Tonya didn't see her staring at Ed.

"Oh, first it was Ed, then Gareth came along, then it was back to Ed, then Gareth, then Ed, then Gareth—"

"Never Keith?"

"*Not on your life*." Tonya chuckled. "He was extremely annoying. Carrie was the only one who ever saw the good in him. And there is good in him—now."

"I've seen it. Sure and he's good ta Carrie."

"Yes, who would've thought?" Tonya said. "So, Maisie, can I ask? You're not that excited to go back, are you?"

"No, but I'll survive. It's been grand ta be here with ya, Tonnie."

Sammy started to cry from his crib. Tonya exited quickly. Maisie looked back out the window. Ed was gone.

And soon, she'd be gone, too.

"Ach, I ferget meself." Maisie suddenly realized how much she'd been caught up in selfish reflection. "Tonnie, let me get Sammy," she said as she hurried to the bedroom across the hall. "Here I am daydreamin' while ya have yer hands full of wee'uns!"

Ed took Mabel out for a jaunt the following day and found Maisie standing by the stream at the edge of the cornfield. The rain fell gently and was cool on the skin. Maisie's hair lay damp about her shoulders and its deeper shades were magnified by the wetness. Ed tried not to notice.

"It's like a grand soft day in Ireland," Maisie said.

"Yes, it is," he said as he slid off the horse. "You don't seem to mind getting wet."

"Ya know what I'm talkin' about, so you do? A grand soft day?"

"I've heard the others use that expression, yes."

"Sure and there are things like this that remind me of home."

"Maisie." When he said her name, it sounded good to her. She turned to look at him and he could see the remnants of tears in her eyes. "I need to apologize—"

"About what?"

"About making the trip possible to return to Northern Ireland."

"Have ya popped yer clogs? That's a silly thing ta apologize fer."

"I know, but hear me out. I was just trying to help you, Tonya, and the children get home. I thought you'd be excited to go back, but Tonya told me you're feeling just the opposite."

Maisie nodded slightly. "She's right, ya know—good friend that she is. But yer not ta blame. It was goin' ta happen eventually."

"I'm sorry."

Maisie furrowed her brow. "Why? Why is it yer fault? And why did ya need ta rescue us in the first place?"

Ed took a step back. He didn't know how to answer that. A soft breeze stirred up and whipped past them. Maisie shivered and Ed wished he felt free enough to give her his jacket. But he didn't.

"Ya think all us poor Irish need rescuin' by all yer rich Americans, do ya?"

"No! No, not at all."

"And that we need yer Yankee assistance?"

"No, but—"

"Then why do ya take it on yerself ta help—"

"I didn't mean to offend you by it."

"Ya know, maybe it's a good thing yer comin' with us ta see how we manage over there. We're survivors, Eddy—people yer age and mine. We've been ta hell and back and we haven't needed ya before!"

Ed never experienced such a strange rebuke in return for his kindness. Once again, he didn't know how to respond.

"I see I've upset you. I'll—I'll just go." Ed mounted Mabel and rode off into the field.

Maisie watched him leave. It was a fine picture of him sitting deep and with ease in the saddle. He leaned back slightly, and she watched the rhythmic movement of his body as he disappeared into the back woods. She bit her lip. What possessed her to snap at him? Sure and she wished he hadn't volunteered to get them back to Northern Ireland so soon, but did she really need to lay into him like that? The sadness in his eyes haunted her. Those eyes. Definitely blue. She knew that now.

Why was he being so nice to her? She wasn't used to such kindness. Michael would never have apologized to her for anything. None of the guys she ever knew were this nice. Why was she actin' the maggot? And to a nice guy like Eddy, of all people?

Phyllis, Haley, and the children stood at the edge of the driveway in tears as they watched Tonya climb into the back seat with Erin and the babies. Ed hugged Alma one more time and with a tearstained face she joined the other women and children. Gareth and Ian gave Ed great big man-hugs and said their last words of wisdom before Ed slipped into the front seat next to Maisie. Fred started up the car and soon they were out of the driveway and disappearing down County QQ.

Ian stood by the side of the road, waving and watching the car vanish out of sight. Phylllis wrapped her arm in his.

"Another goodbye, dear. Are you going to be all right?"

"I'll be fine. I'm sad ta see them all go. I just got reacquainted with my long-lost niece—and got ta meet that bonny grandniece, too—but I'm glad that me son will be reunited with his wife and wee'uns."

"And are you worried about them going back?"

"Ya know me well. How can I not worry? I fear it's still unsafe in Norn Iron. The news reports are always—"

"I keep telling you, dear, that you should turn off the TV in the evenings and stop reading the newspapers."

"Yes, my love. I'll try harder." Ian smiled mischievously.

"Oh, you will not." Phyllis patted his arm and laughed.

Fred helped them unload the luggage at arrivals at O'Hare Airport in Chicago. Their flight from Chicago would take them to Edinburgh, avoiding the three cities across the Atlantic—Belfast, Dublin, and London—where IRA were active.

"Well, this is it, son," Fred said to Ed after he gave the women and children their last hugs. "Your momma and I are proud of your willingness to, as your momma says, 'rescue the girls and help out'. You've always had such a sacrificial soul."

"Thanks, Dad." Ed's face turned red at his dad's words and he didn't dare look at Maisie, but he knew she heard his father because of the slight groan that escaped her lips.

As they stood in the security check line Maisie teased, "Such a *sacrificial soul,* so he is."

"Never mind what my momma says," Ed said, embarrassed.

"She *worships* the ground ya walk on," Maisie said as they moved forward.

"Who are you talking about?" Tonya asked.

"Ed's momma."

"She does dote on her children. But can you blame her? Every mom should dote a bit on their children."

"Thanks, Tonya," Ed said.

"No, I don't blame her. She should be a proud momma," Maisie said and Ed turned in surprise.

"First you tease, then you compliment." Ed looked away. "I don't get you, Maisie MacCauley."

"I don't get ya neither, Edward Wagner."

Once again, she sounded like she was teasing. He pulled the luggage ahead as the line moved and sighed. He never felt such agitation and fascination at the same time from one woman. Even Haley in all their years together never brought him to this point. This trip could be a true test of his patience.

***

They were met by the McGilroys and Eoin in Edinburgh. When the travelers exited the sky bridge, Eoin ran up to Tonya to embrace her and Sammy. While he studied Sammy's little face, Maisie stepped up and put Seamus in his arms. Tears ensued as the baby boy studied the new face hovering over him. But it wasn't Seamus who was weeping.

CHAPTER 19

Aggie McGilroy, Johnny's wife, brought out tea for her guests in their traditional tenement home in Ballantrae, Scotland. The rooms were slightly larger than Ian's cottage and the ceilings were higher with tall sash windows. The chimney rose up high and majestic. Tonya and Maisie appeared from the small room off the sitting room.

"Are the wee'uns abed?" Aggie asked.

"Both boys are already asleep!" Tonya said.

"The twins are amazin', so they are!" Maisie said.

"Best wee bairns ever," Eoin said proudly as Tonya sat down beside him. He didn't waste time pulling her close and she snuggled into him. It had been too long.

"No prejudice there." Ed laughed.

"As long as they're close to each other they sleep well," Tonya added.

"Erin is still awake." Maisie frowned. "She's excited, anxious, and cryin' softly, but she should fall asleep soon."

"I noticed she didn't eat much at dinner," Tonya said. "Should I ask Aggie for some biscuits and tea?"

"She'll not eat nothin'," Maisie said. "Says her wee tummy hurts."

Ed's heart melted. "Do you mind if I go in and see her?"

Maisie nodded. "Away with ya. She seems ta like ya best anymore."

Ed stepped into the room where the babies slept soundly, sharing a make-shift crib out of a large box. Erin lay on a small cot, whimpering softly. Ed knelt on the floor and rested his arms on the thin mattress. Erin turned to face him, the fullness of her dark curls feathered about her head on the pillow. Her wide eyes were watery, her cheeks wet with tears.

"I can't go ta sleep, Uncle Eddy," she said in a pathetic, quiet voice. "But I'm just cryin' softly so as not ta wake the wee babes."

"How come you're crying?" Ed whispered.

She sniffed. "Sadness is on me."

"Why?"

"I liked yer farms an' all the people there. I liked Miss Alma's pretty dishes and the way she talked. I didn't want ta leave. I hate our place. I don't want ta go back."

"You've seen some things that aren't so happy where you live."

"Bloody people cryin' in the street. Children screamin' loudly. Scary soldiers."

"I'm sorry, Erin." Ed's heart hurt to hear her talk like that. "I don't think your ma wants to go back either. I think she has as much 'sadness on her' as you do."

"Surely?"

"Surely."

"But she doesn't act sorry like me."

"Well, I think she knows that going back is what she has to do right now, so she's pretending that it's okay." Ed caressed her arm. "Sometimes, grown-ups just do what has to be done, whether they like it or not."

"I don't want ta be growed-up."

"Me either."

"But ya are, *ya stook*."

"Oh, right. I suppose I am." Ed acted surprised and Erin smiled slightly. "Erin, we can pray about it, you know. God loves you and can either change where you live, or help you be happy in the place where you live now."

"I would like Him ta do just that." Erin reached over and took Ed's hand. His throat tightened. He paused a moment before he could pray. Her little white hand in his big tanned one endeared her to him even more. *God, I don't want to leave this child behind in a dangerous city!* After he prayed, he quoted Psalm 4:8, a verse his mother had always said to him at night when he was a child: "I will both lay me down in peace and sleep, for Thou Lord only makest me to dwell in safety." Erin's eyes closed. And then he sang a quiet good night song:

"Goodnight, goodnight, goodnight.

We'll meet in the morning bright.

May angels guard you while you sleep.

Goodnight, goodnight, goodnight."

"Again," Erin said softly, half asleep.

After Ed finished singing the song a second time, her eyes opened slightly and she mouthed, "again." After the third time, she was breathing deeply and sound asleep.

When he walked out into the sitting room, everyone stopped chatting and looked up at him.

"So?" Maisie said.

"She's asleep."

"Why am I not surprised? Erin is in love with you, Eddy," Tonya said. "I think she'll do anything you tell her to do."

"So what'd ya do?" Maisie said, pleased that Erin took such a liking to Eddy, and pleased that he went out of his way to be so kind to her.

"We talked, prayed—"

"What'd ya talk about?" Maisie put her cup down.

"Oh, just stuff." Ed didn't want to burden Maisie with her daughter's sadness. He felt the pain in Erin's little soul and in Maisie's too. But he knew Maisie didn't want to hear it from him. She'd already made it clear that she didn't need his sympathies.

The next morning after Aggie fed her guests a light breakfast of porridge and rowies, croissant-like rolls, but salty and flat, with a generous amount of butter, she stepped up to the table to clear the food and insisted that the four young adults go out sightseeing before they headed to Northern Ireland the following day.

When Aggie returned to the table to take more dishes and saw that Eoin was in turmoil about which place to go—since he had so many favorite places—she spoke up.

"Why don' ya gae and show 'em one o' yer favorite wee hills, Eoin?"

"Ah, yer talkin' about the Knockdolian Hill and the Castle, are ya? Ya call that 'wee'?" Eoin laughed.

"Aye." Aggie smiled. "An' ya aught tae be goin' a stoat aboot the Ballantrae Beach!"

"Aye, good memories there!" Eoin said. "What about the wee'uns?"

"Leave 'em wehth me."

"Are ya sure?"

"Aye." Aggie turned to Tonya. "Ye want tae gae now, dae ye, Tonnie?"

"Yes! Please!"

Ed's head was spinning. "I couldn't follow all that. What are you guys talking about?"

Tonya explained. "Eoin used to love walking along the Ballantrae Beach. He took me there on our honeymoon. Aggie was saying we should go for a walk there."

"Sounds nice," Ed said.

"I'm in," Maisie said. "Yer okay keepin' Erin? She can talk both yer ears off."

"And you'll be okay with the boys?" Tonya asked.

"Aye, I've got me daugh'er, Josephine, comin' tae help fer the dee. Make sure ya dress warm. In Scohtland, we only got two seasons, June and winter!"

Ed laughed and Eoin nodded in agreement.

"Thehs ehs fantastic! Thank ya, Aggie," Eoin said after Tonya fed the boys and he led the way out the door.

They pulled into the Ballantrae shore car park and got out. Eoin took Tonya's hand. "Follow us!" Eoin and Tonya were obviously glad to be with each other after so many months separated. Now they walked together like two newlyweds, hand in hand, arms brushing against each other, leaving the other two behind. Ed looked at Maisie, wondering what the two of them should do—walk together? She looked at him and stepped on ahead. He shook his head and followed.

They headed north along the coastal path and the beach. Suddenly Ed exclaimed, "A seal!"

"Ya win first prize namin' the animal," Maisie teased, looking at him behind her.

"I'm just surprised to see one, that's all."

"Ya don' see them in America?"

"Only at the Brookfield Zoo or the Lincoln Park Zoo in Chicago. They're not in the Great Lakes that border the Midwestern states."

Tonya glanced back at Maisie and said loudly, "I believe you can find them on the west coast of the US and definitely in Alaska!"

"How do you even know these things?" Ed yelled back.

"How else? TV!"

"I should have guessed that!" Ed laughed.

Maisie looked at Ed questioningly. Tonya stopped quickly and when Eoin felt the tug of her hand he stopped, too. They turned and waited for Maisie and Ed to catch up to them.

"When we were kids," Ed explained, "Tonya was known for watching a lot of TV."

"Why was that?" Maisie asked.

"Remember when I told you my dad was gone a lot?" Tonya said. "Mom and I were lonely at home, so we sat in front of the TV every night together. Whenever I could, I'd go over to the Becketts' and hang out with Haley. But there were many alone times for me. When I was older and Mom started to get busy outside the home, I got into photography and that helped fill in the lonely days."

"She used to know all the shows. Us farm kids were clueless."

"But see how it paid off?" Tonya laughed. "Now I'm so smart."

"Okay, *smarty*." Eoin pointed. "What is that large bird sittin' on a rock with his wings spread and flappin'?"

"Um. Well, I don't think I saw the TV show about that one." Tonya laughed.

"It's a cormorant," Eoin said smugly. "And I didn't have ta watch the telly ta know that!"

"You're a man of much experience!" Tonya slid her hand back into his.

They continued on their walk, watching the white waves and stopping here and there to inspect things like the remains of an old fishing boat or a piece of driftwood. They came upon a drystone dike and stopped.

"Check out this old stone wall!" Ed ran his hand across it.

"The farmers use them ta create boundaries around their property and ta create shelter fer the sheep," Eoin explained.

"But it's so high," Ed said.

"Sheep can jump!" Maisie smirked.

"So how are we going to get past it?" Ed asked.

"Aye, what now?" Maisie asked.

"We cross it," Eoin said.

"You say that like it's so simple, but there's barbed wire on both sides," Ed said.

"Just be careful. I'll go first. I've done this a million times," Eoin said as he started across. Tonya followed and copied Eoin's twisted movements. Eoin took her hand and helped her jump off. Ed went next and Maisie followed. When she came to the end she looked at the ground below her and hesitated. Ed reached up and took her hand. She looked at him for a brief moment and then came down with ease.

"Thank you," Maisie said curtly, as she quickly drew her hand from his. "But I think I coulda gotten down on me own."

"Is it a crime to be a gentleman?" Ed said and walked on ahead of her. The enjoyment of feeling her soft, delicate hand in his was cut short by her brusqueness. They continued across a bog until they came to firmer ground, but then the slopes grew steeper.

"Just when I thought it was getting easier," Tonya whined.

"You're a bit knackered, are ya?" Eoin said.

"I never got back to my old self after the twins."

Eoin took her hand. "I'll help ya, me bonny lass," he smiled. "Yer doin' great."

Ed noticed Maisie struggling. He held out a hand to help her but she refused his assistance, "I don' need mollycoddlin'," she said and continued on without him. When she started to slip and stumble a few more times, Ed grew frustrated. *Stubborn girl*, he thought.

Finally he said, "Just take my hand, Maisie. And don't argue it."

"I don' need a man ta come ta my rescue all the time."

"Well, *good.* Because I don't need a woman who wants rescuing all the time *either*. I had enough of that in the war!" He was forceful in his words and she looked up at him, surprised. She didn't want to succumb to his help, but a strong hand would solve the problem. She found herself reaching for his hand and putting hers into his. She didn't want to admit it felt good. Did Michael's hand affect her like this?

Eventually, they came to a farm track that took them down the lower slopes of Knockdolian. They walked through grasses, bell heather, and a variety of fungi. There were sheep on the slopes, starlings in the skies above them, and wildflowers at their feet.

"Brilliant!" Maisie suddenly exclaimed as she slipped her hand away from Ed's. "See the white flowers? They're called the Grass-of-Parnassus. I love these!" She bent down and picked one, then turned to Ed to show him. "See the petals? They're heart-shaped. Parnassus means 'loving marshes.'"

"They're pretty," Ed said, enjoying the simple delight in her eyes.

Eoin picked a few and gave them to Tonya.

"I love these. They're so dainty," Tonya said.

"Dainty and bonny." Maisie smiled.

Dainty and bonny. The words ran through Ed's head as he watched her put the flowers in her hair.

But he wasn't thinking about the *flowers*. And he wasn't comfortable that his mind went there so quickly.

After an hour, they arrived at Knockdolian Castle at the top of Knockdolian Hill. It would have been difficult to find, but Eoin knew his way and the others followed. At the foot of the castle, they studied the ancient build of mortared rubble with a parapet at the top.

"It's different than I thought it would be. It's so tall and slim," Ed said as he walked around the old castle. "How old did you say it was, Eoin?"

"It was built in the sixteenth century. It's called a pele—a small square defensive tower."

"In the US the oldest buildings aren't much older than 200 years!" Tonya said.

Ed came up behind Maisie when he saw that she had stepped away from the castle and was looking off across the water in the distance.

"The view here is gorgeous. What is that island way over there?"

"Home," Maisie said as she walked closer to the edge of the hill. Ed followed.

"That's Ireland?"

"Aye."

"Are you excited at all to get back home?"

"I look forward ta seein' me broders again."

"That's it?"

She turned, gave him a look he couldn't define, and started to walk back to the castle.

"Wait." He grabbed her arm. She stopped and looked down at his hand.

"What d'ya want?"

He took his hand away. "What was that look for?"

"Why do ya care so much?"

"Why do you avoid certain topics with me?"

"Do I?"

"Yes. And I'm getting weary of it."

"Yer keepin' count then, are ya?"

"So far," Ed said with his hands on his hips, "I think you've done it about seven times."

She paused and studied his face. Wait. *Was he serious?* She stared into his eyes. Was he smiling behind that look?

Ed enjoyed the child-like way she studied him, the innocence that showed itself despite her guarded ways. But he couldn't hold a straight face much longer. Suddenly, a glint of a tease showed in his eyes and she responded with a wry smile.

"Yer pullin' me leg!" She smacked his arm and started back to the castle.

"The look on your face was priceless." Ed laughed as he followed her. "You seriously thought I was keeping count?"

"Naw, ya didn' have me fooled at all."

"You're a big fat liar, Maisie."

"Who's the liar?" She pushed him. "Ya were lyin' ta me a minute ago, that ya were."

"I was just kidding."

"Semantics."

"That's a big word for such a—"

"Such a what?"

"For such a—such a—" Ed hesitated. *What did he really want to say?*

"Come on." She nudged him again. "Say yer mind, Eddy Wagner, rich farm lad from America."

"Okay." He turned, faced her, and smiled despite the name-calling. It was having a different effect on him lately after it occurred to him that no one else had been given a nickname by Maisie. She stopped walking and waited, watching him. "For such a person as yourself," he said with a twinkle in his eye. It didn't get past Maisie.

"That was it?" She smiled at him. "That was what ya were goin' ta say ta me?"

"You don't want me to really say it." Ed smiled back.

Maisie stepped a little closer. "Are ya ascared o' little ol' me?"

"Sometimes." Ed nodded, taking a breath.

"That would be me own fault." She started to walk again and he stepped beside her.

"Yeah, you're tricky, but I'm not really afraid of you." Ed nudged her.

"Soooo?" Maisie nudged him back. "What were ya really goin' ta say?"

"Fine. What went through my head was this; for such a pretty head as yours."

"What?" Maisie drew back. "Pretty heads can't be smart?"

"You're trying to look angry, but I can see right through you, Maisie MacCauley! You liked what I said!" Ed laughed and Maisie laughed with him but she shook her head.

"As if ya really have a clue what I like."

"It's so beautiful here," Maisie said as they walked back along the beach.

"It really is," Ed replied. "Eoin, do you miss Scotland? I would miss this here."

"Aye, but it's just as beautiful where I was born. No matter all the trouble my country has had, I've had a yearnin' ta go back the last few years. It's home ta me, ya know?"

"I know what you mean," Ed said. "When I was in the Middle East I missed Wisconsin badly. I missed the green landscape and the cooler weather. When I returned home though, things weren't the same there. My sister, Peggy, was off to a mission field and Keith had a pastorate. I suddenly felt like an outsider. Mom and Dad are empty nesters now and I'm like the third party. I need to move on."

"Where will ya go?" Maisie asked.

"That's a good question. One I'm not ready to answer," Ed said.

"Tonnie, do ya miss Wisconsin?" Maisie asked.

"Sure. But where we're at, the rolling hills and the greenery is enough like home that I don't miss it much. Oh, and the changeable weather. I like it when the weather keeps me guessing."

"The weather is a bit more crazy here, don' ya think?" Eoin picked up a piece of driftwood, flung it out into the water, and then took Tonya's hand again.

"Definitely. If I'd grown up in a state like California, this kind of life and this kind of changeable weather would've been more drastic."

"But didn't you always want to move to California, Tonya?" Ed said.

Tonya laughed. "Ah, what are old friends for but to remind me of the olden days when I worshiped all the movie stars in Hollywood?"

Suddenly Eoin released Tonya's hand and motioned to Ed. "I'll race ya down ta the car."

"Even with a bum knee?" Ed laughed.

"Aye, it's stronger now!"

And off the two men ran.

"Men. They always find somethin' ta compete in, don't they?" Maisie said.

Tonya smiled and sighed. "*Life* is a competition."

"Me broders will peacock whenever the occasion calls fer it."

"I'm not surprised," Tonya said. The women continued walking down the beach, keeping an eye on the men.

"Did Eddy compete a lot with his broder?"

"Um—" Tonya thought for a minute. "I don't really remember much of that going on, but I do remember Keith and Haley competing a lot. In their younger years they literally stood face-to-face with palms down, measuring their heads, fighting about who was taller. Of course, then there were the years *Eddy and Gareth* were in competition for Haley! That got a bit tricky and awkward for the rest of us! We didn't know how to respond or how to help them."

"Did Eddy always have a glad eye fer Haley?"

"A crush?"

"Aye."

"Ever since I can remember. As early as grade school."

"Did she ever return his affections?"

"Oh, yes. We all thought Haley and Eddy would end up together, until later in high school when something clicked between her and Gareth."

"Poor Eddy."

"Yeah, we all felt bad for him—including Haley."

"So, when did Eddy give up on her?"

"Let's see, we had all graduated from high school by then. Gareth went back to Northern Ireland for three years and while he was gone Eddy pursued her. He was there for her while she mourned what she thought was the loss of Gareth to his homeland. And well, you know Eddy."

"Aye, the rescuer. Why does he do that? Sure and ta put on airs. Does he have ta be in control?"

"No. Eddy just has a big heart and hates to see people suffer."

"Sure and there wasn't an ulterior motive ta save Haley? He wanted her fer himself, so he did."

"Well, yeah, he did and he wasn't going to give up easily."

"And that's what hurt him in the end."

"Yeah. When Gareth returned and apologized for what he put Haley through by leaving, the two were back together in no time!"

"Poor lad."

"Yeah. It was hard. He's a pretty passionate guy."

"Did he get over Haley? Does he still feel fer her?"

"He got over her—finally—and now Gareth, Haley, and Eddy are the best of friends. But I think that's why he's so cautious now. He's been hurt twice and he feels it deeply."

Tonya glanced at Maisie when she realized her Irish friend was smiling widely. "What a craic! I think Eddy won!" Maisie said.

"Be careful. You said that like you're his cheerleader!" Tonya looked down the beach in the direction of where the guys ran and saw that Maisie was correct. Eddy was doing a victory dance while Eoin was bent over huffing and puffing.

"Promise me ya don' tell him!" Maisie said. "I'd hate fer him ta think I've set me cap on him."

Tonya nodded. "You used to think he was a loser. So, have you changed your tune?"

"Maybe. He comes across at first like a smooth, rich American lad who is a people pleaser and one ya could lead around like a horse if ya act sorrowful enough. But gettin' ta know him, I've begun ta see his strong side.

And he has a big heart, so he does. Some people take that fer weakness, ya know? But I don't."

"I'm glad you've finally gotten to see the real Eddy that we all know and love," Tonya said.

CHAPTER 20

The Northern Ireland-bound gang said goodbye to the families in Ballantrae. They traveled down in Eoin's van to the Stranraer terminal to take the Sea Cat ferry and cross the North Channel to Belfast. The waters were smooth and the view was breathtaking. Seamus and Sammy slept in their new carseats in the van most of the trip, making it easy for the young parents. Maisie sat with Tonya and Eoin on the boat while Ed and Erin walked around hand in hand taking in the view and feeling the mist of the water on their faces. Three hours later they debarked in Northern Ireland.

As they drove through West Belfast, Maisie withdrew, but Ed sat up straight, experiencing for the first time the world he'd heard about so much but had never been to. The smell of car exhaust, the constant noise of traffic, the gutters clogged with soggy trash, and crowds rushing by with shopping bags weren't any different than the big cities in the US. But the presence of Royal Irish Constabulary in their Black and Tans—dark-green tunics that looked black and khaki military trousers—reminded him that this was not a peaceful place. The Edwardian architecture was scarred with the violence that had haunted the city for the last thirty years. They passed by a burnt-out building still smoldering, and, as Eoin veered the van around the debris in the road, a blackened car. "What happened here?" Ed asked.

"Probably a bomb," Eoin said.

No one else acted surprised or thought anything of it. Except Ed.

They passed by cheap row houses unlike the nice workers' cottages, Victorian homes, and bungalows that he'd seen back home in the big cities. They drove past a peace wall near the Shankill Road covered with graffiti, lined at the top with barbed wire, and other buildings here and there destroyed by bombs. It was a stark reminder to Ed that he was in the war-torn country that he had seen appear again and again on the *Evening News* and that Gareth had told him so much about. As they drove slowly by another peace wall Ed read aloud, "Ulster will fight, and Ulster will be right."

Eoin motioned to the buildings. "See the flags wavin' outside random windows—there are only Ulster flags in this part of the city. See the red-and-white cross? And the crown?"

Ed ducked slightly to look out the van window. "Oh, yeah, I see them."

"The graffiti here and the Ulster flags are a clear sign that we're in Protestant—or Loyalist—territory. On the other side of that Peace Wall is Catholic territory—the Republican side—and there are Republican flags—the tricolor flag: green, white, and orange—flying out the windows and graffiti slanderin' the Prods."

"Prods?"

"Protestants."

A surreal and sad wave of emotions swept through Ed. This was the city where Gareth experienced that horrible outing with his family, July of '72, when the Provisional IRA set off twenty bombs in Belfast as a response to the breakdown of talks between the British and the IRA. It was later called Bloody Friday. The MacCauleys, as well as so many other people, had gone for a day in Belfast to go shopping and see the city. It was a terrible disaster and the IRA suffered much backlash from it.

Even though the sun was pushing through heavy clouds, sending random rays across the busy streets, Ed felt the darkness that existed outside the vehicle. He saw the tense faces of the people rushing by on the sidewalks and the women hurrying their children.

Finally, they arrived at the rundown tenement building on Shankill Road where Maisie and Erin lived.

"Well, this is yer stop," Eoin said as he parked. "It's good ta have ya back."

"I'll help you with your suitcase." Ed started to get out, but Maisie shook her head. Eoin saw her response in the rearview mirror and stopped Ed.

"It's not necessary. I'll help her," Eoin said.

"That's okay, I can get it," Ed insisted.

"No, Ed, *stay in the van,*" Eoin said through his teeth.

Tonya turned around from the front passenger seat. "Better do as he says, Eddy. This isn't the safest area."

"And you live here?" he said to Maisie in astonishment.

Maisie's cheeks turned bright red. She didn't respond but got out of the van. "Goodbye, Eddy. It was nice ta know ya," she said abruptly, and shut the door.

After Eoin, Erin, and Maisie were gone. Tonya turned around in her seat. "Okay, I lied. It's not so much that it's not safe, albeit it *is* Belfast. It's more because Maisie doesn't want you to see her place, Eddy."

"Why? I wouldn't be judgmental."

"Eddy, are you daft?"

"Daft? *Nice touch, Tonya.* Northern Ireland is growing on you." Ed tried to joke but he really didn't feel it at the moment.

Tonya let out a long sigh. "Think about how wealthy your parents' home is and then look at these tenement buildings. Maisie was blown away by your folks' house: the furniture, the dishes …everything. I think it made her feel inferior to you."

"But I don't act condescending—do I?" Ed asked in frustration.

"No, not at all. But it doesn't matter. To her you're rich and you're American. Two strikes."

"Yeah, I've gotten that from her. I thought she was just being her typical sarcastic self."

"Remember the saying, 'Too much truth in jest'?"

"Okay. I get it." Ed sat back in the seat. "Thanks for the eye-opener, Tonya—or as everyone here calls you, *Tonnie*."

Tonya smirked. "That would be Eoin's doing."

When Maisie, Erin, and Eoin reached the door to the flat, Maisie got her key out and tried it in the lock but the key didn't fit.

"I don't understand," Maisie said as she threw her hands up in frustration.

"What's wrong?" Eoin asked.

"My key won't go in the lock!"

Eoin tried the key himself but to no avail.

"See, I told ya!"

Eoin knocked on the door several times before a stranger opened it.

"What's all the noise fer?" a middle-aged man grumbled. "What d'ya want?"

Maisie stepped close and shouted, "What are ya doin' in me flat?"

"Yer flat? What are ya? Thick as two short planks? Away off and feel yer head!"

"Hold yer hour, man!" Eoin stepped between the two. "This was her place but she's been gone fer a few months. A friend o' hers was supposed ta be stayin' here and keepin' it fer her."

"Ya'd have ta talk ta the landlord. I don' know nuthin' about it." The
man slammed the door shut and they heard the bolt turn inside. Maisie wanted
to cry. Erin had a look of horror on her face.

Eoin squatted down on his haunches and held Erin's hands. "Ye'll
stay with us, lassie, until we get this figured out, ya know?" He stood up and
looked at Maisie somberly. She nodded thanks, took Erin's hand, and bravely
walked out of the tenement building and back to the car. Eoin followed
quietly behind. Maisie and Erin climbed into the vehicle while Eoin put their
luggage back in the van. Tonya and Ed watched with confusion. Maisie's face
was completely flushed by now and she sat in the seat, quiet and stoic.

"What's going on?" Tonya asked.

"Not sayin' too much with wee ears on alert, but Maisie and Erin get
ta stay at our place tonight!" Eoin tried to sound enthusiastic.

"Ma, does that man have all me toys?"

"Hush, agra, we'll not take that worry on us, aye?"

"Aye."

"Well, Erin, looks like you get to hang out with me a bit longer." Ed
hoped to distract the bewildered child now sitting in her seat with her arms
crossed and lips in a pout. Meanwhile, he felt it wise to avoid saying anything
to Maisie at the moment.

"Are ya goin' ta stay at Uncle Eoin's house, too, Uncle Eddy?"

Tonya caught Maisie's sudden look of dismay.

"Yer house might be a bit tight fer all o' us," Maisie said. "Maybe ya
ought ta drop me and Erin at Callum's house."

"Oh, it's okay, Maisie. You and Erin will take the other bedroom.
We'll keep the boys in our bedroom and Ed can stay down on the sofa. I
wouldn't mind having another woman in the house for a while yet with these
little guys."

After they got back to Eoin's place, Maisie made some phone calls and discovered that the friend she left to keep watch over her flat had stopped paying rent and left the place a few weeks after Maisie left for America. Meanwhile, the landlord leased the place out to the grumpy man who met them at the door. Of course, she couldn't really blame him for being upset at them. Much to their disappointment, Maisie and Erin's possessions were put out on the street a month ago and by now were long gone.

That night, Maisie had a hard time sleeping. She worried about what she was going to do and where she was going to live. Tonnie would only need help with the twins for a short time, after all. Maisie's mind wouldn't stop spinning. She needed to get up and clear her head, so she put on her bathrobe over her nightgown, stepped out of the bedroom, and moved down the steps as quietly as possible. She tiptoed past Ed on the couch and went into the kitchen. She moved the tea kettle carefully, pouring water into it, hoping to make herself a cup of tea without waking Ed. When the water came to a boil, however, she wasn't fast enough to stop the whistling of the steam through the spout of the kettle. Ed stirred. She froze, hoping the noise hadn't woken him. But it was no use. Ed sat up and squinted sleepily. "Who's out there?"

"It's me, Maisie," she whispered, "just gettin' the tea things out. Sorry I woke ya."

"It's okay. What are you doing?"

"Havin' tea."

"Well, I figured—what time is it?" Ed stepped into the kitchen, raking his hand through his hair, hoping to smooth out some of the mess. Maisie looked him over. The grey sweatpants and old tee shirt with the US Army logo that he wore were obviously clothes he'd had several years. And was that a hole in the knee? He wasn't the perfect man anymore with this sloppy, fresh-from-sleep look. She lifted one side of her mouth, trying not to reveal a smile of satisfaction.

"What are you smiling about?" he asked.

"Half four in the marnin'," she said, answering his previous question and avoiding his last.

"What?"

"Ya asked me the time?"

"Oh, right."

"Would ya—would ya take a cup o' tea in yer hand?"

"Sure."

"What do ya take?"

"*Lots* of sugar."

"I thought *Northerners* in the US took tea without sugar."

"My momma's from the state of Georgia, making her a *Southerner*— and they like their tea sweet."

"Bless yer sweet ma. She talked so differently than the rest o' yer family." Maisie brought out a tray with a teapot and two cups out to the sitting room while Ed built up the fire. He watched as she poured the tea, her delicate fingers wrapped around the handles of the porcelain. They sipped quietly at opposite ends of the couch with the sound of peat crackling in the fireplace. After a while Maisie sighed and set her cup on the end table. Ed watched her as she pulled out the loose braid she had put in her hair for bed. She started to play nervously with the waves between her fingers and Ed felt the impulse to reach over and calm her hands and feel the luxurious strands that fell about her shoulders. He checked himself. It was a weakness of his to appreciate such beauty in a woman and it was what got him into trouble before—falling so easily for Cassandra when he had resolved to be single. He looked at the weave in the rug instead.

Maisie needed to talk to someone and, as much as she tried to avoid baring her soul to Ed, the rich American farm boy, he was the one who was available. He didn't seem so intimidating in the middle of the night, however, looking so normal and all.

"Worry is on me," she said.

"About where you'll live?"

"And work, and care fer Erin, and—"

Ed put his teacup down. "You don't think you could get another job waitressing?"

"Sure an' it would probably land me back in Belfast. I just don' want ta live there anymore, ya know? It might force me ta live on the bru."

"What's the 'bru'?"

"Government help. Sure and I hate ta take it, but it would only be for a while. I just know I don' want Erin ta live in the city anymore. I know she hates it. She told me."

Ed nodded. "Yeah, she told me, too."

Maisie perked up with a troubled expression. "She did?"

Ed bit his lip. He shouldn't have let that slip out. "Um, yes."

"When?"

"Well, it was that night in Scotland when I helped her go to sleep."

"And all this time—ya never told me?"

Great. Was he going to be in trouble with this woman again? He never knew when she was going to disapprove of his actions or his words.

"Well? Why did ya keep it ta yerself? She's me own daughter."

"I didn't think you wanted to hear it."

"And why wouldn't I then?"

"You made it pretty clear you didn't want me talking to you about your troubles."

Maisie took a sip of her tea and stared blankly at the floor. How could she argue that? She let out a long sigh.

She looked at him meekly. "An' that would be me own fault, so it would. I'm sorry, Eddy."

He wasn't expecting that from her and a chuckle rumbled from his throat.

Her eyes widened. "Are ya laughin' at me apology?"

"I was a bit surprised, is all. But then, what's new? I never know how you're going to react to what I say."

"I know I've been a bit of a crazy cailin around ya, but—"

"The 'frogs in the box' analogy fits here."

"It's 'mad as a box of frogs,' fer yer future usage." Maisie laughed quietly. "Yer a real craic, Eddy."

"See? I *can* be funny."

"Without the tryin'."

He smiled at her. "Look, I feel like I bring out a certain side of you that—"

"A fightin' spirit?"

"You said it, not me. I'm not sure why I do, but I'm sorry—for whatever it was I did—or said. I don't always understand women and I always want to help. I used to think it was one of my charms—"

Maisie laughed quietly as she settled back into the sofa.

"See what I mean? And sometimes, I stumble over my own two feet trying and then I read your reactions wrong."

"Ach, yer not that clumsy!"

"No, I am. I don't read women well at all," Ed said as he slouched down and leaned his head back on the couch.

"Is that why ya don't want ta get involved in another relationship?"

He sat up straight again. "Who told you that? Wait—Tonya? Or was it Haley? Those girls—they talk all the time."

"Tonya told me. She told me about Cassandra and how you were there for her during the war."

"Yeah, that one backfired." He slumped back on the couch. "No pun intended."

Maisie's expression softened. "Do ya still have feelin's fer her?"

"No." He turned and looked at her. "And I suppose you know the other story? The 'love triangle,' as the girls like to romanticize it—"

"With yerself, Haley, and Gareth? Of course. A grand love story, so it is."

"Not if you're at my end of the story."

"True. I'm sorry fer it, Eddy."

"What are you sorry for? You had nothing to do with it."

She startled at his question but when she looked at him he was grinning. "Ach, I deserved that."

"Okay, seriously, thanks. That's kind of you to say."

"I can be cordial."

"I like that side of you."

Their eyes met briefly, they gave polite smiles, and then turned away from each other.

Ed stared into the fire. "Well, Tonya's right. I've been burned twice now and I'm not ready to go in for another scorching any time soon."

"I understand. I've been hurt a bit differently, so I have, and only by one person, but it was enough heartache that I don't want ta ever put myself in that position again, ya know?"

"What happened, Maisie? You never talk about it."

"I don' like ta reminisce about me past."

"I noticed. Is it that you don't remember or that you're trying hard not to remember?"

"That."

"What?"

Maisie smirked. "Both."

"There's wisdom in putting the past behind you, as long as you've dealt with it, forgiven the people who caused the hurt, and moved on from them."

Maisie sat up straight. "Forgive them? Forgive who? The men who shot me parents and left them bleedin' in front of our burnin' house? The man who abandoned me and Erin ta fight fer a useless cause and then lost his life tryin' ta get away from all the fightin'?"

"Is that what happened with Michael?" Ed watched her.

Maisie shook her head. "I didn't mean ta say all that."

Ed lifted one eyebrow and said carefully, "Maisie, do you remember any of what you saw as a child?"

Maisie turned away from him and watched the fire. She tucked her teeth into her lips and jutted her chin to keep the tears from coming. "I didn't mean ta pour my life out like that!" She swallowed hard. "It's just so late and me feelin's are so—" In what felt like a natural move, Ed scooted closer to Maisie on the sofa and rested his hand on her shoulder.

He shouldn't have done that and he shouldn't have moved closer, Maisie thought, *because it felt nice, and I will surely melt and fall apart more.* She stood, took a few steps, and shook her head. "I should be off ta bed."

Ed rose and came up behind her. "Why can't you talk about it?"

"You don' know what it was like!" Maisie sensed his closeness behind her and told herself to step away. But she didn't.

Ed realized the lack of distance he impulsively put between himself and Maisie, but to step away now wouldn't feel right. Of course, being this close to her late at night didn't feel right either. His momma used to say, "*no one thinks right late at night.*" "I have a pretty good idea, Maisie. I used to listen to all the horrible things Gareth lived through. Gareth saw what happened at your folks' house, too, you know. He was with his family in Belfast on Bloody Friday. He was across the street when his friend, Dennis, died in a pub explosion. He'd sit up in the loft of the barn with me, talk it all out, and I'd just listen. He used to have horrible nightmares, but eventually, they died away."

"Maybe I'm not like Gareth," Maisie said. *And maybe I should move away from you.*

"No, you're definitely not like Gareth," Ed said, admiring how the light from the fire made golden highlights in her hair. "But you might want to consider talking about all you've been through with someone, instead of bottling it up inside. When Eoin came to the farm, he was holding in a lot of stuff and a lot of guilt for his mother's death. He was so tense, very bitter and a bit of a pain in the neck. Tonya couldn't stand it and she pushed him to talk about it. It was such a relief—and he was so much happier and at peace when he finally told the whole story of what happened on the beach to him and Anna."

Suddenly, she felt like Ed was trying to coerce her to talk. She turned around and faced him. "Why do ya care so much? Why do ya keep pesterin' me ta talk about it?"

"Look, the whole MacCauley family has become such a part of me. And you and Erin, well, you're part of that special family that I love and I care—" Ed's voice cracked and he felt his throat tighten. They stood too close now and he knew Maisie could see his eyes water. He felt embarrassed, but he had to finish what he started to say. "I care—well, I care about you and Erin, too. I guess—I guess I just can't help it."

Maisie felt the tears start to come and she was mad she couldn't stop them. *Why did he have to be so kind? It makes me feel weak.* Her shoulders shook and Ed wished to take her in his arms. But he didn't.

"I wish there was some way I could help you, Maisie—not rescue you, of course, because you don't need rescuing." He enjoyed her chuckle amidst her soft crying. "And I'm not looking to be your knight-in-shining armor because you don't want a knight to rescue you." She laughed a bit more and the crying nearly ceased. "I've had that blow up in my face too many times anyway. This is just me as a friend, wanting to help a friend."

She looked up at him and they locked eyes. She patted his chest and he automatically put his hand over hers. "Ya have a special kind of heart, Eddy. Thank ya, but—me and Erin—we'll find a way. I do appreciate yer kindness and see it fer what it is now, so I do, and I appreciate it."

Perhaps it was the lateness of the night and the emotions that moved freely about the space between them, but the momentary pause spoke of something more than friends. Maisie let her hand slip away and took a step back. Ed was afraid of what he felt. He turned away from her and watched the peat crackle in the fireplace. It wasn't supposed to go this direction. Surely they were talking and he was comforting her as good friends do—just like he would with Tonya or Haley. Surely that was all.

"I should go ta bed, so I should," Maisie said.

"Yeah, you should. It's late. Thanks for the tea."

"Goodnight, Eddy."

"Goodnight, Maisie."

CHAPTER 21

It was the weekend. The weary travelers took a long morning to relax, but by the afternoon they were all ready to go see how the MacCauley homestead was coming.

When they arrived, Eoin yelled out to his cousins and the McGilroy crew working on the house. "The lassies are back and we've brought the twins and Ed Wagner. Step down from all yer hard work and come say hi!"

Callum and Johnny climbed down off the ladders while their sons, Duncan, Graham, and Tommy put their tools down and came over to greet everyone.

"This is Eddy," Tonya said excitedly after naming everyone for Ed. "He's an old friend from Wisconsin and a very *close* friend of Gareth's."

"It's fantastic ta meet ya, Eddy—"

"It's great to meet all of you, but you can call me Ed. It's these girls. They can't get away from calling me by my childhood name." Ed smiled as he shook their hands.

"Och!" Johnny laughed. "Then I'll be sure tae call ye Ed! I wouldna want tae be though' a lass!"

"An' I'll be doin' the same, ya know," Callum said with a smile.

"And this is Sammy." Maisie lifted the infant in her arms.

"And this is Seamus." Erin pointed to the baby in Tonya's arms.

"Well, if it ain't two wee bairns ya have there, cousin! God blessed ya double!" Callum said and Eoin nodded in agreement. "Molly will be sore that we got ta see the wee'uns first, won't she, Tommy?!"

"Aye, sure and ma will give ya a look as icy as the wind that blows across the loch!" Tommy said and everyone laughed. "But come, look at what we've got done, then." Tommy pointed and they all stepped carefully into the cottage.

"The walls are framed in and, as ya can see, the trusses are almost all up. It's taken us longer than we'd hoped because of our jobs durin' the week and delays with supplies," Eoin explained.

"It's beginning to look like a home," Tonya said. "I can just picture living here. I love it!"

"This is amazing. I can't believe I'm standing on MacCauley land after all the stories I've heard!" Ed said. "You guys are doing this all yourselves?"

"Fortunately, since Brodie has been in hidin', we've gotten more help from the McGilroys," Callum said.

"I'm impressed." Ed looked around and then turned to Tonya. "I'm so happy for you and Eoin. Things have really gone well for you two. Who would've thought when Eoin came to Wisconsin, and struggled watching everything going so well for his brother, that this would be his lot?"

Eoin came up behind Tonya and put his arm around her. "Thank ya, Ed. I wouldna ha' guessed it meself!"

"Neither would I." Tonya snuggled into his grasp and smiled.

"Okay, cousin Eoin, give her a snog and get it o'er with so we can get back ta work!" Tommy said.

Eoin didn't hesitate, but followed through and kissed his wife dramatically just to irritate Tommy. It worked. The boy turned away in mock disgust.

Margaret was beside herself when Eoin's family, Maisie, Erin, and Ed came to the McGilroys for dinner. She moved her short, pleasantly plump body out the door, her stout arms waving excitedly.

"Whar ayr they? The wee'uns? Ah've ben wai-ten' sae long tae see 'em!"

As soon as Tonya and Maisie stepped out of the car with the boys, Margaret was inspecting each child with "oohs" and "aahs" while they all walked up to the house where George stood with a huge wrinkly smile and squinty eyes, holding the door open, welcoming everyone in.

"An' who ehs thehs lad?" George motioned to Ed.

"This is Ed Wagner—Ed, meet George and Margaret McGilroy."

Margaret heard her name and turned to Ed. "Och, Ah've lost me heid! Ed Wagner, wehl ye pardon me rude behavior?"

Ed just laughed as he shook Margaret's hand. "No problem, ma'am, I think these two little ones deserve all the attention, too!"

"Yer tae forgehvehn, that ye are."

Ed smiled and Margaret's face showed a look of pleasure. "My, what a fayne-lochin' fella ye are! Yer ma must be that prood. Any lass who faynds ye fer a mate ehs one lucky lass."

Ed's cheeks turned crimson but Margaret didn't notice. She wrinkled up her face in a big smile and said, "Weel, let's all come on ehn tae the kehtchen. Ah've got a braw meal of neeps and tatties and haggis." She turned to Tonya, who was still chuckling at Ed's embarrassment. "Ye said, 'Feed 'em a tradehtional Scohts meal,' dehdna ye?"

"Yes, I did!" Tonya answered.

"What's haggis?" Ed asked.

"Haggis is the innards of a sheep mixed with onions, oats, suet, stock, seasoning, and herbs. They're boiled inside the lining of a sheep's stomach," Tonya said proudly. "I just learned that one."

"Oh?" Now Ed's face turned pale. Maisie guffawed and smacked his arm.

"C'mon, farm boy. Ya grew up eatin' yer southern momma's liver and onions, so ya did."

"So I did. What about the other things?"

"Neeps and tatties are root vegetables and potatoes, boiled and mashed. The Irish call it colcannon," Maisie explained.

"Oh, I've had that!" Ed put his hand on Maisie's shoulder and let out a sigh of relief. "And I'll give the haggis a try!"

"Ye've no choice, laddie!" Maisie teased as she patted his hand.

"Don't I?"

"Ya have ta set the example fer Erin, so ya do. Ya know she'll be watchin' ya, so she will."

"I can't believe you're using your child to pressure me into eating strange food."

"But it's workin', isn't it?"

"Yes."

Margaret watched the exchange between Ed and Maisie, glanced at Tonya, and winked, but Tonya thought Margaret was reading into their conversation. There was nothing between Eddy and Maisie. They had both firmly sworn off relationships with the opposite sex.

When George found out Ed had served in the Persian Gulf War, he asked him about his time overseas. Ed excitedly began to relay the stories of his time in the service and then George shared his own.

"I served ehn the Fifteenth Scohttish Ehnfantry durin' World War Two. We were called the 'Black Watch' and wore our name proudly. The Germans were afraid o' us."

Erin's ears perked up. "Why were they so ascared o' ya?"

"Well, lassie, our tartans were dark colors—black, dark blue, and green. Originally, the Black Watch had the role of keepin' watch over the Highlands. I must say, we were quite savage-layke ehn our fightin'. They called us 'Ladies from hell'—"

"Nay, George, not sae dramatic there wehth the lassie!"

"Oooo," Erin said, wide-eyed.

"Where did you fight, Mr. McGilroy?"

"Belgium mostly, and Hong Kong, Ed."

"I appreciate your service." Ed nodded.

"All this time and I never knew that about ya," Eoin said. "Thank ya fer yer service!"

"Yer good lads." George's face wrinkled up in a grin. "Ah, those were some hard years but we had music tae lehft our spirits. Always eht were music. We had aer songs tae keep us goin'."

"Can ya sing us one?" Erin asked.

Without any hesitation, George broke out in an old song, his baritone voice still strong, "Every road through life ehs a long, long road fehlled wehth joys and sorrows tae. As ye journey on how yer hairt may yearn fer the things most dear tae ye. With wealth and love 'tehs so, but onward we must gae. Keep right on tae the end of the road, keep right on tae the end. Though the way be long, let yer hairt be strong. Keep right on 'round the bend."

"Och, good auld Harry Lauder," Margaret said. "Didnae he write that one after his son was killed in the war?"

"Aye, he dehd." George nodded.

"We used tae lehsten tae hehs songs all the day long!" Margaret smiled.

"Oohhhh, eht's nayce tae get up ehn the mornin'." George belted another Lauder song. "But eht's nicer tae lie in bed—"

"Enough, auld mon!" Margaret scolded. Erin giggled and the others broke out in laughter. George smiled widely.

"An' how's the haggis findin' ya?" Margaret asked Ed.

"It's delicious!" Ed said. "It reminds me a lot of the sausage I've had back home. It's all so good. Thank you, Mrs. McGilroy."

"Och! Call me Margaret, lest I feel layke an auld womon!"

George laughed. "Ye aer that, me love!"

Tonya smiled broadly and wished she'd had her camera ready. She loved the exchange between the McGilroys and felt quite delighted to have an American friend here in this new country where she was settling down and making a home.

The following day, after attending the First Lurgan Presbyterian Church on High Street in Craigavon where Eoin and Tonya were married, they had a big dinner with Callum's family. Later, they left the twins with Molly and Shannon and went for a long drive to Waterfoot.

They traveled along the Causeway Coastal route through Carrickfergus, Whitehead, Larne, Glenarm, and then Glenariff. They passed through charming fishing villages and valleys covered in gorse—thorny evergreen bushes that produced yellow flowers. Ed was wide-eyed and made many exclamations at the beauty of it all, but Eoin grew quiet as they drew closer to the village of Waterfoot and the beach. Tonya put a hand on his knee and watched him carefully. He glanced down at her and she could see in his expression the fight to stay emotionally detached. She was glad they had left the twins behind so she could be attentive to her husband. Eoin put his hand over hers momentarily before putting it back on the steering wheel.

Certainly they all felt the somberness of the trip but when they pulled into the parking lot, the realization of the kidnappers pulling Eoin and Anna out of the van on this very space hit them all with a fresh sadness.

Eoin walked ahead of everyone through a field of wildflowers and looked out toward the water. Fog had rolled in over the North Channel and dissipated across the soft sand. The shape of a garret diving for mackerel could barely be seen and the water was heard lapping and swishing in the murky air that was as thick as pea soup.

Eoin led the unusually quiet group to a spot and stopped. Tonya caught up to him and clung to his arm.

"Here," he said, "it was about here where they found Ma. They searched and dug fer hours and days on end. They had cadaver dogs, ground-penetratin' radar, and heavy diggin' machinery."

"It's so surreal," Tonya said.

"What a vast beach, Eoin," Ed said.

"Aye. 'Tis a grand beach," Eoin said. "We were very blessed ta find Ma. Others have had searches on other beaches, bogs, etc. It's very hard ta do these searches and it's traumatic fer the family ta get their hopes up and then get told the search was unsuccessful."

On impulse, Ed started to sing "Praise God from Whom all Blessings Flow" and the others joined in, their voices echoing over the waters and through the fog. When they finished singing, Eoin asked Ed if he'd offer up a prayer.

"Dear Lord," Ed began. "May we never forget this place where Anna MacCauley drew her last breath. She had a big heart for others, gave herself to a people not her own, loved her family, and showed the love of God in a country where love was hidden only in the safety of the homes. We know that her death was not in vain and that you have reasons we may never know about as to why she died. Life and death are such mysteries to us. As Job said, 'Man comes out like a flower and withers—he flees also as a shadow and continues not.' May we be ever content to leave these mysteries with you, Lord. Perhaps, some day in heaven we might learn the reasons, but if not, then so be it..."

When he finished praying, Tonya and Eoin thanked him and started to take a stroll along the beach. But Maisie didn't move.

"Is there something wrong?" Ed asked.

"Ya have no right ta say what ya did!" Maisie said.

"What are you talking about?"

"Sure and it was a nice prayer but how can ya say Auntie's death wasn't in vain? A lot of people suffered because of what happened on this beach. An' I ain't feelin' the contentment of leavin' it all unanswered!" Maisie punched her words.

"I said it because I believe God has all of our lives planned out. He's never thrown off by someone's sinful actions."

"Ya mean sure and He knew these guys were going ta kill me auntie?"

"Yes. If He didn't, He isn't an all-knowing God, is He?"

"So, He just let it happen?"

"Yes."

"And I s'pose ya'd say the same about my folks?"

"Yes."

"How can ya say that, Eddy?" Maisie's voice tightened. "I can't—I can't put God in the same equation as those bad men who kilt me folks! I won't!"

"It's not for us to decide that, Maisie. Can't you see that?" Ed reached out and touched her shoulder but she pulled away.

"I don't think we worship the same God, Eddy!" Maisie snapped, turning and walking away. Ed felt the pain of her words deeply. They walked separately along the beach, lost in their own troubled thoughts, until Ed caught up to her.

"Maisie, look, I didn't mean to come across as cold and unfeeling about your folks or Anna."

"Sure and it sounded like it!" Maisie walked a little faster.

"I'm sorry. I think we do worship the same God, but life has taken us down separate paths and our views are a bit different." Maisie stopped to listen. "But I don't want this to ruin our friendship." He looked at her pleadingly.

"I s'pose. And maybe y'are more right than I want ta believe at this time in my life. I just see so much death, so many victims of tragedies here and I wonder why God is allowin' it in our country. I just want it ta stop."

Ed nodded, his hands out open before her. "Look, Job was tested by God and he lost all of his children, everything he owned, and had disgusting, painful boils to deal with all at once. But his faith in God was so great. He said, 'shall we accept good from God and not trouble?' And then Solomon said in Ecclesiastes, 'When times are good, be happy; but when times are bad, consider: God has made the one as well as the other.' Trust me when I say I understand, Maisie. I really do. When my brother and his wife lost their first child I went through a period of questioning it all. I saw how much Keith and Carrie suffered and how hard it hit my parents to lose their first grandchild. During that time I came upon these verses that I had written years ago in an old verse journal. It reminded me that I had to leave the answers to God and accept whatever came my way—good or bad. It's not an easy thing to do and I understand how you struggle with it, too."

"I believe ya, Eddy. But back in Wisconsin, I wouldn't have believed ya."

"Yeah, you wouldn't have." Ed started to walk on with a slight strut, his head held high. "I was too handsome and too rich to be able to understand someone like *you*."

Maisie caught up to him. "*What* did ya say?"

"You know you heard me."

Maisie smacked him on the shoulder and laughed, but then she took his arm, walked with him, and began to ask him more questions about unjust deaths, victims of crimes, and God's hand in it all. And Ed was ready and willing to try to help her find some peace in all the sorrow and confusion.

"Uncle Eddy, do ya have ta go back tomorrow?"

"Yes, I'm afraid, I do," Ed said as he put Erin up on his shoulders for the third time and swiftly took her down the hill behind the house. She yelled with glee. His pent-up sadness at having to leave Northern Ireland and the people here was funneled into his playfulness with Erin. Her laugh was like a happy song to him and it made him smile. He couldn't even think about when he'd see this little girl again. She had pushed her way into his heart. How could he say goodbye? Maisie caught up to them, out of breath and smiling from ear to ear.

"What a craic, Eddy! I thought surely the two o' ya would go rollin' down the hill together."

"Can we do it again?" Erin asked.

"Erin, don't be a bother!"

"It's okay, Maisie. Sure, Erin. One more time!" Ed pushed up the hill with his happy load and came down the hill not quite as fast as the first time. He let Erin down, bent over, and put his hands on his knees huffing and puffing. Maisie guffawed. He looked at her with feigned angst. "Really? I'm dying here and you're laughing?" That only made her laugh harder. He plopped down on the grass to rest.

"I'm sorry."

"No, you're not." He smiled up at her as she stood over him and she smiled back.

"Well, I am sorry of one thing."

"What's that?"

Maisie sat down beside him. Erin tugged at his hand. "Come, do it again, Uncle Eddy!"

"Erin, be a good lass and nip along and play. Ya have a wee bit of time before bed," Maisie said. They watched as Erin skipped away toward a small garden of flowers.

"What are you so sorry about?" Ed asked lightly.

"I'm sorry yer leavin'."

"Oh?"

"Aye."

"Why? Because you won't have anyone to harass anymore?" Ed nudged her.

"Well, there's that. But it's goin' ta be sad—"

"Why is that?"

"Erin. She loves ya, so she does. I would send her with ya if I could part with her. She would be in a better place over there in America, growin' up on a farm in Wisconsin. I dream of that fer her, ya know?"

"And I would take her! But what about you?"

"Norn Iron is me home. I need ta stay here. But I'm sad ta hold Erin back from a better life. Sure an' Erin will miss ya." Maisie couldn't say the words that would be the start of some kind of commitment for herself. She couldn't tell him she'd miss him too. Just as a friend, of course. She could barely say it to herself.

"I understand. I'll miss Erin too."

The words weren't spoken, but Ed knew he was going to miss Maisie. He wondered if she'd miss him, but dared not ask for fear of implying anything that might indicate he was interested in her. He really didn't want to step into those waters again. Already he knew he'd gotten his toes a bit wet and was dealing with unwelcome feelings.

After giving hugs goodbye the following morning, Eoin's family, Maisie, and Erin all stood outside and watched Ed take his luggage out to the taxi. Crying, Erin ran to Ed for one more goodbye hug. When Ed saw the tears on her face he knelt down, whispered something in her ear, and kissed both cheeks. Then he got into the taxi and the car pulled away. Everyone watched and continued to wave as it disappeared down the road. When they went back into the house, Maisie said, "Sure and it was sweet that Eddy kissed ya goodbye."

"Ach, he weren't kissin' me goodbye, Ma. He were kissin' me sadness away."

"And did it help ya, lass?"

"It took it right away, so it did."

Maisie looked out the window at the driveway where the car had just left. She turned toward the sitting room where Ed had slept. The reality of his departure made her feel empty and she thought to herself, *I wish he would have kissed me sadness away, too.*

As Ed sat in his seat on the airplane he felt a small piece of paper in his shirt pocket and pulled it out. It was in Maisie's handwriting. She must have slipped it in his pocket when he wasn't paying attention!

Dear Eddy,

I want to thank you for the fun times we had—the three of us. I told Erin that maybe we could write letters and she could send pictures to you. I think it will make her feel better to stay connected with you. Would you mind?

All the best,
Maisie

Ed looked out the window of the airplane and smiled for the first time after leaving everyone. This relationship with Erin and her ma was different than anything he'd ever experienced before. There was a connection that drew them together and, though Maisie didn't come right out and say it, he knew it wasn't just Erin who wanted to exchange letters with him. She was using Erin to speak for herself while being careful not to come across with stronger feelings. It was good they could be friends—like the friendship he had with Tonya and Haley. He was tempted to open up to a deeper relationship, but the protective layer he'd created around his heart guarded him from succumbing. He let his thoughts go to the following day when he'd be back working with the horses and with Gareth. Back in Wisconsin he could just be himself and not think about anything or anyone else.

For now, while he was alone, he took time to pray for all the people in Northern Ireland whom he'd met, people who were struggling and hurting there, and for Eoin and Tonya settling into a new life together in this unusual and beautiful country. He found that his prayer list had grown a bit longer.

CHAPTER 22

Dear Eddy,

First of all, Erin wants me to tell you that today she saw a rabbit and it told her to say "hi" to you. We're doing fine and glad to be living here with Eoin, Tonya, and the boys. Erin is a sweet big cousin to the wee ones. I finally gave in and signed up to get government help. But only until I can figure out what Erin and I are going to do. I love living out here. The air is so fresh, although it sometimes smells of sheep dung when the winds blow across the hills just right...

How are you cutting? Write when you can,

Maisie and Erin

***

Dear Maisie and Erin,

I'm doing fine. We're starting to get busier as the weather warms up. Please tell Erin to tell the rabbit "hi" for me when she sees him again. We have another new boarder. His name is King. He's a black Appaloosa. He's called a Black Leopard because he's white with black spots. I think you and Erin would think he looks funny. I do.

I think it's great that you are getting some help financially. I respect your morals to work for a living, but right now it's good to get assistance. I wish we lived closer. I'd like to help you—not rescue you—just help you. Haha…

I look forward to your next letter,

Eddy

***

Dear Eddy,

Erin drew a picture for you of the rabbit and told me I needed to, also, so I did. It's not very good, but Erin thinks my rabbit is better than hers. Sure and I can claim that I draw better than a seven-year-old anyway. What a craic that is.

It would be grand if we lived closer. Erin says she would walk over to your house every day. She misses you…

Bye for now,

Maisie and Erin

***

Dear Maisie and Erin,

I loved the pictures. I taped them up on the wall of my bedroom. Don't tell my mother, though. She'll be afraid I'll ruin the paint!

Erin, your drawing of the rabbit was awesome and please tell your ma that her rabbit was awesome, too. You both should draw more often! I don't draw, but maybe I can get a picture of that Appaloosa so you can see how funny he looks…

I miss you, too, Erin. And I miss someone else, but I don't think I'm allowed to say. Do you know who it is?...

   Bye,

   Eddy

                                    ***

Dear Eddy,

   Erin drew a picture of a horse and I'm sending it to you. She says it's an "Applapoosa." We both laughed at her picture so hard we couldn't stop. Of course, the way she said his name made me laugh harder. What a craic! I just drew some special flowers for you. Do you remember where we saw these? If you don't remember, you'll have to wait until my next letter for me to tell you what they are...

   By the way, that time we had together in Scotland was grand. I look back on it fondly...

   Yours truly,

   Maisie and Erin

Ed took a break from work and sat under the coolness of the willow tree, a letter and a few sketches in his hands.

"Is that from Maisie again?" Gareth came up from behind and plopped down in the grass beside him.

"Yes. And this." Ed held up a small crumpled piece of paper. "Another picture that Erin drew."

"What is that? Is that a horse?" Gareth grinned.

"Yeah, King."

"I love kids' drawings. Such a different take on life." Gareth laughed. "What's the other picture?"

"Oh, this? It's a pencil sketch of flowers that Maisie drew," Ed said, but didn't explain the memory behind the picture of the Grass-of-Parnassus flowers. The walk they had taken in Scotland was a special memory and Maisie was reminding him of it. He couldn't bring himself to tell this to Gareth lest he smile too much and Gareth suspect something.

Of course, he told himself, there was nothing to suspect.

"Wow, she's quite the artist. How's she cuttin'?"

"Fine. Maisie and Erin are going to remain at your father's cottage when Eoin's family moves into the homestead."

"I hear that's happening pretty soon!"

"Yes. Hopefully, Eoin and Tonya can move into their new place before too long."

"How will Maisie support herself and Erin?"

"She's regretfully decided to get government help."

"Our MacCauley folk are pretty proud, but she's a single mom trying to make ends meet. She shouldn't feel bad."

"That's what I told her. Gareth, has Eoin said anything more about finding the people who were behind the murders of your families?"

"No. Eoin wishes Maisie would remember more. She had to have heard or seen something."

"She's blocked a lot of it out."

"Aye, but you don't forget some things."

"Do you remember much about those guys coming to your place?"

"Certainly." Gareth looked off to the west and noticed how the sun was not coming down as soon as usual. The days were getting longer and that meant longer work days. He remembered how the sun was high in the sky when he rode his bike furiously to his aunt and uncle's house that awful day so long ago.

"Gareth?"

"Sorry. Yeah. Um, if I heard their voices I think I'd probably still recognize them—like when the O'Grady brother broke into the Becketts' house years ago—I knew right away who it was. And I would testify in a heartbeat. But people over there don't want to talk, don't want to be labeled as informers. They're still scared. This year alone there were twenty bomb alerts in Belfast—"

"I'm so glad Maisie and Erin don't live there anymore."

"Me too. I'm concerned about Collins. The Royal Ulster Constabulary is not looked upon favorably by either side. There have been stories of at least four RUC officers who have been shot and killed or beaten to death this year."

"I know better how to pray for them after being there, that's for sure."

"They need all the prayer they can get! There's a new support group, Widows Against Violence Empower, to help people suffering from traumatic losses of loved ones during the Troubles. Tonya and Eoin have spoken with some of the people there. They're hoping this can be a safe haven to get more people talking about what happened to their loved ones. So, um, back to you and Maisie—you've been exchanging letters since you left over a year ago?"

"Yeah, that's right."

Gareth winked.

"Oh, don't give me that look. It's not what you think. We're just good friends, Gareth."

"Ed, my man, are you sure there's not more to this relationship then you two are willing to admit?"

"She made it very plain to me that she's been hurt once and doesn't want to take that risk ever again. I basically let her know I'm not interested either."

"Are you sure she still feels that way?"

"Until she says differently, I'm going with that. I won't ever push her—she's not one to be pushed!"

"Yeah, I know that about her. But how do you feel about that?"

"I can't handle getting my hopes up for another relationship."

"That's not what I'm asking. Do you have strong feelings for her, Ed?"

"Well, certainly I *care* about her or I wouldn't keep writing to her."

"Well, maybe that goes both ways."

"I guess we're not going to find out any time soon, are we, friend?"

Ed folded the letter and pictures, put them in his pocket, got up, and went back to work in the barn. Gareth followed.

"Wait! Are you going to leave it at that?"

"Yessir." Ed grinned, picked up a shovel, and walked away.

Gareth and Haley sat at the dinner table with their four children seated around them. Liam made a mess in his high chair while the other three ate ravenously. It was rare to order pizza, but the day had been pretty hectic for Haley and Gareth knew she needed a break. Home became their school of choice for the children, living so far away from the city. For Haley, farming, homeschooling three children, and watching a toddler, life could get pretty crazy—even with the help of Phyllis.

"I always thought I wanted six children," Haley said, "but now, I'm beginning to question that dream."

"I've been wondering the same thing, honey."

"Have you?"

"Yes. I've been praying about it."

"Same here."

"And?"

"I think we have our quiver full right here."

"I'm glad to hear you say that. I think so, too." Gareth took a swig of his pop and set his glass down.

"Momma, can I have another piece?" Fiahd asked.

"Are you already done? You ate that first piece fast!" Gareth said as he looked at Annie's plate with not even half of the pizza eaten.

Haley put another piece on Fiahd's plate. "Did Ed get another letter from Maisie and Erin today?" she asked.

"Aye, they've been corresponding all year. I'm thinking there might be something more than a friendship going on."

"This is *you* suspecting something? *Matchmaking?*"

Gareth laughed. "No, no, just making an observation."

"I don't think you're right, though. Ed doesn't want to get mixed up in a relationship again and when Maisie was here she basically gave off that impression, too."

"Yeah, you're probably right." Gareth took a bite of his pizza, finished chewing, and swallowed. "So, Eoin and the cousins are making some progress in the investigation."

"Are they?"

"Aye." Gareth stared down at his plate. He wished he could be a part of it—he knew he could help—he *wanted* to help. He also wished he could see his cousins. It was frustrating to think of his brother and his cousins meeting together, eating, laughing, and sharing good times without him. And then two of his friends, Tonya and Ed, got to meet his cousins and were able to see his old homestead. It didn't seem fair, but his life here held him back, and Haley would never speak to him again if he went back—even for a brief visit.

Haley knew that look of yearning on his face. She sighed. "So, what have Eoin and the cousins come up with?"

"Just more names to look into right now. We didn't talk long. It's too expensive."

"I've told you that you and your brother should email each other."

"You know how handicapped we are at those computers, Hale. Do you know how poor I am at typing?"

"You could learn. It would help with corresponding with Eoin more, you know."

"I know. I'd just rather be—"

"I know, I know. You'd rather be there. And leave me here with four kids, not knowing if you'd ever make it back. It's dangerous over there, Gareth, and you know it. You left once and I thought I'd never see you again. I just can't go through that one more time!" On the verge of tears and not wanting the kids to see her like this, Haley dropped her fork on her plate, got up, and went to the bedroom to have a good cry.

Gareth sighed. "Annie, will you sit over here by Liam and keep an eye on him for Daddy?" He went into the bedroom, and found Haley sitting on the edge of the bed, weeping. "Hale. I didn't say I was going to go, did I?"

"No, but I can tell you really *want* to go."

"Of course I do!" Gareth's voice rose in pitch.

"Shhh. The children will hear you!"

Gareth shut the door. "It's my broder and cousins over there trying hard to investigate my ma's murder! Don't you think you'd want to be a part of that if it were your ma? I've not seen Brodie and Callum since that horrid day when our folks were taken away from us!"

"But you have me and four children over here. Doesn't that hold you here at all?"

"Why do you think I haven't gone before this?" Gareth sat on the bed next to Haley and carefully put his arm around her. "But I think you're being a bit selfish."

"How can you say that?" She turned toward him and pushed his arm off her shoulders. "Your children need you! I need you! Is that so selfish of us?"

"Well, in some ways, yes, it is, Haley."

"That's so wrong, Gareth! Just go away." She turned from him. "I don't want to talk to you right now."

"No, I won't just go away. Look, you have your momma and my da here. You know they'd help you here if I was gone."

"But what if something happened and you were killed?"

"That could happen to me anywhere! I could get brutally hurt on the farm by animals or machinery. If it's God's timing for me to go, I'm going to die wherever I am."

"Well, if you're going to leave this earth I'd like to be by your side, not far away from you in a country across the Atlantic!"

Gareth groaned. Fiahd knocked on the door.

"What is it?" Gareth asked impatiently.

"Gareth, watch your tone. The children aren't part of this argument," Haley whispered.

Gareth opened the bedroom door. "What do you need, Fiahd?" he said as nicely as he could.

Fiahd looked up at her father for a minute and studied his face. Gareth caught the hesitancy in her expression.

"It's okay, baby. Daddy will help you."

"Annie says to get Momma. Liam is crying and Bobby spilled his pop-water."

"I'll take care of it." Gareth went out and shut the bedroom door behind him. He was done trying to talk sense into his wife. It was hopeless. He wasn't going to go over to Northern Ireland anytime in the future. He stood in the hall to get a better grip on his frustration before he took it out on the kids. He put the conversation in a box in his mind, shut the lid, and went out to the kitchen. The children looked at him wide-eyed, unsure what to think.

Suddenly Gareth got a twinkle in his eye and said, "So, do ya want ta hear a story about my piebald pony?"

"The one named Murphy?" Annie smiled.

"Aye!"

"Yeah!" the children said in unison.

CHAPTER 23

Callum motioned for Eoin to have a seat in the sitting room of his home in Glencairn while the women chatted in the kitchen. Shannon and Tommy played with Seamus and Sammy on the floor.

"Collins told me they brought in Billy O'Grady fer questionin'," Eoin said. "He's bein' implicated in the murders of yer folks and the burnin' of our homes, but he's not givin' out any information about who was with him or who ordered it. These guys are ascared of the higher-ups. But we did get one thing out of him. He had nothin' ta do with my kidnappin' and Ma's murder."

"The mystery remains, so it does." Callum sighed as he poured them both some tea.

"From what I've learned about the people who kidnapped Ma and me, I don' believe it was anyone goin' rogue. I believe that the woman involved was part of a group called the 'Unknowns' an' that that group was a part of the IRA." Eoin took his cup and set it on the side table.

"Do ya think we stand a chance at findin' out who was really behind it?"

"Barely. But I'm still willin' ta try. You?"

"Aye. Did ya hear about the RUC who was shot dead in Belfast by the Irish National Liberation Army?" Callum said.

"Are we okay talkin' about this in front of—?"

"I'm afraid me children have heard it all by now, Eoin. Sadly, nothin' really shocks 'em, ya know?" Callum said.

"I s'pose we knew a lot at their age, too."

"Sure and we did!" Callum said. "There was an RUC beaten ta death by a loyalist in Ballymoney."

"Weren't there more RUCs shot down in Lohrgan?" Eoin added.

"Aye."

There was a pause in the conversation while they watched Seamus toddle over to his da. Eoin picked him up and put him on his lap, bounced him, and made him giggle. When Sammy saw that Seamus was having so much fun with Eoin he wanted to bounce, too. He grabbed his father's leg and said, "Dadadada!" The children laughed at him.

Callum smiled. "Who would've thought we'd all be gathered here in my house and I'd be watchin' me cousin's wee laddies play?"

Eoin nodded. "Sure and I didn't think it! Have ya heard from yer broder?"

"Shannon and Tommy, take the boys upstairs ta play now, would ya?"

Callum waited until they were gone before speaking.

"Me children are worried about their uncle and they don't need ta know any details lest someone ask them on the street. Did ya see them pause in their play and see their ears perk up when ya asked about him?"

Eoin nodded.

"Brodie came by late last night after the young'uns were in bed."

"Where is he livin'?"

"I can't say fer now."

"Isn't Joe in jail?"

"Aye, but some of the other men are takin' up Joe's cause."

"Even though it were Joe who kilt that Catholic girl, right?"

"Don' ferget, worse than killin' is being a tout."

"So in their eyes, Brodie is worse than Joe?"

"Ta be sure."

"How's he doin'?"

"He misses everyone, but he doesn't want ta put anyone in jeopardy. He feels bad they threatened me family."

Eoin sighed. "It all gets so wearisome, all this—this life that our family has been livin'."

"So it does."

"For once, it would be nice ta not talk about soldiers, murderers, loyalists, and IRA."

"Sure and it's such a part of our daily lives here—always in our face."

"I miss me days in Scohtland and even Wisconsin."

"Do ya wish ta leave here, Eoin?"

"Nay. I'm determined ta rebuild our home and help other families who had a loved one disappear."

"How're ya gonna help 'em?"

"First, keep visitin' them and let them know someone cares. Second, get people involved ta convince the government ta set somethin' up ta help find the remains of the missin'."

"Think that'll happen?"

Eoin shrugged. "It ought ta, is all I got ta say."

Maisie, Tonya, and Molly stepped out of the kitchen. "Dinner's ready." Molly announced. Tonya could tell by Eoin's face that the men's conversation was serious.

"What were you guys talking about before dinner?" Tonya asked later as they drove home.

"I was goin' ta ask the same question," Maisie said as she kissed Seamus, asleep in his car seat.

"Is Erin asleep?" Eoin asked.

"So she is and the boys as well."

"Brodie came by late in the night."

"He did? I wish we could see him," Tonya said.

"Me broder. He's an eejit hangin' with these guys. They get bloodthirsty and seek revenge at every turn. I wish he hadn't joined. Once they join they're not able ta leave." Maisie tried not to think of Michael.

"Why not?" Tonya asked.

"Once ya join, it's impossible ta get out."

"Why? What would they do?"

"Shoot ya. Beat ya ta death," Maisie said.

Tonya was surprised Maisie could talk so matter-of-factly about it. "It's such a different world here," Tonya sighed.

"Are ya sorry ya came?" Maisie asked.

"No." Tonya glanced at Eoin, who was obviously waiting for her response. "No, I'm not. This is where I'm supposed to be."

Maisie watched Eoin reach over to the passenger seat and take Tonya's hand. She thought of Michael then. She missed his comfort—at least, when he was available to give it. Their early days were wonderful, full of romance and new love. And then, when things got more intense with the paras, he was gone more. How many nights had she sat alone in their little sitting room with the noise of the telly to keep her company, waiting for him to come home, hoping he'd make it safely out of the skirmishes? She was glad her broder had left the group but still feared for his life. She didn't think he'd ever really be able to escape alive. Some para, someday, would find him and that would be the end.

CHAPTER 24

Gareth came in from a long day of work. When he stepped into the kitchen his face was forlorn. Haley looked up from the potato she was peeling.

"This is about Buck again, isn't it?"

"The arthritis in his limbs is worsening," he explained. "He's just getting so old."

"I'm sorry, Gareth. Is there anything you can do?"

"I can only make him comfortable. Keep him in familiar surroundings. He's just so lethargic and takes longer getting his legs moving. I hate to see him this way. The vet is coming tomorrow and he may suggest we put him down." Gareth left the room and went to get a shower. When he returned he passed the children playing on the floor. Instead of getting down to romp with them, he slumped down on the couch. Haley put the boiling potatoes on simmer, sat down beside him, and took his hand in hers. As if on cue, Rusty came to his side and Gareth put his other hand on the dog's head.

"He's been a good horse, honey," Haley said, "and he's lived a good long life."

"I know. But it's just that he's such a part of this farm and he was here for me when I first came."

"I remember how you loved him from the start."

"I did. I used to scoff at your pouting long over an animal dying when we were kids. I had seen so much of people dying in my home country that it seemed so petty to me at the time. But now, I'm feeling like doing my own pouting."

"You didn't scoff at *all* the animals dying. I remember how you were there for me when Jake and Beauty died. You were very compassionate and sweet to me. I understand how you're feeling, Gareth. And horses are just like dogs in many ways, aren't they? Buck was a godsend for you when you came over here so angry and sad. We couldn't connect with you in the beginning, but Buck did."

"He was a good, faithful companion."

A few weeks later, Gareth and Ed used Fred Wagner's small backhoe to bury Buck in the acreage beyond the cornfields. Ed put his arm around his friend and stood silent as Gareth shed some tears.

It was just an animal, he told himself, but he couldn't help feeling sorrowful for days afterward. Haley watched him push through the day and then make great efforts to look upbeat in front of the children. She wished she could cheer him up. She knew what would—going back to his homeland. But she couldn't bring herself to offer that suggestion.

***

On a rainy day Maisie and Erin took a cab to see Molly and the kids at Glencairn Estates. After a fun afternoon of baking and watching movies, Maisie called another cab to return home. As they were pulling out of the Estates, the cab driver cursed, "Blast dis rain! Don' it know I got miles o' drivin' ta do 'fore ta day is o'er!" Maisie's ears perked up. The man's voice stirred her memory and made her stomach flip. Where had she heard him before? As she listened to him complain about the weather, her gut wrenched and she started to feel nauseous. With red lights flashing in her brain she felt a surge of panic. She needed to get out of this car! She needed to get Erin away from this man! She took in a deep breath and calmly asked the man to turn around and take them back to the place he picked them up, making up some story about how she decided to stay at her friend's place after all. He shrugged and did as she asked—as long as he got paid. As soon as Erin and Maisie stepped inside her brother's apartment, Maisie started to hyperventilate. Erin looked up at her mother, frightened.

"What's goin' on, Maisie?" Molly asked, but Maisie couldn't talk. Instead, she took long gasps for air, her hand on her chest.

"What's wrong with Ma?" Erin asked, her eyes wide.

Molly led Maisie to the sofa in the sitting room. "Erin, agra, go upstairs and play with Tommy." Erin obeyed. Maisie put her head in her hands and rocked back and forth. Molly tried to console her but Maisie refused the comfort. Molly was relieved when Callum came home from working at the docks. Molly looked at him, worried, and pointed to his sister pacing the floor.

"Maisie? I thought ya'd be gone by now." Callum waited for an answer but there was none. "Molly, lass, what's wrong with me sister?"

"I don' know. She won' talk. I think she's had a panic attack. She and Erin left ta go home, but came back five minutes later and she's been like this fer a while, so she has. See if she'll sit back down and I'll go make some tea." Molly went in the kitchen.

Callum went to his sister and she folded in his arms. He cradled her and talked softly. "Did somethin' happen ta frighten ya, wee sister?" She nodded. "Did someone threaten ta hurt ya or hurt Erin?" She shook her head. The questions continued until she finally spoke.

"I—I heard him. I heard him, so I did."

"Who? Who did ya hear, lass?"

"The cab driver."

"You heard the cab driver?"

"Aye."

"What about him? Did he say somethin' wrong?"

She nodded. "He was there."

"Where? In the car?"

She shook her head.

"He was there." She paused and looked past her brother. "He was there."

"Let's sit down, lass," he said gently as he led her to the sofa.

Seeing his concerned face, the tears started to trickle down Maisie's cheeks.

"Hey," Callum said. "What's goin' on?"

"I don' know."

"Do ya want some hot tea? Molly has some fer ya."

"Grand, just grand," she said softly. Molly poured her a cup of tea, brought it out to her, sat next to her sister-in-law, and rubbed her back. Callum got up and made a phone call.

"Can ya talk ta us, dearie?"

Maisie took a sip of tea slowly.

"That's it, just drink fer a bit, ya don't need ta talk about it."

Callum stepped out into the sitting room. "I just called the taxi service and got the man's name who drove ya. They said it were Thomas O'Malley. He goes by Tommy."

Maisie felt a numbness course through her body and she let the teacup click down clumsily in the saucer. Tea spilled everywhere and Molly rushed to the kitchen for a rag.

"I'm sorry," Maisie said.

"No worries, I've got it!" Molly yelled.

Maisie didn't want to think any more about that man in the cab. She didn't want to hear his name. That name. She'd heard it before, just like she'd heard the voice. She stared at the carpet and followed the design with her eyes.

"Maisie, does that name sound familiar ta ya?" Callum asked.

But Maisie couldn't answer. Or wouldn't answer.

***

"I talked to Eoin today," Gareth said, as he sat around a bonfire with his friends. "Maisie isn't doing well."

Ed looked up quickly from gazing wearily at the dancing flames. He told himself his fatigue was exhaustion from work, but he knew better. He was dealing with a conflict of emotions over someone who was making him lose sleep and he knew exactly who it was. And now, hearing her name perked him up. "Why? What's going on? Is she sick?"

"Not exactly. Something or someone has upset her. Callum and Molly think a traumatic memory from the past has been triggered. She and Erin were taking a cab home from Callum's house but she had the driver turn around and bring her back. She had a panic attack, but won't speak of what triggered it to anyone. Something about the driver—his voice, they think—set her off. They found out his name is Thomas O'Malley. Collins looked into the man's background and it turns out he has history with Billy O'Grady—"

Ed sat up straight in his chair. "The man who broke into your home years ago?"

"Aye."

"What do you make of it?" Keith asked.

"Well, there's good reason to believe—judging by Maisie's behavior—that this cab driver was in on the murders of my aunt and uncle and burning down our homes. But there's no proof. I mean, it could be something totally different."

"Can't Maisie give any more details? Couldn't she identify him?" Penny asked.

"She probably could." Gareth looked at Ed. "But she won't. She's not talking much or doing anything lately but sitting around the house. They're all concerned about her. She's fearful and won't leave the cottage. Tonya and Eoin are worried because they're hoping to move to the homestead pretty soon and they don't want to leave her and Erin alone—not when she's had such a scare."

Ed bit his lip. He'd never felt more compelled to rescue someone in his life, all the while knowing his attempts would be futile and he'd be humiliated by her scorn. He leaned his head back in the lawn chair and looked up at the night sky, lost in his thoughts.

Carrie watched Ed carefully and wrapped her blanket tightly around her shoulders. "Gareth, do you think you'd recognize these men—"

"I doubt it. They were wearing balaclavas—"

"Explain again, what are balalacla—?" Scott said.

"Balaclavas are ski masks—you can only see their eyes," Gareth said and then continued, "but I heard them speak at my home and at my cousins' home. I recognized O'Grady's voice when he broke into the big house here and started yelling and cursing."

"Are you thinking of going—?" Scott asked and Penny nudged him. He looked at his wife questioningly and she glanced Haley's way. He didn't complete the question, but it was too late and he sensed the awkward tension. Gareth let out a big sigh and poked the fire with a stick.

"No. I'm not," he said curtly as he side-glanced Haley.

Haley jumped up. "Does anyone want some hot chocolate? It's getting a bit chilly and it sounds good to me!"

"It sure does." Carrie stood up and followed Haley into the little house. Penny joined them.

Keith waited until the girls were out of sight.

"She still doesn't want you to go, does she?"

"Nope," Gareth said. "And we're avoiding the subject to keep the peace."

"Sorry," Scott said.

"Don't be."

"It sure seems like you could help Maisie, and the rest of your family, get this mystery solved," Ed said.

Gareth let out a long sigh and looked at his friend. "I *know* I could, Ed. But my relationship with my wife is more important to me. And, by the way, I've noticed how your affections have transferred, old friend. Years ago you would have rubbed it in my face about how it tore *Haley* apart the last time I went to Northern Ireland. And then, you would lecture me about even considering leaving *Haley* like that again. Hmmm. But now, you're thinking I should go over there to help *Maisie*—oh, yeah, and the rest of my family, too." Gareth smirked. Slightly embarrassed, Ed got up to gather more kindling for the fire.

"I know Carrie would say Ed should go over there to help Maisie," Keith teased.

Ed turned and looked at his friends sadly. "Carrie's wrong. Maisie wouldn't want me to do that."

"Are you sure?" Gareth stopped grinning.

"*Yes, I'm sure,*" Ed said.

"Why wouldn't she?" Scott asked.

Ed threw a few sticks into the fire and looked at Scott. "You don't know this girl like I do. She doesn't *want* to be rescued or what do they call it over there?"

"Well, they use the term 'mollycoddling.' It means to pamper or baby someone," Gareth explained.

"Yeah, I've heard it from her mouth directed right at me before," Ed said.

Gareth laughed. "That Maisie, what a corker."

"And why would Carrie think I should go over there to help Maisie anyway, brother?"

"You know Carrie. She's got this perception—or women's intuition—or whatever you call it, and she thinks you two have a thing for each other."

"I think Carrie's a bit off on this one, Keith," Ed said. "We're just good friends and we both don't want to get into another relationship."

Meanwhile, the girls watched Haley hover quietly over the stovetop, stirring several cups of milk into a heated paste made of cocoa powder, sugar, salt, water, and vanilla. Carrie looked at Penny and Penny looked at Carrie.

"We can tell you're bothered by something, Haley," Carrie said.

Penny nodded. "Yeah, out with it, girlfriend."

"Gareth wants to go back to Northern Ireland and I don't want him to go."

"Well, *we all knew that*," Carrie said, "but I think there's more to your frustration here."

"That's what *I'm* thinking," Penny added. "Like maybe there's some guilt involved on your part?!"

"Guilt?"

"Perhaps, dear friend," Carrie said sweetly.

"Ouch. That hurts."

"Spoken in love by your friends," Penny said. "Well, spoken in a loving way by Carrie, at least."

Haley rested the spoon on the counter and turned around, leaned against it, and crossed her arms. She groaned. "Why do you girls have to be so *insightful*? Like you can see *right into my soul*! I just don't want to lose him." Her voice cracked slightly and she swallowed hard, trying not to cry. Suddenly her hands flew out dramatically. "What if something were to happen to him?!"

Carrie put her arm around her friend. "Maybe, Haley, well, maybe you should trust the Lord for that and let him go. Gareth would be so glad to go back and you would be happier giving him your blessing, don't you think?"

Haley looked at her girlfriends. She sighed.

"I need to think about it." But deep down, she knew her friends were right and she knew Gareth should go.

After all the friends were gone, Haley and Gareth started to get ready for bed when Haley plopped down on the bed and sighed.

"What's wrong?" Gareth sat down beside her, put his arm around her, and she leaned into him.

"I need to apologize."

"For what?"

"For holding you back."

"From?"

"From going back to your homeland, from meeting your cousins again and from helping solve the terrible crimes against your family."

"What are you saying?"

"I'm saying you should go back to your homeland."

Gareth's eyes grew wide. Was he hearing her correctly? "You mean go back to Northern Ireland?"

"Yes."

"Are you sure? Because if you don't want me to go, I won't."

"I know." Haley choked on her words as tears streaked down her cheeks. "Oh, I've been so selfish!" She put her head in her hands.

"No, please don't say that about yourself." He pulled her hands away from her face and kept them in his. "You've had to deal with a lot marrying me. You've done all the work giving birth to our four children, nursing each one and carrying the load that comes with a big family. I won't have you feeling selfish in this. I was wrong saying it before. I'm just so stunned to hear that you're okay with me traveling back to Northern Ireland now. I wouldn't go if you weren't okay with it, ya know."

"I know that. And, I know that you need to go back—you *want* to go back. And I *want* you to go back, too."

"Are you sure about that?"

"Yes. I'm sure."

"What made you change your mind?"

"More like 'who.' It's good to have friends who are honest and unafraid to speak the truth."

"I'll agree to that!"

Gareth tipped Haley's chin upward and she looked into his eyes like a pathetic child. He leaned down and gently kissed her tear-soaked lips. "I love you, Haley girl."

"I love you, too."

Ed went back to his parents' house in turmoil. Alma saw it on his face as soon as he entered the kitchen where his parents were relaxing to a Mantovani record while putting together a jigsaw puzzle.

"Son, you sit yohself down he-ah and tell yoh momma and daddy what's going on in that fine head of yohs."

Ed sat at the table and looked over the half-finished puzzle. "Maisie isn't doing well."

"Oh no, what's going on?" Alma asked.

"What's happened, son?" Fred looked up after putting one more piece in place.

"Is little Erin doing okay?" Alma looked worried.

"Yes, Momma, Erin's fine," Ed said. He then repeated all that Gareth had told him.

"So?" Fred leaned back in his chair. "What are you going to do about it?"

"What do you mean—going to do? What can I do?"

"Land sakes, Edwahd! You should go the-ah and be with her!" Alma got up and put on the coffee.

"I can't just pick up and go, Momma."

"Why evah not?"

"She has made it very clear that she doesn't want to be rescued. She takes a lot of pride in being a survivor of the Troubles over there. And besides, we're just friends. This is a very personal thing she is going through. I'd feel like I was invading her privacy."

"I think we all know she'd welcome your coming over there," Fred said and Alma nodded.

"It's too much of a risk. I can't just spend that kind of money to have her freak out and turn me away. Besides, what will Gareth do here without my help?" Ed started to get up. Alma looked at Fred.

"Sit down, son. Your mother and I have something to say."

Reluctantly, Ed sat back down.

"Look, you've been hurt a few times by girls. We get that. But that doesn't mean you give up on every other girl who might be interested and who might be the one for you. You and Maisie have been writing letters for over a year now. And how do you feel after you read one of her letters? Be honest."

Ed looked down, contemplating his words. He looked up. "Her letters are the best part of my day."

"That's all I needed to hear. Your momma and I are going to pay for your flight. You need to go after this girl."

"But what if she rejects—"

"You'll never know unless you go there and find out. Besides, this girl needs some counseling and you've had a lot of experience giving spiritual advice to those who have suffered trauma! Tell you what. You just pray about this tonight and give it some more thought. But we've given you our counsel on the matter and we will make this trip happen if you are willing to go."

"Thank you. I love you guys."

Alma poured three mugs of coffee and put out a plate of cookies.

"It's late, dear. I don't know if I should indulge," Fred said.

"I think we have cause ta celebrate, Frederick. Besahdes, this puzzle isn't going ta put itself togethah all bah itself."

Ed stayed up with his folks, drank two mugs of coffee, ate six cookies, and helped finish the puzzle. He knew he wouldn't be able to go to sleep anytime soon anyway. There was too much to think about!

The following morning Ed and Gareth met in the barn. Both were smiling widely and consequently looking at each other with curiosity.

"What's got you looking so happy?" Gareth said.

"Why are you smiling?" Ed asked.

"You first."

"No, you first."

"Okay. Haley gave me the okay to go back to Northern Ireland!"

"That's *awesome,*" Ed said as his heart sank. Gareth needed to go to Northern Ireland much more than he did and that meant he would need to stay behind to take care of the horses. There was no way Ed would tell Gareth to let him go instead. He relinquished the rights to the trip immediately. It wasn't meant to be after all.

"Okay, now what about you?" Gareth asked.

"Oh, well, it was just a beautiful sunrise this morning—"

"That's it?"

"What? Can't a guy be happy about a sunrise?"

"I think the war did something to your brain, my friend." Gareth smirked.

"Yeah, probably," Ed said as he walked away so Gareth wouldn't see the huge disappointment on his face.

CHAPTER 25

Gareth had some reservations of his own when it came to traveling back to his homeland. The last time he went back to Northern Ireland he wasn't married and didn't have any children who depended on him. Now, he felt the need to be more cautious with what he did and where he went. Going back to Northern Ireland was a risk and his da didn't let him forget it. On the other hand, would he ever forgive himself if he didn't go back and try to find some justice for what happened to his family? *Please God, keep me safe in Your hands!*

But, once he landed, all lingering fears vanished. On his journey in the taxi from the airport to his father's cottage, Gareth found himself smiling broadly at things as simple as the drystone walls that bordered narrow lanes, making boundaries of the fields for the sheep and cattle to graze. When they passed through a narrow road through misty wooded hills he knew they were drawing close. It opened up again into rolling green hills. Ah, the drumlins! When he stepped out of the taxi and took in his surroundings, he breathed in the thick, damp air and took in the sheep grazing along the hillsides surrounding his da's cottage. Was that the rattling of a corncrake he heard in the distance? It all felt surreal. It felt like home. Even this little cottage where he lived with his da for three years was home. How many years had it been since he'd been here? Almost ten? The cottage looked nicer now. The outside clay walls had a fresh coat of white paint, the window frames and the door had been repainted red. The roof had been redone and the drystone walls around the property repaired. Tonya and Eoin had made so many improvements! Suddenly, the couple burst out the door, each holding a twin, followed by the cousins.

"Gareth, broder!" Eoin gave him a huge hug, followed by Tonya. Gareth checked out his little nephews and marveled at how fast they'd grown. Then, he took a step back and took a look at Callum, Molly, Maisie, and the children in the background.

"It's a bit of a shock, eh, broder?" Eoin said as they all stared quietly.

Gareth looked at Callum again. "Last time I saw you—"

"We were all runnin'," Callum said. "Sure and it's grand ta see ya now, cousin." His voice broke. "Standin' here healthy and strong."

"It's fantastic to see you, too!" Gareth choked out, surprised by the strong feeling of emotion that welled up suddenly within.

"Will ya listen ta him talk? We have another Yank in our midst!" Callum said, and it broke the emotional tension. Everyone laughed.

"Someone's gotta remind everyone that there's American blood in the family!"

"And proud of it!" Tonya said and Gareth winked at her.

Suddenly a small voice broke from behind them. "I can' wait no longer!" Erin pushed through and gave her cousin Gareth a big hug. "We have a surprise fer ya!" she said. Gareth looked at Eoin puzzled.

"Well, I thought ya might want ta see this," Eoin said.

Erin took his hand, led him to the side of the house, and showed him a small garden. There were vines climbing in between a strange, twisted piece of metal.

"My bike?!" Gareth laughed as he got down on his knees to examine it. "It's in pretty rough shape but it's—it's my bike?!"

"I couldn't throw it away when Tonnie and I moved back here. It was the connection that brought us together, ya know? So, Tonnie made it an art piece in the garden now."

"What a craic! I love it."

Later, when the cousins had gone home, Gareth pulled out a letter and handed it to Maisie.

"A hand-delivered letter. I feel like the queen," Maisie said dryly.

"You two have been corresponding over a year now, eh?" Gareth said, noticing her gaunt cheeks and the dark circles under her eyes.

"Aye. Sorry ta hear about Buck. Sadness was on us, as well as many tears."

"Thanks." Gareth paused. "Ed misses you, Maisie. He does. I can tell."

"Hmmm."

"It's too bad he couldn't—"

"I can' deal with much right now, cousin." Maisie turned away and walked up to her room.

That night, Maisie sat with Erin and read Ed's letter aloud.

Dear Maisie and Erin,

Hi, you two! How are you doing? We all miss you here, including the animals. The other day I was in the barn and I heard the horses talking. Mabel was chatting with Princess and Blackie. She told them that if she could, she would fly all the way over to Northern Ireland and pick up Erin and take her for a ride across the ocean and back home again. (Erin giggled.) Princess and Blackie were jealous, first of all, that she could fly, and second, that Erin loved her best. Mabel talked about the time that Erin brought her a very delicious apple and how happy that made her. (Erin giggled again.) *She said Erin was a very kind and thoughtful girl who must have a very wise and loving ma.*

Lucy, the retriever, is pregnant again and will have puppies soon. I remember a very romantic story of Eoin and Tonya's about when Lucy had her first brood—one of them was Rusty. Remember Rusty? You'll have to ask them about it!

I saw a beautiful sunset a few weeks ago—one with pinks and yellows scattered across the horizon. I thought of you both and wondered if you saw it? On another night I saw the full moon and thought that maybe you saw the moon, too. It was beautiful. Even though we're so many miles apart, the moon is very big! So, sometimes, when I look up in the sky I wonder if you've seen the very sky I look at several hours later. It makes the world seem smaller and the distance between us feel shorter!

I love all the pictures you send, Erin, and you need to tell your ma she is a good artist, too, and should keep drawing pictures like you do. I think it's a good thing for her to do and that it would be a great distraction from the hard things in life...

Yours truly,

Eddy

Maisie could tell he was thinking about her, even though he never was very direct in his letters about it. She couldn't deny that that thought alone brought her a fragment of joy in her numbed state. The feelings lasted throughout each day. And the next. And then, she'd pull out his letters and read them over again. Next to her daughter, it was what kept her feeling anything at all.

The following day Eoin and Tonya took Gareth over to see the old homestead. Gareth stepped out of the car and couldn't believe his eyes. The last time he'd seen the place, it was going up in flames. Now, it looked almost the same way it used to, only with newer stonework, a new roof, windows, a second floor, and a bright green door. An overwhelming feeling of happiness and hope that things were changing in his old country coursed through his veins. For the first time, he felt a bit jealous that his brother would be living here, in this house, on their property and in their homeland. He went out in the back and sat in the garden. Eoin and Tonya followed.

Gareth got a far-off look on his face. "Eoin, remember the days we used to sit here together with our plates full of fried potatoes and sausages, telling funny stories?"

"I do."

"I missed that when I left home."

"Same."

"When do you think you'll be moving in?"

"Well, we hoped ta move in next week." Eoin looked at Tonya. "But Tonnie isn't sure Maisie can be on her own with Erin yet." He looked up at the dark clouds moving overhead. "Her moods are like this weather— unpredictable."

Tonya and Gareth looked at the sky too. Tonya was worried about the possibility of rain and getting her clothes wet, but she wanted to be a part of the conversation so she stayed. "Some days she seems to be doing fine," Tonya said, "but then other days she just sits around looking sad. I try to talk to her during those sad days, but it's like she's not really there."

"We suggested that it might help for her ta get herself a job instead of living on the bru or help out with a charity while Erin's in school. But right now she's not in any condition ta do that," Eoin explained.

"I noticed how sickly she looks."

"I wish Ed had come with you, Gareth."

"Do you think Maisie would respond to him, Tonya?"

"I think so. She reads his letters all the time. She even carries them around with her and hugs them to her chest. I think they're a bigger comfort to her than she'd ever let on to anyone."

"Who knew? I mean, did you guys ever think there was something more to their friendship? Something deeper?"

"I was oblivious," Eoin said.

"Keith said something about Carrie suspecting there was more, but none of us really saw it," Gareth said.

"Carrie saw that there was more?" Tonya said, feeling droplets of rain on her head.

"Aye, but you know Carrie."

"I trust her intuition." Tonya stood up. "I think Eddy needs to get over here! And I think we need to go inside!"

"He was goin' ta come over," Eoin said, not moving from his spot.

"What do you mean he was *going to*?" Gareth said, staying where he sat, too.

"He was ready to, but when you decided to come, he thought he'd better stay to watch the horses." Tonya shrugged.

"What? He didn't tell me that!"

"He didn't?" Tonya put her hands out and felt the soft rain.

"No." Gareth suddenly remembered the conversation in the barn. Ed wasn't just smiling over some sunrise. He was thinking of traveling here to

Northern Ireland to help Maisie. "I'm a stook! I think he was going to tell me—ach! He should've said something. We could have hired extra help with the horses!"

Suddenly the rain came down fast and hard.

"Do you think you can get him to come over here?" Tonya yelled as she started to run toward the back door.

"I'm calling Haley tonight," Gareth yelled as he got up. "I'm going to tell her to make Ed get on a plane and get—"

But his last words were drowned out by the storm.

***

Haley, Carrie, and Penny sat outside on lawn chairs watching the children play a game of Red Rover. Their high-pitched shouts and screams echoed across the farmstead and brought Phyllis out on the porch to soak in the sounds and watch.

"How's it going, Haley?" Carrie said and took a sip of her lemonade. "Are you surviving okay on your own?"

"I'm fine. The kids and I miss Gareth like crazy, but Momma and Ian are constantly checking up on us and offering to take the kids, so I can go do the grocery shopping or just have some time to myself. I sat at Mullen's Dairy by myself one time."

"You did? Seriously?" Carrie said.

"I'm jealous!" Penny laughed. "I love Jonathan and Angie, but I'd love to have some moments like that to myself!"

"It was so peaceful and I enjoyed every spoonful of my butter pecan ice cream uninterrupted."

"Heavenly! Oh, but I do love my Benny."

"Well, of course, you do, Carrie!" Haley said.

"So, I heard about Eddy," Penny said. "He's going back to Northern Ireland?"

"Yes," Haley said.

"I felt so bad for Maisie," Carrie said, "but I was so happy when I heard Eddy was going over there!"

"Why? You really think Eddy will be able to help her?" Penny asked, puzzled. All she could recall was Maisie's smug but funny remarks to Ed and his quizzical expressions at anything she said.

"Do we even have to ask that question?" Carrie said.

Penny looked at her funny. "What are you talking about, Carrie?"

"You should have seen Eddy's face light up when Haley called him and told him that Gareth was ordering him to come over to help Maisie."

"You saw that, Carrie?" Haley asked.

"We were over at Mom and Dad Wagner's when you called." Carrie smiled. "He acts so aloof whenever Keith and I talk to him about his time with her on the last trip. Well, *he* may think he's not in love—but *I* know better."

"So, the two of them?" Penny tipped her glass and drank the last of her lemonade.

"Apparently," Haley said. "According to what Tonya says, Maisie seems to be taken with him, too."

"And Eddy?" Penny asked. "Does he seriously feel that way about her?"

"I'm still not completely sure."

"I am," Carrie said.

"How did we miss this?" Penny was still puzzled. "I thought they were both determined to not get involved in any other relationships?"

"Oh, quiet, girls, here he comes," Haley said when she saw him walking toward them from the barn. "Hi, Eddy. Are you done showing the men around who are taking care of the business while you're gone?"

"Yes, I am."

"Here, sit down for a minute." Haley stood. "I'll go get some more lemonade. Don't talk about anything important until I get back!"

When she returned, she found Annie and Fiahd trying to pull Ed into their game.

"Girls, let Uncle Eddy rest. You go on and play!"

"So, when do you fly out, Eddy?" Penny said.

"Tomorrow."

"Are you excited to go?"

"Of course, Carrie. I'm impatient to get there. I'm concerned about Maisie."

"Is she doing any better?"

"She's still in quite a state of high alert."

"Has she written you since this all happened?" Penny asked.

"Her last letter was shorter than usual, but there were several pictures that she and Erin had drawn."

"Do you miss her?"

"Of course, Penny. And Erin, too. That little girl has my heart."

"What about Maisie?" Haley said.

"What do you mean?"

"Does she have your heart, Eddy?"

"We're good friends, Hale." Ed took a long drink of lemonade.

"But Eddy, she has your heart, doesn't she?" Carrie said.

He stopped drinking and looked at the girls. "Well, just like you all have my heart, I guess."

The girls glanced at each other. They could see right through him. Ed scanned their faces and grew uncomfortable. He stood up. "Well, I should get back to work. I need to check on Lucy and the puppies, too. Thanks for the lemonade, Haley." He walked off quickly.

"Wow, now I know what to do if Eddy is ever annoying me. Just mention Maisie's name." Penny joked and Haley laughed.

"As if Eddy was ever annoying." Carrie pooh-poohed the idea completely.

"Right. That was his brother's job," Haley said. Penny guffawed. Carrie smiled sweetly. She could never say anything bad about Keith, but even she knew Haley spoke the truth. Keith had been the annoying one of the group in their younger days. But life had matured him and losing their first baby had sobered him up more than anyone had realized.

"I'm praying this trip will help Eddy and Maisie open their hearts again to love," Carrie said.

"Amen," Haley said.

"Miracles do exist," Penny said. "I mean, look at me and Scott."

***

Gareth sat with Maisie on an old stone bench behind the cottage.

"I know why ya brought me out here, so I do," she said.

"I knew you weren't an eejit."

"I can't help with identifyin' anyone, Gareth."

"Can't or won't?"

Maisie didn't answer.

"I could use the support, Maisie."

"Yer not sure o' yerself, then."

"I don't know how I'll do."

"I'm sorry."

"I am, too. But can I ask you a question?"

"What?"

"What stops you from trying to remember—you came so close—"

"The memories are like a big, dark monster waitin' in my head. Every time the memory of it all comes too close, I shut it out. If I don't shut it out—if I go back there, I feel like I'll lose my mind—I'll go crazy—I'll go down inta a deep hole, never ta come out again, so I will."

"I don't think you—"

"How can ya know what will happen, Gareth? How can anyone fix this? Sure an' it's better ta leave it all be."

Gareth sighed. Though he understood Maisie's fear of digging up the past, it was still frustrating. He really wanted her to come with him to help identify the men who burned down their houses and murdered their family. But he hardly knew his cousin anymore, so how could he push her too far? If it were Haley, Tonya, Penny, or even Carrie, he could possibly make them think differently. But not Maisie. She was cut from a different cloth. He really didn't know if Ed could make a difference either, but it was worth a try. Meanwhile, in a few days, Gareth would go to the constabulary in Belfast and try to identify O'Malley's voice on his own.

Two days later, Constable Collins explained the procedure for identifying a criminal. The officers put balaclavas over the heads of ten men and then filed them into a lineup. Gareth watched in another room through a one-way mirror. Then, one by one, an officer ordered a man to speak and to yell a phrase. Gareth listened intently and watched each man as they spoke. He prayed for two things: First, that he would be able to identify the right man and place him at the scene of the crime. Second, that he wouldn't fall apart while being reminded of the traumatic events that happened so many years ago.

Gareth narrowed it down to four men and had Collins tell the officers to have those four repeat the phrases they had been ordered to say. He sat down and closed his eyes. He pictured the men coming into his house and pictured them standing outside his uncle's house. And he heard a voice in the midst of the four that matched those pictures. *Thank you, Lord.* He stood up and told Collins which man's voice he recognized. Gareth looked at Collins and Collins smiled.

"You identified O'Malley, lad. Good job."

"Fantastic! What's next?"

"O'Grady and O'Malley go ta trial fer the war crimes done ta yer families."

"What about the kidnapping, the murder, and the disappearing?"

"Once these men are informed that they're lookin' at heavy sentences, we'll try ta get them ta talk fer a lesser sentence."

"Is that even a possibility? Most would rather die than be known as a traitor."

"We shall see. I'll keep ya posted."

That night around midnight, Maisie heard a noise. She got up out of bed and walked softly to the door so as not to wake Erin. She stepped out into the tiny hallway and listened. It was coming from downstairs where Gareth slept on the sofa. She tiptoed closer to the stairs and listened. Was he talking in his sleep? He sounded angry. "No! No! Ye'll not be takin' her with ya! I'll not let ya, if I have ta—" And then he started to groan. And then weep and moan. Maisie didn't know what to do.

Eoin stepped out of his room, concern masking his face.

"Should we wake him?" Maisie said quietly.

"I don't know." Eoin shrugged. "I wish Haley were here. She'd know what ta do." His countenance fell as they heard more groans and mumbled talk. "Haley knows more of me broder than me." Maisie patted his shoulder. She understood. All of the children of Ian and Sean had been separated from each other and consequently had to get reacquainted when they were brought together again. It was strange what this civil war in their country did to people.

"It's troublin' ta me," Eoin told her. "From what I was told, he stopped havin' these nightmares after he came back from that first visit here ta try ta find Ma and me. That was years ago. I hate ta think that comin' back here now will bring on the nightmares again."

"I'm sorry, Eoin. I hope it doesn't bring it all back either. Maybe he shouldn't have come."

"Nay, he was glad ta come. He needed ta do this."

But Maisie wasn't sure she agreed.

Everything got quiet. They both stood in the hall and waited awhile. Eoin nodded, indicating all was good.

"He's peaceful again. Go back ta bed, cousin," he whispered, motioning to her bedroom door.

Maisie took a deep breath, released it, went back to her room, and climbed into the bed next to Erin. She lay there for a while. She had heard that Gareth used to suffer from nightmares when he first came to America. Did the events earlier in the day trigger one? Why would he volunteer to identify someone like O'Malley if it would just bring them up again?

The following morning Gareth walked into the kitchen, his dark curls pressed flat on one side, his eyes half-closed and his feet dragging.

"Ya didn't sleep well, did ya?" Maisie asked.

"No." Gareth sighed. "Not at all."

"I heard ya."

"You did? Did Tonya and Eoin? Was I yelling out?"

"I know Eoin did. We both stood in the hallway fer a bit. Ya were yellin'. Did yesterday bring that on?"

"Most likely."

"So, are ya goin' ta give up bein' a witness?"

"No, Maisie, of course not."

"But—"

"It's not all about me. Our folks and our siblings all need some semblance of justice and I'll do whatever it is I need to do to help bring that about."

"I don't have the guts ta do what yer doin', Gareth."

"Just do what you're capable of, *Gingerbap*."

Maisie smirked at her nickname and stuck her tongue out.

"Ah, I see the old Maisie is still in there. I've missed her."

Eoin and Gareth met late at night with Callum and Brodie at Glencairn Estates.

"Cousin!" Gareth said to Brodie as they embraced. "I didn't think I'd get to see you!"

"Me neither. Look at ya!"

"Look at you." Gareth laughed.

"Ya talk like Tonnie, cousin!" Brodie laughed too.

"Yeah, yeah, that's old news by now," Gareth said, and then explained what happened at the constabulary.

"For once I feel like we're on the right track ta justice," Callum said.

"Aye," Eoin said. "There's hope that the Provos will pay fer what they did."

"Are Joe Campbell's men still looking for you?" Gareth asked.

"Not really. My buddy Paul tells me his group is plannin' an attack on the IRA and that's got them distracted fer now."

"How big is this group?"

"Not more than a bit over twenty."

"And they think they'll beat the IRA? Without their leader?"

"These paras think they're goin' ta bring down both the British Empire and the IRA with sticks and stones." Brodie laughed again as Molly brought out the tea.

"A bunch o' stooks," Callum said. "One time, when these guys battled against the British, both sides stopped at six o'clock fer tea time." Callum took the cup and saucer from his wife's hand and nodded thanks to her. "They resumed at seven."

"Are ya kiddin' me?" Eoin said.

"You're talking about the loyalists, right? So they fight against the British, too?" Gareth asked.

"Aye. It's crazy what the British government's done. It's not just the Catholics who see it. Catholics, they think us Protestants support the British and all that they've done, but we don't. British could've handled things much better," Callum said.

Molly came back out with a hot pot of tea to refill their cups.

"Thanks, lass," Callum said. "We're probably goin' ta be up late. Yer lookin' weary. Why don' ya set that pot out here and we'll take care of it ourselves."

"I'll leave ya a plate of biscuits and then I'll be goin' ta bed, so I will. Good night, all."

They all wished her a good night and, after she left a plate of biscuits on an end table, she went on up to the bedroom.

"Sure an' it's funny how so many on both sides—Catholic and Protestant—believe the same as far as politics go," Brodie said. "Yet not all the Protestants carry the same politics as other Protestants."

"Not all the Catholics believe the same as each other, either," Callum added. "Ya can't believe everything ya see or hear on the telly. Most people outside Northern Ireland think this war is a religious war but it's not, it's political. The media is powerful and tainted, so it is."

"In the US they made it look like it was a religious war," Gareth said. "When I came back here years ago, I learned differently." Everyone nodded and took a drink of their cold tea. Callum got up to put the kettle on again.

"By the way, Gareth," Eoin said, "the Divis Flats—where Ma and I were last seen, and where ya scouted out when ya first came back, are gone. Only the tower remains."

"Really?"

"Aye, and the top two floors are controlled by Sinn Fein and the IRA."

"The IRA," Callum said in a low, disgusted tone as he stood in the doorway of the kitchen. "They're the worst thing that happened ta Northern Ireland. People think our country is full o' terrorists because o' them. The IRA's left a filthy path o' ghosts behind us, pullin' us down and continually draggin' us backward."

"What ever happened ta Paul's brother, William?" Eoin asked.

"Is he the one you dragged into a home after getting shot?"

"Aye. He got released and is layin' low at his folks place," Brodie said. "Paul keeps me posted."

"Gareth, have ya made any headway with Maisie?" Callum asked.

"Not really."

"I wish she could get out of this country with Erin and live a different life," Callum said and then went into the kitchen to get the tea kettle. He poured the hot water into a tea pot with tea bags and brought it out to warm up everyone's cup. "Sometimes I ask God why He let her see what she saw."

"There are so many other places in this world where we all could have grown up—where there are no terrorist flags flying," Gareth said somberly.

"Why did God let us grow up here in this awful place?" Brodie asked.

"It took me a while to accept what happened to me, being taken so far away from my family, wondering if I'd ever see any of them again. But then, I fell in love with Haley and then she gave birth to our four precious children. God took away many things from me, but He gave back in return. Sometimes, we focus too much on what we have lost and not on what we have."

Everyone took a sip of their hot tea and didn't speak for a while.

CHAPTER 26

Ed took a chance and flew from Milwaukee to Belfast. When the plane landed, the pilot announced over the intercom, "Welcome ta Belfast. Sure and ya can turn yer watches back 300 years." The passengers roared with laughter, especially those returning home. Ed nodded. After his first visit, he got the joke.

Ed was thankful that the airport was west of Belfast and that the first part of his trip to Northern Ireland this time could be a lake scene and country instead of the city. On the drive to the cottage they passed through Lurgan, Craigavon, and Portadown. The names of the towns were all familiar to him now as his taxi continued on south to Laurelvale. Ed tried to enjoy the interesting and beautiful scenery, but he was too nervous. He had no idea how he'd be received by Maisie. As far as he knew he'd be getting to the cottage while she was alone at the house. Eoin told him that he would be at work and that Gareth would be taking Tonya, the boys, and Erin in his rental car over to the homestead to unpack more boxes. He said that no one told Maisie that Ed was coming. That worried Ed, but the family decided it was better this way. Maisie had a tendency to get so worked up over the littlest things lately; it would make her sick to her stomach, anticipating his visit. He said a prayer as the cab driver drew near to his destination.

Maisie sat at the kitchen table dressed in an old floral dress from the '80s. Her slacks were too baggy now and wouldn't stay up on her hips. She sipped a cup of tea and took small bites of a piece of toast. She wasn't eating much and found that this simple fare set well in her stomach. As she munched slowly, she heard a car pull up in front of the cottage. She got up and peeked out the sitting room window. Her heart lurched. It was a cab! "He" was coming to get her! Surely it was O'Malley! Why else would a cab be in front of the house? Frightened, she grabbed her jacket, slipped out the back door, and ran barefoot, moving as quickly as her fragile body would let her. She wasn't thinking where she could run, she just ran—like the day she saw her folks, bloody and dying. She moaned and cried, frustrated her legs wouldn't move as fast as she wished. She was too weak.

Ed stood outside in the cool misty air, wondering why Maisie wasn't answering the front door. When he heard a woman's voice in distress beyond the house, he ran to the back and looked out over the rolling fields that continued into the other farmlands around them. And then he saw her, frantically trudging up a hill just beyond Ian's property.

"Maisie!" he called out, but she didn't respond. His long legs carried him at a quick pace as he headed toward her. He yelled her name again as he drew closer. She glanced behind her at the sound of his voice, but turned and ran again.

He stopped and gave pause. Maybe everyone was wrong. Maybe this was a bad idea. If he kept chasing her, what good would that do? But then, he saw her crumple to the ground. "Maisie!" He bolted and caught up to her.

She had curled up in a fetal position, her waves of auburn hair fanned about the dark purple heather and when he leaned down and touched her arm, she flinched and pulled away.

"No! No! Leave me alone! Don' kill me, please," she cried.

"Maisie," Ed said gently. "Look, it's *me, Eddy*. I would never hurt you."

She pushed herself up and looked at him, her hair falling about her face, her eyes wide with fear.

"It's me." Ed's voice was hoarse. She wasn't the same healthy girl he'd left a year ago. He knelt down and pushed her hair carefully away from her face. "See?"

"Eddy? Is thatchoo?"

He put his hand out. "Yes—yes, it's me."

"What are ya doin' here?" She didn't reach out for him, but put her hand to her chest and started to gasp until she began to hyperventilate. Ed knelt down beside her and put his arms out tentatively. She finally succumbed to his grasp and he relished it with great relief. "Take deep breaths. Here. Breathe with me, like this." He took in air slowly and let it out carefully. She tried to do the same with a few hiccups of air in the process. "That's better. Slow your breathing. It's okay." He rubbed her back. "You're okay now. I've got you and you're safe." She tipped her head up and looked at him sadly. The dark circles under her eyes and her sunken pale cheeks melted his heart.

"I thought ya were the taxi cab driver coming back ta get me! Why did ya come here?"

"I came—" Ed felt his throat tighten. "I came for you."

Ed waited for some kind of response but she just played with his fingers, quietly processing what he said. The iciness of her touch alarmed him. "I need to get you inside by the fire," he said, *"if there is a fire."*

He helped her to her feet, but she was unsteady.

"Can you walk?"

"Aye." She faltered. Without asking, Ed scooped her up in his arms, cradled her and carried her back to the cottage. He was too aware of how her hair fell about his arm now, swishing and tickling his skin as he walked. Her head and hand rested on his chest. Her forehead, just inches from his lips, tempted him to place a kiss on her cold skin, but he refrained. He was also aware of how thin and light she was to carry. She'd truly been suffering inside. Kissing her would be a mistake. Bad timing. He was not, as these Irish folk would say, an *eejit*. All the same, he held her tightly and wondered if this closeness warmed her heart as much as it warmed his.

They sat together in the sitting room for a while talking of surface things: the horses at the farm, the garden, Erin's schooling, and the twins. Maisie started to liven up a bit and Ed was glad to see it.

"Where are my manners? Will ya take a cup of tea of in yer hand?"

"I'd love it. But let me get it. You need to rest."

"What? Ach, no. I'm feelin' better now." But when she tried to stand, her balance was off after such an excursion outside. Ed caught her quickly and helped her sit. She forced a laugh. "I'm fine, Eddy. Sure an' I don' know what just happened! I'm not langered." She tried to make light of it, but Ed saw through it all. She was weak and wasn't herself at all. He was glad he came and thankful there was no fight or protests about him coming.

"You probably just got up too fast," he said. "Let me make the tea." And before she could answer, he was headed to the kitchen.

Ed had just poured them cups of tea when he heard the front door open and the noises of children and adults. He stepped out into the sitting room. Gareth was helping Tonya with one of the twins, putting them down on the floor to play. Erin was the first to see that Ed had arrived and she cried out with joy, "Eddeeee!" Ed hurriedly put the tea cups on an end table, knelt down, and put his arms out for her. She ran to him and hugged him tightly, nestling her face in his neck. "Oh, it's just grand, just grand ta have ya here, so it is!"

"It's so good to see you, too, Erin," Ed said, fighting the emotion that comes with a sweet reception from a child. "You've grown so much!"

"I'm almost nine! How long will ya be here? Are ya stayin' here with us? How'd ya get here?"

"Erin," Maisie said, "let him breathe."

Erin went to her mother and took her hands in hers. "Ma, is happiness on ya then, ta have Eddy here?"

"It is, surely."

"Sure an' it will make ya feel so grand—havin' Eddy here now," Erin said and mixed emotions welled up in Maisie. She felt embarrassed at the comment about Eddy and sad that her daughter would have to hope for her to feel grand. Had she appeared that miserable to her daughter? She fought to keep the tears at bay. "But won't it, Ma? Ya've had a face *even longer* than a Lohrgan spade." She turned to Ed. "Sure and she has fer days and days and days."

Sensing Maisie's inner turmoil, Ed went to her, sat beside her, and put his arm around her. "It's made me happier, too, to be here with yer ma and all of you. I've missed everyone here."

"But surely 'specially ta me and Ma," Erin said as she pushed herself up onto Ed's lap.

Gareth and Tonya looked at each other knowingly, picked up the twins, and took them upstairs to the bedroom to play.

At dinner that night Eoin pulled up some benches and extra chairs and they all crowded around the table that Ian had built so long ago. Eoin felt a keen sense of satisfaction that his house was full. The two bedrooms upstairs held his family and Maisie and Erin. Gareth had volunteered to sleep on the floor by the fire with several blankets layered beneath him while Ed slept on the sofa. Some hosts might feel cramped and wish for guests to leave their house after a while, but Eoin's heart was full of love for all the people who gathered here. Gareth saw him smiling as the stew and soda bread were passed around the table.

"What's going on in your head, broder?" he asked.

"Just feelin' mighty grand and thankful ta have ya all here." Eoin grinned from ear to ear. Tonya reached over and patted his hand.

"Someday, maybe I can afford to bring the whole family over!" Gareth said.

"That would be grand, broder! Just grand."

"I think Da would love to come."

"I'd like to get my folks over here, too," Ed said. "I know they would love it."

"Maybe. Someday," Gareth said. "We never know what God has planned for any of us. I mean, look at us now—all of us sitting here. Who would've thought Tonya would be married to my broder and have cute wee twins? And who would've thought my best friend, Ed, would be with me in Northern Ireland? And I could've never imagined I'd see my cousins again." Gareth looked lovingly at Maisie. "It's unfathomable what God can do in our lives."

"Amen to that!" Ed said, as he slipped his hand over Maisie's.

And she didn't take her hand away.

That night, Ed was woken by footsteps on the stairway. He opened his eyes and in the darkness could make out Maisie's form descending the steps, clad in her bathrobe over her nightgown. It brought back memories of being here over a year ago. He watched her tiptoe into the kitchen and then waited to hear the sound of the tea kettle on the stove. But there was no such noise to be heard. He slipped out of his covers and walked quietly past Gareth. "Maisie?" he whispered as he entered the kitchen. Maisie stood with her hands on the edge of the sink, staring out the window at the night sky. "Hey, are you okay?" he asked as he lit the candle on the table and went to her side.

When she looked up at him he could see the sheen of tears on her cheeks.

"You've been crying?"

"It's nothin'—just frustration. When I can't sleep I come down here and look out at the night sky."

"Does this happen often?"

"Often. My mind won't shut down in the night, so it won't."

"You're probably on high alert—it's a sign of fight or flight. I saw this as an army chaplain."

"I hate it."

Ed put his hands beside hers on the counter and they stood together quietly, looking out the window. She moved her hands closer to his and he rested his over hers.

"Eddy, remember that night when Erin couldn't get ta sleep and ya helped her?"

"Yes. She was so precious."

"What did ya do? Ta help her, ya know?"

"I quoted Scripture, prayed—and sang."

Maisie rested her head on his shoulder. "Do ya think ya could do some of that fer me?"

"You want me to?"

"Will you?"

"I'd love to." Ed put his arm around her. "Where can we go? It's not my normal protocol to go into a woman's bedroom but Gareth is out in the sitting room."

"Erin's in the bedroom and it will be proper, so it will. She sleeps like a log, we won't wake her."

They ascended the stairs quietly and tiptoed into the bedroom. Erin lay sleeping, cuddled up into a corner of the bed. Maisie kept her robe on and slipped under the covers. Ed grabbed an extra quilt at the foot of the bed and sat on it on the floor beside Maisie. He leaned his elbow on the mattress, his head in his hand. Maisie slid her hand out from under the covers and put her hand on his forearm. The connection she felt brought a comforting sense of security. Ed smiled.

"When I was a kid and I had a hard time sleeping at night my momma would say this Psalm: 'I will both lay me down in peace, and sleep; for Thou, Lord, only makest me dwell in safety.'"

"I miss Ma comfortin' me like that," Maisie said sadly.

"So you remember that of your ma?"

"I do."

"That's sweet. Do you remember anything else of your ma?"

Maisie thought for a minute. "She used ta read stories ta the boys and me on Saturday nights. I used ta fall asleep before she got ta the endin's." Maisie smiled. "And in the mornin's, Ma would sing a happy good mornin' song ta us ta get us out o' bed."

Ed was enjoying her sudden spurt of memories and egged her on. "What else? What of your da?"

"Well, Da made us laugh, so he did. But sometimes, it made Ma upset because she'd just get us settled inta our beds and quieted down. Then, Da would come in from a long day of farmin'. He'd come in ta say goodnight and then he'd do somethin' like run inta the wall and act like he got hurt. We'd laugh so hard in our beds. Ma would say, Sean, I just got them quieted, so I did! Now, ya laloo, ya have ta get them quieted yerself!"

Ed and Maisie chuckled softly together.

"Such good memories, Maisie."

"I haven't thought o' those in a long time. I miss them so much." Maisie started to weep quietly. Ed gently caressed the dainty fingers that rested on his arm.

"It's okay to cry. Often, crying helps relieve the emotion you've got all built up inside of you. Your folks sound like they were wonderful people. Hold on to those precious and good memories you have, Maisie. At night, when you have trouble sleeping, think of the people who have loved you and those who love you now. That alone can bring peace."

Maisie smiled through her tears and started to breathe easier.

"I used to quote this verse often to the soldiers: 'Thou wilt keep him in perfect peace, whose mind is stayed on Thee, because he trusteth in Thee,'" Ed said. "See, if we trust in God, our mind is stayed on Him—our mind is steadfast—and that will give us perfect peace.'"

"I need that, so I do," Maisie whispered. "I need perfect peace. I don't have it."

"Here's another verse on peace: 'Great peace have they that love Thy law and nothing shall offend them—or make them stumble.' Maisie, you need to let go of your fears and all that is turning you away from totally trusting God—hatred, offenses—"

"I never thought all that could affect me this way."

"It can."

Ed started to pray. He heard her start to breathe deeper. When he finished praying, he thought she was asleep and started to move, but her eyes fluttered and she looked up at him sadly.

"I was almost asleep," she said softly, "but then, I get this jolt in my body that wakes me back up. It makes me so mad and—"

"Shhh." Ed put his finger to her lips. "It's okay. Don't fret about it. Don't get irritated. That just ignites your nervous energy again and will keep you awake longer." He got up and sat on the edge of the bed. He caressed her hand and her arm as he sang softly:

"So precious is Jesus, my Savior, my King,

His praise all the day long with rapture I sing;

To Him in my weakness for strength I can cling,

For He is so precious to me.

For He is so precious to me,

For He is so precious to me;

'Tis heaven below, my Redeemer to know,

For He is so precious to me."

Maisie focused on the song. The vibration of his tenor voice and the feel of his touch on her skin soothed her. He continued singing softly until he was certain she was asleep and remaining so. He slipped off the bed, wrapped himself up in the quilt, and slept on the floor next to the bed. If she woke again, he'd be there for her.

The following day there was a slight dampness to the air, but Maisie insisted she'd be fine outside and, in fact, stated it would help lift her spirits. Ed took her for a stroll about the gardens. She hung on his arm and the longer they walked, the more heavily she leaned on him.

"Let's stop a minute. You're worn out already," Ed said.

"I didn't eat much this mornin'."

"And you didn't sleep well last night."

"Sure an' I did get some good hours of sleep in, thanks ta you. But ya didn't sleep well either because of me. I'm sorry."

"Don't be. I'm fine. I was glad to help. How long has this been going on?"

"I've not felt the same ever since—ever since—"

"It's okay, I know what happened." They sat down on a stone bench. "You have a hard time talking about it?"

"Aye."

"Maybe some time you can talk to me about it and get it all out of that pretty head of yours that seems to be filled with so much turmoil."

"It ain't much of a pretty head no more."

"I beg to differ."

"Well, ya need a pair of glasses then, ya stook!" It was good to hear the energy in her voice, but then it softened. "Do ya think talkin' would truly help?"

"First of all, I don't need glasses. You're beautiful, Maisie. Even in the middle of the night," Ed said. "But I do think it would help to talk it out. I dealt with a lot of soldiers who saw terrible things in the war. If they kept it all bottled up in their heads they'd suffer more with nightmares and trauma. Somehow, talking it out and then leaving it in the past seemed to help them. But everybody's different. I do know this: you've kept everything bottled up all these years and it doesn't seem to make it go away, does it?"

"No." Maisie rested her head on his arm.

"Should we go in?" Ed asked.

"Let's not. It's just mizzle driftin' in."

"It makes all the shades of green out here like a deep blue-green."

"I love it."

They sat quietly, watching a few hooded crows hunt for food.

Maisie finally spoke. "Did Gareth talk ta ya a lot like that?"

"Like what?"

"About what happened ta him—what happened here."

"Yeah."

"It helped him, so it did? But it didn't make his nightmares go away, did it?"

"As far as I know, he's not had one in a while."

"After he identified O'Malley, that night he had a nightmare."

"Oh? He didn't tell me." Ed frowned. "I'm really sad to hear it."

"He was loud—yellin' somethin'—it didn't sound good an' it sure brought back the Irish in 'im. But he's going ta keep pursuin' this justice thing and testify when he needs ta."

"I'm not surprised. It will be tough for him, but in the end I think it will help him and all of you, actually."

"Do ya think so then?"

"I do."

When they returned to the house Maisie went right to her room to lie down.

Tonya looked at Ed. "How'd it go?"

"I think I had her out walking too long and talking too much about her issues. I probably shouldn't have pushed her."

"I think she needs this, Eddy. And getting out and exercising might help her sleep better, too. Just give her some breaks between the pushing. If anyone can do it, it's you."

"I'm not sure you're right about that, but thanks, Tonya."

"I saw that you slept on the floor of Maisie's bedroom last night."

"That sounds scandalous!" Ed laughed. "Please don't tell my momma!"

"So scandalous." Tonya laughed. "Except for the fact that you were on the floor! And there was Maisie, sleeping well in her bed. That's a good step in the right direction already—her sleeping well. You're helping her, Eddy."

Tonya was right and she made it a point every so often to be sure Ed realized the effect he was having on Maisie. He sat with her at every meal, lifting her spirits and making sure she ate. He pushed her to go out for walks, the cool moist air bringing health back to her skin and overall countenance. And he sang to her at night, quoted verses, and prayed. She was sleeping better and eventually, she began eating well and feeling more herself. Her cheeks were rosy, her eyes brighter, and soon her true character returned.

They were sitting out in the back garden on a bench talking when suddenly the white clouds overhead turned grey.

Ed looked up. "The weather changes faster here than back home!"

"That's our island!" Maisie laughed. "Sure and the rain will follow soon."

"Do you want to go inside?" Ed asked, admiring how her eyes twinkled and her freckled nose scrunched when she laughed. He was drawn to stare at her today, but he tried not to be obvious.

"Ach! Rain never hurt a soul."

"I just don't want you to get chilled."

His sweet look of concern for her changed her breathing pattern and she felt overwhelmed with emotion. But she couldn't show it. Not now. "I'll be fine, but what about youse, rich boy?" she taunted him as she leaned into him. "Is the rain too cold fer yer spoiled self?" There was that familiar tease in her beautiful green eyes. It was something Ed hadn't seen in a long time and his heart warmed. "What?" Maisie asked when he didn't say anything.

"Nothing," Ed said, trying to suppress the feelings that stirred. How could he explain to her the contrast of her present appearance and attitude to how she was when he first came back to see her? How could he tell her that even a bit of teasing made him rejoice because it meant she was getting back to her old self—that piece of her that he treasured so much and missed while they were apart? He was afraid to say much, lest he scare her away. He may not ever have her love, but he could at least survive with her friendship.

"Tell me what yer thinkin', farm boy," Maisie said, looking at him in anticipation.

Ed smiled. "It's just that I missed this side of you—this teasing. And you look so beautiful today." Ed reached up and pushed a runaway lock of hair away from her face and placed it gently behind her ear. He hoped he didn't scare her with this simple gesture. He surely yearned to kiss her, but he'd already been bold in his words and actions.

Suddenly, the rain started to fall. Maisie jumped up and ran farther into the gardens and away from Ed. His heart sank. There it was. Just as he feared. He'd frightened her off.

He ran after her and when he caught up to her she was staring out at the drumlins in the distance. He stood next to her, observing the beauty before them. They didn't say a word. The rain continued to fall on the rolling green landscape. He felt her cold hand slide into his and he warmed it with his. He felt relieved, assured she was not running from him. When he heard her let out a little gasp he looked at her. "Maisie? Are you crying?"

She turned and looked up at him, her tears mixing with the rain on her cheeks. "Sadness is on me."

"I don't understand. You were happy a minute ago. Was it something I said?"

"Sure and it was."

"I'm sorry."

"I'm the one ta be sorry, so I am."

"For what?"

"Fer ya havin' ta come all the way from yer home fer me and fer what I put ya through."

"You don't need to be sorry at all. You didn't push me to come here and you didn't put me through anything that I wasn't willing to go through. I did it for you, Maisie. I hope you can see that. It was all for you—and for Erin. She needed her ma back."

Maisie wept at his words and turned into him. He wrapped her up in his arms. She calmed, feeling the warmth of his chest and the beating of his heart. She knew what she felt then—sanctuary. She wanted to be with Eddy forever. But he lived in America and he'd been hurt too many times to give his heart away. She would just enjoy this moment while it lasted. Eddy was a rescuer, and right now, she was the damsel in distress. Nothing more.

It was the perfect day to make the final move to the new homestead. Maisie was doing much better and Tonya felt better about leaving her alone. The sun was shining and the billowing clouds passed by without a drop of rain.

Everyone stood in the new kitchen while Eoin balanced on a stool over the sink and hung the tartan wool and lace knotted together that Eoin and Tonya had made when they said their wedding vows.

"That's perfect!" Tonya said. "I want to see it every time I'm in the kitchen making meals for my family."

"Which is every day," Eoin said.

"That's exactly right." Tonya smiled.

"She's a grand wife who cooks me fantastic meals now. Especially after Da taught her some of our traditional meals and Margaret taught her some Scohttish dishes."

"Ach, poor Tonnie! Ya shouldna pick on yer bonny wife, cousin!" Maisie said.

"It's all good. I needed to learn. I grew up on Chef Boyardee, SpaghettiOs, and Banquet frozen dinners!" Tonya smirked.

"I don't know what all those are, but I'm guessin' not grand!" Maisie said. The others laughed.

"It's amazing how you two have given our old home a new life," Gareth said to Eoin as he helped him carry in Eoin and Tonya's mattress.

"It's got a new feel along with the old one, eh?" Eoin said.

"That's a good way to put it, broder."

"When we're done settin' it all up, Tonnie will take pictures ta send ta Da."

"He'd like that and Haley will like to see pictures, too."

"How much longer do ya think you'll be stayin' here?"

"Just after the trial is over. The VWCU—Victim Witness Care Unit—will let me know when the court date is and will keep me posted on the details. They said they can't give any guarantees how long it will take so I'm not sure how long I'll be here," Gareth said as they carried the mattress up the stairs.

"Are ya worried?"

"About what?"

"About bein' threatened?" Eoin asked.

"Well, on one hand, Collins says it seems that the IRA won't care if these guys get put in prison."

"And on the other hand?"

"The Provos might. It all depends on who they were really working for."

"I don' like it when they enter inta the picture."

"No, broder, neither do I," Gareth said. "Is this where you want to leave the mattress for now?"

"I s'pose."

They leaned the mattress up against the wall and left the room.

"The more I hear about the Provos and the loyalist paras from our cousins, the more I think I'd rather deal with the IRA!"

"Paramilitary from either side are not even kind ta their own people. Catholics will shoot Catholics and Protestants will shoot Protestants."

"Seriously?"

"It's a lot of our generation, broder. Callum explained ta me that they grew up in this mess, had nothin' ta do but steal cars and go fer joy rides, get drunk and get angry with the fightin' and injustice around them. They were perfect candidates ta get sucked inta becomin' part of a paramilitary and takin' justice inta their own hands."

"It's hard to believe Brodie is a part of it, but I think—what would I have done if I'd have lived here my whole life?"

"You were always the scrapper, Gareth. Do ya think ya would've joined up?"

"Haley would answer that with a resounding 'yes'!" The brothers laughed together as they went down the stairs. At the foot of the steps Gareth stopped and turned to Eoin. "Do you ever think that taking us from this mess the way we were taken was God's way of sparing us from getting too involved in the fight? I mean, I *know* I would've joined up like Brodie."

"I never thought of it that way, but perhaps. God works in mysterious ways. What happened ta us is pretty mysterious."

"We may never know the answers. But that's okay. As long as God has this in His hands, I'm good."

"I believe that too, broder," Eoin said as they stepped outside and found the bedframe in the truck. "However, it would be nice ta see some answers—like findin' out who was really responsible fer it all!"

"It's too bad Maisie can't testify. I think it would help the trial wrap up faster."

"Aye, it would."

"Well, hopefully it doesn't last too long and I'll be out of here. Haley will be glad of that. I miss her and the kids."

"I understand that feelin'."

"I'm sure you do. The distance is unsettling," Gareth said as they carried the bedframe up the stairs. "If there were an emergency with the kids, it would be hard to get back quickly to be with the family."

"I couldn't even think of that when Tonnie was away."

"Yeah, I try not to think about it either. Kids always seem to have emergencies. The older Bobby gets, the more accidents he has in his play. I just hope Haley doesn't have to handle anything alone."

"Maybe we can send some pictures back with ya."

"Good idea."

"I like havin' ya here, broder."

"And I love being back here. My home is in Wisconsin now—but I miss it here. I didn't realize how much until now."

"An' Da's home is over there now, too. I'm glad ta have the cousins here."

"Maybe Ed will end up here. I think he's won two girls' hearts."

They had just finished putting the bedframe together when Ed came in, holding a large box, with Erin hanging on to his back, giggling. "Maisie told me to take these to the main bedroom."

"You can leave that here, thanks," Eoin said. The brothers looked at each other and smiled.

"What?" Ed asked.

"I'm still trying to wrap my head around Ed being such *'good friends'* with our cousin, Maisie," Gareth said to Eoin. "I mean, I knew Haley would've been a handful for him in all her feistiness, but broder, he's going after our wee cousin—"

"With a bit of the banshee in her!" Eoin finished the sentence and Gareth nodded.

"*Brothers*," Ed said, and the brothers laughed together. Ed smiled. "C'mon, Erin, let's go see what else your *sweet* momma says we need to do."

Tonya called Eoin down to the sitting room with a question and Gareth went out to get more household items to carry in.

When Erin and Ed went to the car to grab another box, Maisie was trying to lift a heavy one. Ed came up behind her and took it from her. "You shouldn't be doing that, Maisie. You don't have your strength back yet."

"Yer not me da," Maisie said saucily as she reached into the car and took out another box of the same size.

"Yep, the real Maisie is back!" Ed said dryly.

Erin took a pillow to carry, Ed grabbed a box, and they both followed Maisie to the house. Just before they reached the door, Eoin stepped out and held the door for Tonya, who was fussing at him about something that had to do with the location of the sofa. She walked out, mumbling to herself about how she knew better where things should go. Ed asked her what was wrong but she just continued on. Eoin kept the door open as Maisie and Erin went in.

Eoin looked at Ed when he stepped up to the threshold and rolled his eyes. "*American women*," he said in exasperation.

Ed nodded toward Maisie, struggling with the box she chose to carry. "*Irish* women."

CHAPTER 27

"So, are you ready for this, Gareth?" Ed said as Gareth climbed into the right side of the car and into the driver's seat. He started the car while Ed shut the passenger side door.

"I just want to get it over with and be able to go home to my family, ya know?" He pulled out into the small country lane and headed north to the courthouse in Belfast.

"I can imagine."

"So, we all know *my* plans. What are yours, Ed?"

"What do you mean?"

"I think you know what I mean."

Ed let out a long sigh. "I want to stay a while longer, you know? But when you leave, it will just be me with Maisie and Erin in the cottage. I'd need to stay somewhere else for propriety's sake. I know Maisie feels ready to be on her own with Erin, but I'd like to be with her until the trial is over."

"I'd stay to help if I didn't have my own family back home."

"Oh, of course, I'm not asking you to stay by any means. Haley would have my head—"

"And your feet—"

"And my whole body—in the grave," Ed said. The men laughed. "I just don't want to rush things with Maisie."

"Do you think there's a possibility of you two finally coming together?"

"You mean the two of us—officially dating?"

"Aye."

"I don't know."

"Come on, Ed. This is the slowest I've seen you make a move in your whole life."

"It's just that we're both—"

"I know, you're both being *careful*. Look, for what it's worth, you two should stop using your past relationships to define the one between the two of you."

Gareth's words gave Ed pause.

"I'll think on that one."

"Well, don't take too long."

"Someone should tell Maisie the same thing."

"That's your job, Ed, my man."

"I was afraid you'd say that."

Eventually, they pulled into the parking lot of the courthouse. They paused to pray together and then went in and met Collins, Callum, and Brodie.

Gareth testified in the magistrates court against Tom O'Malley. There was no jury and the judge would decide whether it was a serious enough accusation to go on to the crown court or not. The crown court would include a jury. Gareth stated he recognized O'Malley's voice as being one of the men to come to his home and set it on fire. He believed him to be one of the same men who came to his uncle's home, murdered his aunt and uncle, and burnt their house. But the prosecutor, John Byrne, from the Public Prosecution

Service, told him later it wasn't enough to place O'Malley at his uncle's home. He said they would have to come up with better proof. Were there any more witnesses who could come forward?

Gareth sighed. "We believe my youngest cousin knows and heard more but she's fearful of reliving the past. She's not in the best frame of mind after she recently experienced being in the very taxi that O'Malley was driving."

Callum put pressure on his sister to testify.

"Ya know better than ta talk ta me about it!" Maisie turned from the counter where she was helping Molly wash dishes.

"An' what'll ya do ta me? I ain't ascared to push ya, lass! Sure an' our cousin, Gareth, came all the way from America ta testify and try ta bring justice ta the MacCauley families, but his testimony won't be enough! The least ya could do is ta help the family. It would expedite the case and Gareth could then return ta his kin in the US."

"Leave me be, broder! I wouldn't be of use ta any of it!'"

"I suspect ya know more than anyone but aren't willing ta admit it!"

"Callum, don't be too hard on yer sister," Molly cautioned. But he ignored his wife and pushed anyway.

Molly put out a plea to Ed when she had a moment alone with him later. "I fear fer all the family. Everyone's feelin' the pressure of this court case, Eddy, includin' me husband. He's beyond frustrated with his sister fer not helpin' and I'm ascared he'll push her back into her hole."

"You think he'd push that hard?"

"He can be a bit abrasive and harsh with his family, but it's his way, feelin' the responsibility of bein' the eldest and with the parents gone, so he is."

"I understand. But both Brodie and Maisie have strong minds of their own."

"So they do, but Callum helped Brodie get away from the paras. He was hard on Brodie, but Brodie can take it. Callum's same approach with his sister might do more harm than good, ya know?"

"Yeah, I get that. I'll see what I can do, but you and I both know who I'm up against: a very stubborn and troubled woman."

"Sure and her heart is yers, Eddy. Ya got ta see that. She's just not ready ta show ya."

It was too chilly to go out for a walk, so Ed borrowed a car and took Maisie out for a south easterly drive in the country. The rain continued to pelt the car and the windshield wipers created a soothing rhythm.

"When they say it rains a lot here, they weren't kidding," Ed said as he pulled off the narrow road to let a bigger vehicle pass. "Are those mountains over there?" Ed pointed through the misty view.

"Aye."

"I can just barely see them."

"Of course. That's because you can't see the Mourne Mountains when it's rainin'. When you *can* see the Mournes, then it's *goin'* ta rain," Maisie laughed. "Here." She pointed. "Pull off over here and we can enjoy a good view." Ed did as she directed. She let out a long sigh. "I love it out here."

Ed smiled. She was herself again. He hated to ruin the joy on her face by asking her about testifying. But he knew, for everyone else's sake, he needed to. *Lord, give me the right words to say.*

"It's beautiful," he said.

"Eddy, thank ya fer comin here. Since ya've come I've felt more like the ol' me. Ya bring me a sense of security and comfort."

"Do I?"

"So ya do." She turned and smiled. Never had anyone looked so beautiful to him as this girl. The softness of her fair skin distracted him and the way she looked at him—was that admiration? And then, when they locked eyes, it felt natural to reach his arm up across the back of the seat, and apparently it was natural for her to move under his grasp. It was a special moment in their relationship and Ed could feel his courage to talk about the case shriveling. How could he make her relive horrible memories in order to testify in court? And how could he ruin this perfect moment? She trusted him.

But along with trust came honesty and he had to be honest with her. It might be beneficial for Maisie to get her trauma out in the open, work through it and start to heal from it. If he truly loved her—and he was beginning to understand that he truly did—he would man up and talk openly with her about it.

"Maisie?"

"Hmmm?" she asked, relaxing in the comfort of his closeness.

"There's something I need to talk to you about."

She tipped her head up and looked into his eyes. It melted him. He almost lost courage again.

"I want you to know, first of all, that this is hard for me to say." He paused. "But I'm doing it because I love you, and I want what's best for you. I want to help you recount what happened back in '74." He felt Maisie stiffen. "And hopefully, you can see, like I do, that you are a brave enough person to testify against these men." Maisie pulled away.

"Not the likes of ya, too!"

Ed couldn't believe he'd just let it slip out and admit that he loved Maisie while challenging her to face her fears. And then, to make matters worse, she didn't even flinch when he admitted he loved her. Instead, she tensed up. He felt like a fool. Why did he use this moment to express his feelings? Embarrassment and an old fear of rejection stirred in his gut. Who did he think he was to push this woman to dig through her terrible past and talk about it? Certainly he'd lost her now.

Maisie stared out the window as the rain continued to come down. "Why are ya askin' this of me, Eddy? Yer just like everyone else! Don't ya understand that what I went through hurts me and sends me inta such a dark place? Don't ya care about me feelin's? Doesn't anyone care about me feelin's? Don't they realize what I've had ta live with me whole life? I lost me whole family and me home!"

It was then Ed heard it in her words. He drew in a breath. "It's not just about you, Maisie," he said softly. Her head snapped around.

"What? What did ya say?" Her voice rose.

"Calm down."

"Don't tell me ta calm down!" She pushed the door open and got out quickly.

"Maisie!"

Ed got out of the car and followed her. "You're not the only one who went through this traumatic experience! What about your brothers and your cousins? Didn't Callum, Brodie, and Gareth see much of what you saw that day?" He caught up to her and grabbed her arm to stop her. "Did you ever think about them running in fear, out of the barn, young boys fearful of being pursued by these scary men in balaclavas with guns? And then, your brothers living with the fear and guilt of leaving their little sister behind? And there was Gareth, who lost *his* whole family and *his* house and then got shipped off to a strange country."

"Go away!" Maisie pulled out of his grasp.

"No, I won't! Just listen to me," he begged. "Didn't you tell me Gareth had another nightmare after testifying? What about his feelings? Maisie, you're so focused on *your* experience and *your* pain that it's caused you to only look inward and have terrible anxiety over it. Maybe if you looked at these others who have suffered, it would help you deal better. I mean, look at Eoin—after all the terrifying things he went through at the beach—going to visit others who have suffered with loved ones disappearing? That's been great therapy for him. And look at Gareth, leaving his wife and four kids to come testify and do what he can to bring justice, despite how it affects him personally.

"And then there's Callum trying to hold you all together and get some semblance of justice and peace in your family. Even Brodie has fought to get justice in his own foolish way and has endangered his life. And what about your poor Uncle Ian who sat in a prison for ten years and suffered such loss of his wife and years with his boys? Yet now he's moved on while courageously hanging on to the good memories of the past. I know I'm saying stuff you already know and don't want to hear. I know you may never speak to me after this, but I'm saying it anyway! *Because I love you and it needs to be said.*"

"I don't want ta hear anymore," Maisie said curtly.

"Maisie, if you ignore this battle with the past, you'll lose it. You can't change this fight within if you don't confront it."

Maisie looked away as the tears started to flow. "Take me back ta the house."

Ed let out a loud sigh and went back to the car. Maisie followed behind him.

They rode home in silence. When they pulled up to the cottage, Ed put the car in park and Maisie bolted without a word and went immediately to her room. Ed entered the cottage and found Gareth and Erin playing a card game of Go Fish.

"Everything okay?" Gareth raised one eyebrow.

"*No*," Ed said as he sat down on the couch and crossed his arms, frustrated. "I did what you all wanted me to do. I *pushed* her."

"To testify?"

The men spoke minimally with Erin present.

"*Yes*."

"And?"

"I don't think it did any good except make her mad at me."

Gareth sighed. "God help us. We need her."

"God may have to come up with something else." Ed shrugged. "I'm done here."

Maisie sat stiffly on her bed. She was so mad she couldn't cry at first. Eddy's words hurt. Was she really being selfish all this time? No! She gave up so much of her life to take care of Erin. That wasn't selfish, was it? She thought about it for a while. She was avoiding the past as a protective layer. She couldn't fall apart with a daughter to support, could she? But what was she protecting? Herself. And frankly, she wasn't doing too well at that. She fell apart despite trying to "protect" herself.

And she was pulling away from people she loved by keeping up that layer of protection—including Eddy. Was it worth it? Would she eventually push away her own daughter? She was already being neglectful of her duties as a mother, pampering her anxiety over the taxi driver experience. Was this how she wanted to live? Not really.

"God, help me. Help me dig the details from me head, get them cleaned out and do me part ta help the family like everyone else. I do want ta bring justice ta me parents. But I'm afraid!" she said aloud, and then sobbed.

Erin looked up toward the stairs. "Is Ma okay?"

"Aye, lassie. We'll just leave her to cry a bit and sort things out, but she'll be fine," Gareth said.

After the sobs subsided, Maisie lay down on the bed exhausted, and stared at the ceiling. She let the memories come.

She remembered the day she hid in the big chest in the loft of the barn. She remembered thinking the boys would never look for her there. She was pretty proud of herself. She remembered feeling sleepy and then the next thing she knew she was waking up to strange men's voices. It shocked her because she knew neither one was her da's voice. Was it the neighbors? She listened for a while. She raised the lid of the box and stepped out.

"Where are ye, laddies? Ya have no place ta go."

Maisie saw two men enter the barn, their balaclavas lifted and faces exposed. Quickly and quietly she lay down on her belly.

"Ya Prod brats! Whichever of ya shot me broder will die, surely!"

"Billy, let's get ayt o' here. We done wha' we were s'pose ta do, ya know?"

"Wha' about me baby broder?"

"He's dead and yer O'Grady clan will go dayn in history as martyrs, ta be sure!"

"Look, Tommy, I don' t'ink me ma will look at it dat way! Would yer O'Malley clan t'ink so?"

"Go on, Billy. T'ese boys are gone and will be bringin' back the gardai soon. An' we can' take yer broder, sorry, lad, but we gotta move!"

"Tommy!"

"Are ya daft?!"

The men's voices moved outside of the barn so Maisie knelt on the loft floor and leaned carefully over the edge. It was then she saw the house on fire. She tried not to gasp out loud. She wondered where everyone else was. When the men were gone, she climbed down the ladder in order to get a better look outside. Why was her home in flames? She saw what she thought were three people lying on the ground. She called out for her ma and then da. No one answered. All she could hear was the crashing of the timbers as the house burnt to the ground.

Maisie's mind went black. She lay on the bed, concentrating. There was something about this next part that turned her stomach. What was it?

Maise sat up in bed quickly and gasped. She got up and rummaged through her drawer and pulled out a small jewelry box. Underneath other little treasures and some jewelry, she found what she was looking for. It was a pearl-handled pocket knife. She closed her fingers tightly over it. She'd forgotten this was with her jewelry and now, after being evicted from her apartment, she was glad she'd taken it with her on the trip to America, otherwise it would have been lost in the eviction.

Maisie remembered that she had picked up the pocketknife off the ground near her da that day. The picture was out of focus but she knew what she saw. Her da was lying there, face down in the dirt, and her ma was beside him, also face down. She remembered just standing there silently, staring. Did she know they were dead? She wasn't sure if it actually registered, but living in Northern Ireland during the Troubles meant seeing death on a regular basis if you went near the cities at all. Even for the children.

It had been over an hour when Ed looked up from the three-way game of Go Fish and saw Maisie coming down the steps. She stopped at the foot of the stairs and looked at him with a tear-stained face.

"I don' want ta be selfish," she said hoarsely. "I care about me broders, me cousins, and Uncle Ian." Ed got up quickly and went to her. She nestled into the comfort of his arms.

"I know you do," Ed said. "I know you care about them all. I'm sorry, I shouldn't have—"

"Nay, ya were right ta say what ya said ta me."

"But you were weeping. I made you miserable and—"

Maisie pulled away and looked at him squarely. "You knew what I needed. And I let it come, Eddy. I did. I remembered."

"Let's go sit down," Ed said as he guided her to the sofa.

Erin tapped Gareth's arm and whispered in his ear. "Is Ma okay now?"

"I think she'll be fine, lass." Gareth smiled and hugged her.

Erin came up to her mother and tapped her fist, still wrapped around the pocketknife. Maisie opened her hand.

"Whose is this?"

"Yer grandpa's, agra."

"Your da's? Can I see it?" Ed asked and Maisie handed it to him.

"I found it by his body the day he died," she said softly.

Ed examined it carefully, turning it over, running his finger over the smooth inlay of pearl. When he touched the steel layer beneath the ivory piece, his finger felt a rough spot. He looked at it closely, thinking the scratches he felt were probably the engraved initials of Sean MacCauley. But it wasn't his initials at all. "Um, Maisie, you said this was your father's?"

"I picked it up on the ground where he lay—"

Gareth looked up at Maisie and their eyes met. He nodded slightly. He remembered that awful picture, too. "I saw the faces of the men, Gareth."

"You did?"

"Aye." Maisie's eyes filled with tears again and she broke down weeping. Gareth got up, sat on the other side of her, and put a hand on her shoulder. It was the first time she came face-to-face with what happened. The trauma and grief were strong. Sharing it with Gareth helped her release the pain of it. They sat together quietly while Ed found a piece of paper, put it over the initials on the knife, and rubbed a pencil over it. The initials were T.

O. Ed sighed. How could he tell Maisie, especially now as she grieved heavily, that this pocketknife she had saved as a last memory of her father, was not her father's at all, but probably Tom O'Malley's, one of the men who killed him? She would have to learn eventually, and this could actually help the case.

Ed sat back down and quietly handed the knife to Gareth. He pointed out the engraving and the rubbing on the paper that showed O'Malley's initials. Gareth's eyes lit up and he said exuberantly, "Yes! This may be all we need for proof!"

Ed winced. He was hoping Gareth would help him handle this situation with kid gloves, but no, Gareth's outburst meant that the truth was going to come hard and fast. Maisie sat up straight and asked about it. Gareth bit his lip and Ed rolled his eyes. Gareth showed her. Maisie grew quiet and melted into Ed's arms.

She lifted her head to speak, but barely a sound came out. Ed put his ear close to her lips.

"I want ta talk ta me big broder," she said.

CHAPTER 28

Gareth contacted the prosecutor, John Byrne, and told him that Maisie would identify the men who were at her home the day of the murders. He said that she had heard their names, seen their faces and that she had saved some physical proof that might possibly help their case. Byrne said he'd take the knife to a forensic scientist and see if any small amount of O'Malley's DNA, even if degraded, could be analyzed and identified.

After Maisie met with Byrne and he felt she was ready to appear, he had her testify. When the judge heard her story, saw the knife that Maisie had found next to her father's body and learned that DNA had indeed been identified as O'Malley's, he decided that this case was worthy of the crown court. O'Grady and O'Malley would be tried separately. Everyone was ecstatic and felt hopeful.

During the court sessions with O'Malley as the defendant, O'Grady appeared to testify.

Eoin leaned over and whispered to Gareth. "Did ya know he was comin'?" The cousins leaned forward and waited for his response.

"No. I don't get what's going on."

"Is he goin' ta ruin my testimony?" Maisie whispered to Ed.

"I have no idea."

But when O'Grady testified, he spoke against his partner, putting himself *and* O'Malley at both MacCauley homesteads. He implicated

O'Malley as being the one to pull the trigger on both Erin and Sean MacCauley. Maisie flinched and started to get up, but Ed took her hand in his and kept her seated close to him. He whispered, "You need to see the end of this. No more running."

John Byrne told them later that O'Grady had been carrying a grudge all these years against O'Malley for making him return to the scene of the crime and throw his brother's dead body into the fire of the MacCauley home. O'Grady's mother suffered much from the death, never having a body to bury. Her heart failed too early in life and she was buried a year after losing her son. There was no way O'Grady was going to take the fall for murders he didn't commit. He tried to implicate Gareth in the murder of his brother, but when the jury learned of Gareth's story, how old he was at the time, they dismissed it as an offense committed by a juvenile in self-defense. When they came out of the courtroom, Byrne said he felt confident that this was enough to indict O'Malley on the charges of arson and murder. It took a week of deliberations, but the verdict came in and O'Malley was found guilty. O'Grady was found guilty of arson and accessory to murder.

The trial over, Gareth started to make preparations to fly back to Wisconsin. He was anxious to get back home and Haley and the kids were excited to have him return. Meanwhile, Ed was in turmoil. He wasn't ready to leave. He needed more time with Maisie. But it wouldn't be proper for him to stay alone with her in the cottage.

She brought it up before he could figure things out. They were sitting together by the fire one evening. Erin had been in bed for a while and Gareth took the cordless phone and disappeared in the bedroom to talk to Haley.

"So, when Gareth goes, are ya goin' back with him?" There was no lilt in her voice as she spoke.

"I don't know what I'm doing." Ed took her hand and she wove her fingers between his. "I'm so torn right now. I don't want to leave you and Erin. But I can't stay here forever."

"I don't want ya ta leave either. Maybe ya can stay with Eoin and Tonnie." Maisie gripped his hand. "I wish we had more time together ta sort things out."

"Same here."

"Sure and we both are cautious." Maisie chuckled and leaned into him. "Although ya let something slip the other day when ya were bound and determined ta get me ta testify."

"I did." Ed smiled as he put his arm around her. She had not mentioned his admittance to loving her until now. There was still no response from her concerning his declaration, but he was willing to give that time.

"Why do ya, Eddy? Why do ya care so much about me and Erin?"

"I was drawn to you the day you came to the States. You had me puzzled by your feisty, sarcastic comments but I believe I saw something deeper in you and I wanted to know what it was. You're unpredictable—"

"And ya like that?"

"I do. You make my day exciting and interesting. And you challenge me." Ed paused. "But I have to add, that I am smitten with your beauty."

"Smitten?" she teased.

"Yes, I used that word." He laughed. "When you first came to Wisconsin, I found myself looking for you every time I was at the farm—"

"I watched ya a few times from the upstairs window!"

"A few times, huh?"

"Well, maybe more than a few!"

"Why?"

Maisie smiled. "I know I teased ya about lookin' like a 'Ken doll', but I just couldn't get enough of the tall, handsome farmer in his overalls, workin' with the horses, fixin' the fences—"

"After all that teasing!" Ed complained, but he was glowing.

"It was me way of hidin' how I felt whenever ya appeared—like a teenage girl again with a crush."

Now Ed beamed. "Well, you hid it well."

"I'm not so good at hidin' it now."

"You don't need to." Ed pulled her closer. She put her hand on his chest and fingered the buttons on his shirt.

"I hope we can be tagether longer, Eddy, so I do."

"Well, we have a little while to figure things out."

Gareth came downstairs.

"So, Haley said she just learned today that Uncle Bobby is coming here."

Ed sat up. "Why?"

"Because O'Malley is talking now. He's not going to go down for his crimes without taking others down with him. He feels betrayed by the IRA and the Provos because no one has come to his rescue and no one has threatened us about testifying against him. He knows why Anna and Eoin were taken and is willing to give us some information! Uncle Bobby has jurisdiction over an American citizen being a victim of a crime in another country and can be a part of talking to O'Malley."

"That's awesome, Gareth!" Ed said. "To think you might finally get the answers your family has waited for all these years."

"Right?"

"Does that make you want to stay longer?"

"Yes. And I think Haley will be okay if I do."

"When is Detective Hanford coming?"

"He's coming in a week and I told him he could stay here. I'll go stay with my broder and his wife. Are you willing to stay a bit longer, Ed?"

"Yes, of course," Ed answered all too quickly.

"You could take the bedroom, Ed."

"No, let Bobby have the bedroom! I'm fine out here," Ed said and Maisie smiled.

"I don't know what you two are more happy about: that O' Malley is talking, or that Ed can stay here longer." Gareth grinned.

"A wee bit of both," Maisie said and Ed laughed.

CHAPTER 29

Detective Bobby Hanford traveled with Constable Collins to Long Kesh in Maze, County Down, where O'Malley was being held. He was brought to a private room where the three could talk.

"Tommy, this is Detective Hanford from the US," Collins said as they sat down.

"Why a detective from the US?"

"Sure and it were his sister, Anna MacCauley, who fer no reason got the IRA's feathers ruffled!" Collins said. "But let's get right down ta business. What have ya got ta give us?"

"I want ta get a guarantee dat me life sentence will be reduced first."

"That's not goin' ta happen."

"Then what 'er we here fer?"

"A transfer out of Northern Ireland after you've given us information," Hanford said.

"Dat's it? Why would I need dat?"

"After you've met with us you're goin' ta need a transfer," Collins said, wryly.

"But I haven't given ya anyt'ing yet!"

"Nobody knows that, now, do they?"

"Awright, awright. So, what is it ya wanna know?"

"Who gave the orders ta burn down the MacCauley homes? And who ordered the deaths of Sean and Erin? Who kidnapped Anna and Eoin MacCauley and who killed Anna? And what was behind it all?"

"Dat's a lot o' information ta hand ayt for not'in'."

"Okay, how about ya get a cell all ta yerself?"

O'Malley thought for a while. "Okay. So, dere was a time I woulda taken a bullet fer t'is guy, but nahy, I'd put a bullet in 'im if I could. They called him 'Bodach'—"

"I heard of 'im. Who was it?"

"Why Bodach?" Hanford asked.

"Bodach is the name fer the bogeyman in Irish," Collins explained.

"We just knew 'im by his nickname," O'Malley said. "Rumor has it 'is family burnt all pictures of 'im so British soldiers couldn't identify 'isself. Whoever he was, t'e orders were carried dayn from Sinn Fein ta 'im and he delegated people ta do jobs. He done many murders hisself, too. Word is dat later, he turned on Sinn Fein fer givin' in wit' all t'is peace treaty talk."

"No honor among thieves," Hanford said. Collins agreed. "That doesn't help us much, O'Malley."

"Does it help if I tell ya he's holed up on t'e top floor of t'e Divis tower, just livin' ayt the rest o' 'is life lookin' ayt over Belfast?"

"Isn't that a big complex?"

Collins turned to Hanford. "They tore all the other apartments down except the tower, so they did."

Hanford nodded. "That's easy, then. We can find him."

"Good luck." O'Malley chuckled. "It's well guarded by Provos. He's no use ta anyone."

"Why do ya say that, lad?"

"Word has it he's slowly killin' hisself wit' drugs and alcohol. He can't live wit' all t'e t'ings he's done."

"That doesn't surprise us. But what about the reason the MacCauley families were attacked?"

"O'Grady broders and me were sent ta give a message ta MacCauleys."

"Why?"

"Word was dat two Ms. MacCauleys were helpin' Ms. O'Connelly, who was suspected o' helpin' a British soldier. T'e one, Anna, was seen herself talkin' ta British soldiers. And someone t'ought dey saw dat MacCauley lady sneak a transmitter inta O'Connelly's apartment."

"That's a bunch of baloney!" Hanford snapped. "Knowing Anna and Erin, they were probably bringing some food to the poor family who lost their father."

"But they kidnapped Anna *and Eoin*," Collins said. "And then they punished the whole family? Why?"

"T'e son was just in t'e wrong place at t'e wrong time when t'ey took Ms. MacCauley. Den, we was sent ta send a message ta both MacCauley homes."

"Who is 'they'? Who killed Anna?" Hanford asked.

"Dat was a group called t'e 'Unknowns.'"

"Do they have names?"

"No. Dat's why dey was called *unknown*." O'Malley sniggered.

Collins clicked his tongue and shook his head. "Sure and all this death and sadness was because of rumors and lies—the O'Connelly family, the MacCauley family—innocents caught in the middle of a war. Just sad—all of it."

"I wouldn' call 'em all innocent. Dat American woman, Anna MacCauley, she was keepin' names in a book somewhere, threatened ta expose IRA, and we was commissioned ta find it."

"What book?" Collins looked at Hanford and he shrugged.

"Dat's what we was lookin' fer. It wasn't nowhere. And her brat dat shot dead O'Grady's broder. I wouldn' call dat innocent, neither."

"How did O'Grady know where to find him after he left Northern Ireland?"

"Dey was someone on the inside at t'e time who tipped us off. O'Grady were an eejit ta go ta Americay."

"Yes, he was."

"Ye'll get me transferred right away, den?"

"We made a deal," Collins said as he and Hanford stood.

"By t'e way, lads, rumor has it dat t'e woman who drove and led t'e Unknowns is draynin' in her alcohol, too. Can't live wit' herself neit'er." O'Malley guffawed.

"And you?" Hanford was incensed. "What about you? You shot two innocent people in cold blood and left kids orphaned and without a home! Who knows what other crimes you committed! Can you live with that?"

"It ain't so much as some."

"And that makes you better?" Hanford lunged at the man but Collins held him back.

"Come on, Bobby, let's go. He's sufferin' inside. Sure and I can see it in his eyes. They'll all suffer in their souls fer all eternity, so they will."

O'Malley looked away.

Collins and Hanford got in the car and started down the road. Collins got strangely quiet.

"What is it?" Hanford asked.

"Sure an' we're bein' followed by a black taxi and that's not a good thing." Collins moved quickly from one lane to the next. The car behind them did the same.

"Why do you say that?" Hanford turned around and watched the taxi.

"The IRA are known for their black taxis. Someone must've leaked out information from the prison about O'Malley givin' us info." Collins did a quick turn onto a side street and tried to lose them, but Hanford spotted them shortly afterward. Collins called for backup. Suddenly, out of nowhere, another taxi appeared in front of them and blocked them. Collins put on the brakes and tried to back up, but the taxi was behind them. "They're trappin' us in."

"Do you think your men will get here in time?"

"Here's hopin'!"

Everything grew eerily quiet. "What are they doing?" Hanford asked.

"I don' know."

Then, suddenly, the doors of the taxis opened and men dressed in camouflage, black berets, and black scarves tied like bandits, hiding their faces, appeared and approached Collin's car. They began to beat on the car with clubs, bats, and the butts of their Armalites. The sounds of banging and glass cracking in the car were frightening even to Collins and Hanford, who both had served many years bringing down rough criminals. Never in America had Hanford experienced this kind of attack. Seeing these infamous men in all their life-size violence, eyes looking coldly over the scarves, was disturbing. Though Collins had heard of it happening amongst his peers, he'd never been personally attacked. He wondered if his day had come, and that life as he knew it was about to end for him and for his dear friend from America. Then, one man crashed through the driver's window, yanked the door open, and with the help of two other men, pulled at Collins. Collins resisted them and Hanford strained to get Collins back, but the men succeeded and hauled Collins out of his seat, dragging him into the street.

"Collins!" Hanford yelled, as he looked frantically for a gun or something to defend himself and save his friend. He heard a thud and watched Collins collapse to the ground. It all happened so fast and then, it ended. It was unbelievable how the men disappeared into their cars, skidded tires, and left the scene. Just as Hanford got out of the car to help Collins, three policemen pulled up in separate vehicles and gathered around them. They started asking Hanford questions right away. His first concern was if Collins was dead, but when he saw the man move and groan, a great feeling of relief swept over him.

"Collins! You're alive!"

The wounded constable rolled over and coughed. An ambulance could be heard in the distance.

"Sure and I'm—hurtin'— but I think—I'm okay."

"Did they say anything?"

"They warned me—ta leave off—stop with the investigation—a warnin'—next time—not so lucky—family and especially my *American* friends."

Hanford let out a long sigh of relief, though he still felt shaky. "Do we follow that threat?"

"For now—let things settle—a while."

"What do you mean? How do we do that?"

Paramedics arrived at the scene and pushed Hanford aside to check Collins and put him on a stretcher. As they took him to the ambulance, Hanford chased after them and yelled, "How do we do that? What should we do?"

Collins put a hand on one of the paramedics to stop.

"Go home—America—all three o' ya—act as if—done investigatin'—pursuin' justice—"

"You mean just stop everything?"

"Aye."

"We really need ta get him ta hospital," one of the paramedics said.

Hanford didn't pay any attention. "I'm afraid that's going to be a hard sell for Gareth and the others."

"It's life or death—IRA—not afraid ta send more—messages. Innocents always die."

Gareth and Ed rushed to the hospital as soon as they got Hanford's call.

"How is he?" Ed asked when they saw Bobby in the waiting room.

"They're still doing tests for internal bleeding."

"How you cuttin'?"

"I'm fine physically. But mentally and emotionally? Wow. A bit shook up!" Hanford showed them his hands, still trembling. "I'm so thankful they didn't kill Collins. I thought for sure this was it—for both of us."

The men sat down in uncomfortable waiting room chairs together. "Collins said we need to return to the US and stop investigating."

"What?" Gareth sat up straight.

"Why?" Ed asked, troubled.

"He's concerned that this was just the beginning of the IRA sending brutal messages to us and to the family. They want us to discontinue our search for justice."

"So, just like that we give up and go home?"

"Yes, Gareth, we do," Hanford said.

Gareth slumped back in the chair. Ed was quiet.

"Gareth," Hanford said, "you need to think of your wife and children right now. Your life has been threatened. They know we're here investigating, stirring things up and testifying. Haley would not want to find out that you were forewarned and that you ignored the warning. She'd be mad at that. But then, if something bad happened to you—she'd not come to your funeral."

Gareth hung his head. "You're right."

"I'm staying," Ed said.

"What? Over my dead body!" Hanford said. "Your folks would kill me if they knew I left you here under these conditions."

"I'm not leaving Maisie and Erin," Ed said. "They're in just as much danger, aren't they?"

"I don't know that. I just know that us Americans are in danger and putting others around us in danger too. If the three of us leave, the IRA will think we've given up on the pursuit of justice and leave things alone."

"I can't trust that, Bobby," Ed said. "I'm not leaving."

"Well, we'll see what Collins thinks, Ed."

The doctor came out and explained the test results. "Constable Collins has a robust constitution for his age and some extra fat around him that protected him from the blows. He'll be okay ta go home in a few days."

"Can we see him now?"

"A nurse will come and take ya ta his room."

When they entered the room, Collins was a sight to behold with bandages and stitches, bruised and swollen. His left eye could hardly open but he smiled when he saw the three men.

"Sure an' I've had a bit of a facelift," he joked.

"You're looking like you had a makeover, that's for sure," Gareth said and the others chuckled, albeit a bit sadly.

"Ya told the men what I said, did ya?" Collins said to Hanford.

"Yes. Gareth is going back with me, but Ed has yet to be convinced."

"Ed, lad, ya need ta go back with the others."

"I can't. I can't leave now."

"Don' ya see how that puts ya in danger as well as the others?"

"I'll steer clear of Belfast and the cities. I'll stay quiet in the cottage. I came here to help Maisie and now, well, I just can't leave her."

"Love. Sure and it makes us do foolish things," Collins said. "Well, I can't force any of ya ta go back, but there's my advice for ya."

When the men returned to the cottage Maisie was relieved at first to learn that Ed would stay there. She knew she loved him, although she didn't exactly tell him that yet. There was still a hesitancy to commit to another man and, right now, while she struggled emotionally over digging up her past, it wasn't the time to make that kind of decision. She hoped that, with him staying here, she'd be able to see more clearly. But later the following day, while Ed was outside playing with Erin, Gareth had a moment to take her aside, explain the situation more thoroughly, and ask that she persuade Ed to go back.

"It will be safer for all of us if he leaves, cousin. But he's being stubborn and doesn't want to abandon you and Erin."

"I want him ta stay here, Gareth. He's becomin' such a part of Erin and me."

"It's for his own safety, Gingerbap—and everyone else's. I'm trusting Collins on this one and Ed needs to trust him, too."

"I understand," Maisie said sadly. "I'll say what needs ta be said." Maisie watched Ed and Erin out the window as she thought through what she could say to make Ed go back to America. She knew what his arguments would be and she knew what it would take to make him return to his country.

After dinner that evening, when Erin was put to bed and Gareth was upstairs on the phone with Haley, giving her the happy news of his return, Ed and Maisie sat on the sofa in the sitting room staring at the fireplace.

Maisie turned and looked at Ed. "I need ta explain somethin' ta ya, Eddy." Ed took her hand in his.

"What is it?"

"I want ya ta go back to the US."

"No, you don't."

"That is what I wish, Eddy."

"What? Why? I want to stay here with you. You're still dealing with all these new feelings from digging up your past and life hasn't exactly settled down."

"It will be safer fer all of us and I'm better now. While I truly appreciate yer helpin' me through it all, I need time on me own ta get stronger—by meself, Eddy. Do ya see that? I can't be leanin' on ya me whole life fer strength. I have ta find it first, alone."

"I don't understand. Are you saying you don't want me around?"

Maisie drew in a breath. "Well, don' say it exactly like that, but fer the present, aye."

"Do you even love me, Maisie?"

"This has nothin' ta do with love."

"Sure it does. If you loved me you wouldn't want to get rid of me." Ed sat up.

"It's not that I want ta get rid of ya—"

"Then you're saying it because Gareth and Bobby told you to."

"Your life is in danger, Ed. I can't live with that. I can't keep ya here with me, knowin' I'm puttin' you in harm's way. I won't allow it."

"Then come back with me to America. You and Erin. Come with me, *marry me*."

Maisie sighed. This was going to be harder than she thought. He was persistent and she truly didn't want him to leave. And now, he even made an impulsive proposal of marriage. It was tempting. *But too soon.* "I can't make that decision right now. I need ta get me head tagether. I hope ya can understand that. An' maybe, in the future, we can be tagether and sort that part out. But fer now, I'm not in any condition ta make a commitment. And I don't think yer ready, either. We've both been cautious about our relationship. Let's not do anything impulsive now. I hope ya can understand that." Maisie drew in a long breath and spoke emphatically. "I need ya ta go back with Gareth and Uncle Bobby."

Ed stood. "I don't understand it, Maisie. I thought we had something here—I'm just so blown away by the way you're acting. I mean, I—we—finally let down the walls that our pasts had built and we were finding something special between us. But now, you're just putting the walls up again? Why?"

Maisie stood up and went to him. "I'm not puttin' a wall between us. It's not forever, Eddy."

"I don't know if I can believe that, Maisie."

She took a step back. "Are ya callin' me a liar then?"

"No. It's just that what you're saying all of a sudden isn't making any sense."

"That's offensive."

"I don't know what else to say to you."

"I'm feelin' the same."

Frustrated, Ed walked out the front door and started down the dark road. He'd never felt so stunned. He kicked the stones in his path. He was angry. How could he have fallen for a girl yet another time only to have been sent away? Three strikes and you're out, ole Eddy boy.

Maisie stood and watched him walk down the road. Was that the right thing to do? Should she go after him? No. But it made her feel sick. She knew he needed to go back to the US. She knew how these people in the paramilitary groups worked. They didn't pull punches. He was in danger here and she couldn't let anything happen to him. She couldn't handle the death of another man she loved.

Bobby was able to secure three plane tickets out of Dublin two days later. He and Gareth sat in the rental car waiting while Ed said his last goodbyes. Erin leaned against her ma as they stood by the edge of the road.

"So, this is goodbye, I guess," Ed said, watching, hoping for a fluctuation in Maisie's expression that would indicate a change of mind. But there was none.

"It's goodbye then, so it is." Maisie hoped Ed would finish saying his last farewells, get in the car, and go before she totally lost control of her emotions. Ed leaned in, kissed her on the forehead, and walked away.

Erin, looked at her ma, then at Ed, and then back to her ma. She hoped he wasn't really going to leave and that her ma would beg him to stay. But the reality of his leaving struck her and suddenly she burst out, "No, no, no!" as she rushed over to Ed and hugged him tightly. "Sure and ya cannot go and leave us again!" Tears flowed down her soft cheeks and she wept unabashedly. Ed tried hard not to shed tears, but this was the true test. His eyes watered and he tried to blink the tears away.

"Erin, agra, ya need ta let Eddy go," Maisie said, trying to keep control of her own emotions.

"Why? He *can't* go! You can't go, me dear Eddy." Erin turned to her ma. "I don't want him ta go. Why do ya, Ma? It's not right and ya know it!" Erin stamped her foot.

"Erin, I'm sorry, but I need to leave. I love you, little one. Don't you forget that." Ed gave her a big hug before turning away. "I pray we can see each other again," he added and looked at Maisie. What was her expression? He wasn't sure, but there wasn't the change of mind he'd hoped for. He went to the car and slipped into the front passenger seat, all the while hearing Erin's cries and protests in the background. Gareth reached up from the back and put his hand on Ed's shoulder. Ed motioned for Bobby to drive on. And he didn't look back.

***

Haley and the children were beyond excited that Gareth was returning to America and Gareth was thrilled to have such a reception. The children gathered around him and he marveled at how much each of them had grown in such a short time. They took turns giving them their homemade cards and then they all sat down together in their home for a family dinner. Ian and Phyllis said they'd see him in the morning, wanting to let his family have all the attention first. Haley basked in the sound of his voice at the table, laughing with the children and talking to each of them. When Gareth and she had put the children to bed they had their own special time alone. Haley was glad she had given Gareth her blessing on taking a trip back to his homeland. He seemed revived and very relieved to have done something for his family. They cuddled together on the couch.

"Do you feel like justice has been served?" Haley said as she nestled under Gareth's arm.

"Somewhat. But not all." Gareth pulled her in closer and rested his chin on her head. "There are still those out there who murdered Ma and shot Eoin and there are those who ordered it."

"Was it hard, then, to return home?"

"No. I missed all of you terribly. I'm so glad to be home." He kissed the top of her head. "And finding complete justice—finding all who made us suffer and seeing them all prosecuted—could take months, even years. And even then, it may never happen. I'm not going to wait over there while you grow older and my children grow up and leave home! This is where I belong,

Haley. This is my life now. I have to leave the past behind me or I'll miss the present."

Haley looked up at him. "I don't want to live in the present without you. It was hard to see the children do new things while you were gone. I wanted to save each cute thing so you could see it all, but obviously, I couldn't."

"Well, I'm here now."

"Thank God, you're home safe and sound." Haley turned her face toward Gareth's and felt his lips touch hers.

***

The MacCauleys in Northern Ireland needed to come together after such a tumultuous time with the court case and Collins' attack. They were feeling cooped up while heeding the warnings to lay low, so Tonya invited the family to come over for dinner.

Eoin got everyone's attention after the plates were filled with an American dinner of fried chicken, mashed potatoes, cornbread, and greenbeans. "I was talkin' ta Collins on the phone today."

"How's he doin'?" Callum asked and then took a large bite out of a chicken leg.

"He's recoverin' from his wounds nicely. He'll go back ta work in a week. He's not goin' ta continue investigatin' our case until he feels it's safe ta start up again."

"Waitin' fer the IRA ta back off, is he?" Callum said.

"Aye. And meanwhile, he's cautioned us ta watch fer unidentified packages that might come ta our doors. He also said ta watch fer parked cars that don't belong in our area," Eoin said.

"Are ya thinkin' the IRA would send a bomb in a package or a parked car near us?" Tommy asked, his eyes wide.

"Do ya think the children need ta hear all this?" Molly said, feeling uneasy when she saw Tommy's expression of excitement mixed with fear.

"Aye," Callum said. "There could be a bomb." He turned to his wife. "They all need ta know, lass. They might be the one ta go ta the door and see a package at the stoop."

Molly understood then. Shannon, Tommy, and even Erin acted grown up now during the conversation and nodded knowingly. They'd be careful. This was the world they'd grown up in and they understood it.

CHAPTER 30

Christmas of '97 came and went. The winter of '98 blew across the farmlands of Wisconsin with vehemence. Ed and Gareth stayed busy keeping the horses warm, fed, and exercised. By late winter everyone was ready for spring. One blustery, rainy night in early April, the MacCauley family sat beside a roaring fire in the fireplace at the big house. Haley and Phyllis conjured up a large pot of hot cocoa while Ian and Gareth helped the children roast marshmallows.

"Sure and it's supposed ta be warm here by April?" Ian sighed. He took marshmallows from Annie, nine, and Fiahd, seven, and put them on a long metal skewer with a wooden handle.

"Haven't you been listening to our vice president, Al Gore? Global warming!" Gareth smirked.

"I might be off me head, but it ain't warmin' up fast out there!" Ian said. "Politicians!"

"Speaking of politicians. Did you hear the latest back home? They're pushing harder for peace back in Northern Ireland," Gareth said as he took his skewer from the fire and let the boys eat the marshmallows.

"Daddy, Momma said we had to wait until we had our hot chocolate," Annie said in a big sisterly tone.

"Oh. Oops." Gareth laughed as he watched Bobby, five, and Liam, three, hurry to gulp the treats down. "I guess it's too late now!" Annie sighed at her father's mistake. He turned to Ian. "Sinn Fein was banned from the peace talks because of the recent bombings in February and President Clinton has sent an American statesman, George Mitchell, over to play a big part in forcing a decision."

"Somethin's happenin' over there," Ian said as he held his skewer over the fire.

"Okay, guys, this is a family night, remember?" Phyllis said as she and Haley carried out mugs of hot chocolate.

"Yes, ma'am." Ian winked at his wife and put two roasted marshmallows in Fiahd's mug.

"Did you invite Eddy and his folks to come over tonight?" Haley asked. "Fiahd, sit down with your mug, please, so you don't spill." Fiahd sat, but when she saw where Annie sat down, she stood up and walked in that direction.

"They seem so lost, just the three of them roaming around in that huge house," Phyllis said.

"And you can tell Eddy is heartbroken over the situation with Maisie," Haley said.

"I invited them," Gareth said. "They're coming over soon."

"Oh, good. Fiahd, I said to sit down with your mug, honey. I don't want you to spill it."

"I did, Momma, but I wanted to sit by Annie."

"Liam hasn't stopped wearing the cowboy hat you gave him at Christmas, Da."

"So," Ian said to his grandson, "ya like the hat, do ya?"

"Yeah." Liam's chubby face lit up. "An-an-an if I get oldah—if I get oldah—I will tuhn into a cowboy."

"Aye." Ian chuckled. "That ya will, me lad."

"I like mine, too, Granddad," Bobby piped up, "but Mr. Bear wanted to wear it today so I left it hanging on his ears."

When Fiahd sat down beside her sister, Annie stood up and moved across the room. Fiahd stood again.

"Fiahd, what did your momma say?" Gareth scolded. Tears started down Fiahd's cheeks and her lips went into a pout.

"I just wanted to sit by Annie but—but she moved!" she sobbed.

"I didn't want her to sit by me because she always spills things," Annie whined. Gareth and Haley looked at each other in dismay. Ian and Phyllis tried not to chuckle in front of the children.

"Your Great-Grandpa Beckett used to sing old cowboy songs when he was outside working on the farm," Phyllis said to Bobby and Liam. "I think his favorite one was 'Home on the Range.'"

"I know that one!" Bobby said.

"Do you?" Phyllis was surprised and pleased her young grandson knew an old, traditional song.

"Yes, I learned it in my childhood," he said, very grown-up.

"You did? Why, that's wonderful!" Phyllis and the others smiled.

There was a knock at the door and then the Wagners let themselves in. Phyllis took their coats while Haley poured more mugs of hot chocolate. The women congregated in the kitchen, the men sat in the living room, and the three younger children went off to play while Annie took it upon herself to clean up the messes the other kids had made in the living room.

"I heard that Mitchell set a deadline to make a decision in Northern Ireland. He said it's time to stop talking about peace and come to an agreement," Ed said as he put the warm cup of chocolate to his lips.

"Shhh, talk quietly," Ian said, mischievously. "Don't let the women know we're talkin' politics."

Gareth laughed.

"I believe it will transpire soon at Stormont," Fred added.

"The ninth," Gareth said.

"Do ya think it can happen?" Ian asked.

"Ian Paisley is skeptical about it all," Ed said.

"Of course he is!" Gareth said.

"He thinks that no matter what happens with all the peace talks, there's going to be war," Ed added. "Tony Blair, however, is more hopeful."

"Momma said you shouldn't talk polly-ticks," Annie said before she took the trash into the kitchen.

"Oh, you're exactly right, Annie." Gareth smiled at the other men. "My eldest child has taken on the role of looking out for everyone else." The men chuckled. "She has everyone's concerns before her."

"She takes after her momma." Ed smiled.

"She's so worried about Maisie and Erin and makes sure we pray for them every night. I think she's heard too much."

"She has every reason ta be concerned, bless the lass. Ya should go get yer girls, Ed," Ian said.

"It's not mine to decide, Mr. Mac," Ed said. "Maisie and I are taking a break while she sorts things out."

"What is there ta decide? Ya love her, don' ya?"

"*Da*." Gareth looked at Ed apologetically.

"Yes," Ed answered and grinned at Gareth.

"An' she loves ya?"

"*Da*, ya have a right brass neck!"

"I'm not completely sure," Ed said. "The words haven't exactly been spoken, Mr. Mac."

"Well make sure and then go get me niece and her wee bairn outta that war zone!"

"Da, be careful." Gareth looked to see if Annie, who had returned with a rag, was listening. Fortunately, she was busy wiping up a mess Liam had made on the end table. Gareth turned to the Wagners. "I apologize for my da. He has a heart o' corn and has gotten so worried about everyone over there."

"It's okay, Gareth. I understand your father's concern. I'd like to get them out of there, too," Ed said.

"I have every right ta be worrisome, lad," Ian said to his son.

"It's getting better over there," Gareth explained. "Most of the violence is in and around Belfast or London. Eoin and Maisie's families are out in the beautiful countryside where it's just regular everyday stuff happening. You should know that, you lived there."

"No need to apologize for your father, Gareth," Fred said as he put a hand on Ian's shoulder. "We understand. Alma and I feel the same way about your niece. Why, we thought for certain Ed would be bringing Maisie and that precious little one of hers back to us."

"I'm sorry to disappoint so many of you," Ed said. "Anyone who knows Maisie knows I couldn't push her to make an important decision in such a short time."

Gareth laughed. "Oh, don't I know it!"

"You're respecting her in that way, Edward," Fred said. "Being the gentleman."

"My apologies, Ed," Ian said. "Love, marriage, and all shouldn't be rushed."

If love and marriage were actually an option, Ed thought. He was beginning to wonder. Had he let himself fall for another girl again? A girl whose heart wasn't available?

***

The entire first week of April, 1998, people were talking everywhere in Northern Ireland—at work, at school, at the stores, in the parks—about important men meeting for peace talks in Stormont, the Parliament building in Belfast. Would something really get settled? There was a lot of doubt.

The politicians hoped for an agreement by April ninth, Holy Thursday, but the talks seemed to be failing. That day, the officials could hear a crowd of schoolchildren, from both Catholic and Protestant, gathered outside the gates of Stormont singing a song written by Tommy Sands called, "Carry On." It was an encouraging moment for all the men who were part of this mind-boggling and taxing time to make such an important decision.

Friday, the MacCauley clan met at Ian's cottage. Tonya made a large pan of cottage pie and Scottish shortbread. Brodie had safely taken up residence there with Maisie and now all of the family could meet together and talk. After eating, Callum turned on the telly to watch the news. Even though American statesman George Mitchell had set the deadline at Stormont for the ninth, no agreement was made until the tenth, Good Friday. As the children fell asleep and were put to bed, the adults stayed up and watched the news reports together. They watched a snippet of loyalist politician Ian Paisley, as he gave a stormy press conference but was heckled by the Progressive Unionist Party and the Ulster Democratic Party. One of the politicians yelled out, "Your days are over, dinosaur!"

Brodie guffawed.

"Brodie, keep it down," Callum said. "Ye'll be the one calmin' down the wee'uns and missin' the news if ya wake 'em up!"

"This is goin' ta take forever." Maisie sighed.

"Let's go make some tea," Molly suggested and the two women rose up quickly, glad for something to do besides watching the telly.

"How about somethin' ta eat?" Eoin said.

"There's some shortbread leftover," Tonya offered as she got up to follow the other women into the kitchen. "And we can reheat the cottage pie."

"I have a bag of crisps in the cupboard and some biscuits," Maisie said.

"Ya still gettin' letters from Eddy in the post?" Molly asked as she heated up the tea kettle.

"Some."

"How's he cuttin' over there?"

"Fine."

"Do you miss him?" Tonya asked as she put the pan with cottage pie back in the oven to reheat.

"I do. A lot. So does wee Erin. She cries at night sometimes. An' I want ta cry with her."

"Och, ya shoulda gone back with 'em, Maisie."

"I couldn't. It all happened too fast, him leavin', so it did. An' now, I think I've hurt him."

Tonya remained quiet, but she couldn't help wondering how Ed was doing. Was he taking this rejection from Maisie as a third strike on his dating life? Would he even consider trying to woo Maisie back? She hoped so. She couldn't fault Maisie for it, however. Everything happened for them all in a state of hurried panic after Collins was beaten up. Ed needed to return to the US. Maisie was only pushing him away because she cared about him. Molly's voice broke through her thoughts.

"Maisie, how are you and Brodie gettin' along here in the same house? I don't know if I could live with me broder!"

"As long as he takes care of his own dishes and keeps the place tidy, I won't scream at him." The girls laughed. "Brodie can act the maggot and give the impression he's a stook, but deep down, he's very lovin' and carin'. I know both of me broders love me in their different ways. I'm glad ta have one of them around and I feel safer with a man in the house—as long as Brodie cleans up after hisself!" They laughed again.

As the news continued on, the family kept glued to the telly.

The Loyalists, the Democrats, Sinn Fein, the Republic of Ireland, the British, and the US were all involved in making the proposals and a final decision.

"The Good Friday Agreement?" Tonya said. "But what does it settle? I don't understand what's going on."

"The agreement is acknowledgin' the fact that many people of Northern Ireland wish ta remain a part of the United Kingdom," Callum explained, "and that a good majority wants ta bring about a united Ireland."

"Where are you all at with this?" Tonya asked.

"Well, we've seen where the British have helped our country, but also where they've hurt us. We feel secure in their politics and it's a bit frightenin' ta let that go," Callum continued. "We've been loyal ta the queen. Do we want ta let that go? Not necessarily. Yet, the British have never been kind ta the Catholics and it's been a big part of ignitin' the Troubles."

"The agreement allows fer dual citizenship," Eoin said. "I like that. And, if Northern Ireland wishes ta join the Republic of Ireland, Britain would allow it."

"Do ya think that will happen?" Brodie asked.

"Who knows," Eoin said.

"Do ya think Tony Blair was right when he said he hopes that the burden of history can finally be lifted from our shoulders? Do ya think this will really end the Troubles and the conflict in general?" Molly asked.

"Sure and it's hard ta feel hopeful," Callum said.

"What else do we have but this small ray of hope?" Eoin shrugged.

"Well, we'll see. They said it won't be in effect until the second of December, 1999. But that's a long time yet ta waitin', so it is," Callum added. "They said that political prisoners would be released as part of the agreement. Does that worry ya, Brodie, about Joe possibly gettin' out?"

"Sure an' it does. It ain't right. He murdered innocents."

"Nay, it's not." Eoin shook his head.

"Still and all, there's progress bein' made," Callum said, and the rest agreed.

"But there'll be people who won't be happy at all with the agreement," Brodie said. "There are people—a lot involved with the IRA and the paras—who've listened ta Gerry Adams and Sinn Fein these past thirty years, hopin' fer an independent country. These people murdered and destroyed homes in the name of war and fer the sake of the fight against the British and the Protestants."

"And what about the people who 'disappeared' others—kidnapped, murdered, and buried touts in undisclosed places around the country?" Eoin added. "That's been a brutal, heartless part of the war, not just punishin' the accused, but leavin' innocent families—like ours—in a place of desperation, false hopes, and despair. And now, fer what have they committed these crimes?"

"It makes one wonder if they'll feel that their heinous acts performed fer 'the cause' were all fer naught and now they have ta live with their sins," Callum said. "It wouldn't surprise me if some turn their backs on the IRA and Gerry Adams."

"And what about us? What about all of us who've suffered through it, seen family members and friends murdered? Wondered about missin' loved ones? Watched our homes burnt ta the ground? What do we do?" Brodie said.

"We have ta leave our past behind and go on with our lives."

"How can ya just do that, Eoin?"

"What choice do we have, Brodie?"

"What about seein' all who hurt us pay fer their crimes?" Maisie asked.

"I know there are more out there who should be payin' fer the crimes, Maisie, but what do we do? Sit here and put our lives on hold while we wait? I have two little boys who I want ta give a good, happy life. How can I do that if I'm holdin' a grudge against all these people who hurt me and me family? What I see in the Scriptures tells me that that isn't what God wants me ta do. And I have ta trust God ta take care of these people." Eoin felt Tonya slide her hand into his and give it a squeeze. "These people have already created havoc and disturbed our lives. They can't hurt us anymore. I can't force ya ta feel a certain way about it all, but, look, ya have two children, Callum, ta focus on. And Brodie, ya ought ta find a girl and start a family instead of seekin' vengeance on these criminals!"

Everyone looked at Brodie. For once he was somber, shaking his head. "Ta be sure, ta be sure."

It was June. Tonya was in the mood to do some spring cleaning. There were still boxes that hadn't been sorted through and were piled into a closet that she needed to store everyday things. She pulled them out as the boys toddled around the house giggling, chasing, and playing with each other. As she went through them she pulled out a rusty old metal box and recalled when young Emmet McGilroy found it buried under the floor here. She remembered how excited he was, thinking it was buried treasure, and then how his countenance fell when his dad made him give it up to Eoin.

"Eoin, remember this?" Tonya said when Eoin returned from work at the stables. "Can you get this open?"

"Ach! I fergot all about that!"

"I did too. It got packed away in the closet in a box. I wonder what's in it. I've been shaking it and it sounds like a book clunking around in there."

Eoin got out his tools and worked at the lock until he could pry it open. Eoin carefully took out an old brown leather journal. Tonya sat down beside him. He opened up the cover.

"What is it?" Tonya asked.

"This is me ma's writin'. I think I remember seein' her with it long ago."

"Why would she lock it up and bury it under the floor?"

"I don't know." Eoin opened the worn cover and read the first page. "'The secrets and names behind the civil unrest in Northern Ireland, by Anna Hanford MacCauley, 1966.'" Eoin looked up at Tonya, wide-eyed.

Tonya sat up straight. "Keep reading!"

Eoin turned the page and Tonya looked over his shoulder. "Ma started documentin' the riots and the protests early on. I didn't realize that Ian Paisley was involved in so much at the beginnin'."

"Your ma was writing names and details about so many people!"

Eoin continued to read. "Wait, this name is familiar." He pointed. "I think we used ta talk ta them at the Divis Flats. And this person," Eoin said. "She was writin' down names of people we talked ta there. But why?" Eoin turned the page. "This page is about the O'Connely family."

"When she says 'we went to visit the family,' is she talking about you or your Auntie Erin that went to visit the O'Connelys?"

"Coulda been either of us. But she's bein' careful not ta mention our names."

"Eoin, she was documenting everything she saw and heard going on over there at Divis Flats."

"I'm sure of it. She was suspectin' things, but she never told me. All I knew is that we were visitin' a poor family who lost their ma. She took me along ta help them warm up ta her. Here's a name I heard of and thought it strange—Bodach. It means bogeyman."

Tonya shivered. "That gives me the creeps. And look how she marks certain names—like they were more important for some reason. Do you think the IRA grew suspicious?"

"Maybe so. I want ta show this ta Collins."

"Is he ready to get back to work?"

"I'm sure he's chompin' at the bit!"

"This is so exciting! Let's read some more!"

Seamus came up to Tonya with Sammy at his heels. "Ma, I hungy."

"I hungy too," Sammy said.

"I could ate the twelve apostles, Ma." Eoin winked.

"I ate t'elve possels, Ma," Seamus said.

"I too, I too t'elve possels," Sammy copied his brother, who copied his da. Eoin guffawed and the boys laughed with him.

"Seriously, Eoin. That's a bit macabre, don't you think, honey? Should our children be hearing that?"

"What a craic ye are, Tonnie! They're Irish laddies. Leave 'em be, me bonny wife." Eoin kissed Tonya's cheek and grabbed up his boys around their waists and ran around the room with them, giggling, their feet kicking behind them. "An' what will we have fer a treat tonight, me fine lads, ta celebrate this discovery? Apple crumble or a chocolate Bundt cake?"

"Chocate cate!" the boys yelled, excitedly.

Tonya laughed. "My three lads, all alike and thinking of food. Well, so much for the exciting stuff for now!" She stood up. "Ma will make dinner and a chocolate Bundt cake." She smiled at the innocent faces of her children and the adoring face of her husband looking up at her. "As long as your da keeps reading to me from this special book while I work."

As Eoin read on through Anna's journal, Tonya pulled out the ingredients for the cake. She thought of Anna and pictured her living here with her two young boys, taking care of them and making dinner for the family. She thought of Anna sitting in a corner in the evenings, away from the family, secretly writing in this journal. Anna was so desperate to help others, but she knew it was dangerous. By the looks of this journal and how she hid it, she was trying hard to keep her family safe. If she knew what came of it all she'd be horrified! Tonya felt sorry for her.

Tonya was glad to be in this same place, and hoped that she and Eoin could somehow continue to help the poor people who suffered here during the Troubles. *But*, she prayed, *God protect us and please keep our family together!*

Eoin contacted Collins and invited him to come down to their place the following evening.

"How are ya doin' since the attack on ye?"

"Sure an' I'm a lucky one, I am. No organs were injured, no broken bones—just a lot of bruisin'."

Tonya placed a cup of tea in front of him. He took a sip as he examined Anna's journal.

"This is fantastic, so it is. Sure and this will connect a lot of dots fer us at the constabulary. May I take it with me?"

Eoin looked at Tonya and she nodded. "Ma would want ya ta have it, Collins. As much as it's a piece of me ma, it's a piece I don' want floating around in me own home—fer the safety of me own family. She locked it up and buried it fer a reason."

"I agree wholeheartedly," Tonya said as she held out a small plate. "Cake?"

Collins' eyes grew large as he took in a whiff of the chocolate Bundt cake. "Aye! That would be fantastic!"

"You men get as excited over food as you do a discovery like this journal!" Tonya laughed.

"I haven' had a bit o' homecooked dessert in donkey's years. Thank ya!" Collins licked his lips and took a huge bite. "Yer ma was somethin' else, Eoin," he mumbled as he swallowed the delicious cake. "She sacrificed her life fer her deeds and I hope ta give her some redemption by usin' this book ta bring in some murderers and kidnappers."

"Do ya think ya can still find these people?"

"I do. Ya don' even know how many of them are still walkin' the streets of Belfast and other cities around us—as if they never did a blessed thing wrong in their lives! The children of the O'Connely family have seen 'em around. It's an awful thing ta see a person who had somethin' ta do with yer loved one's murder, livin' their life like a regular citizen in the shops and pubs."

With the testimony of O'Malley and now Anna MacCauley's journal, Collins went with his men and stormed the Divis tower where the man called "Bodach" was hiding out. There was hardly a soldier to be found as they climbed to the top. When they found him, his figure was hunched over, emaciated, and his demeanor forlorn. He was sitting in an old stuffed chair, looking out over the city of Belfast, a cigarette in one hand and a beer in the other. He had an unkempt beard and, wore an old jumper and sweatpants that hadn't been washed in days—maybe even weeks. The room reeked of filth and stale smoke. He didn't flinch when they came in, but sneeered, "Ach, youse finally ha' come fer me," and his shoulders shook as if he were laughing, but no sound came out. "All fer nutin'," he wheezed. "It were all fer nutin'."

When Collins sat with him in a prison cell days later, he confessed to so many murders and named so many names that Collins had to hire a secretary to come in and help record it all. The names in Anna's journal matched many of the suspects. Bodach obviously didn't care anymore whom he implicated and felt no threat on his life since his bodily functions were about to expire from all the heavy drink and nicotine he consumed. Collins asked him about Anna MacCauley and the family. He looked away.

"Me people was just supposed ta threaten—ta give her a scare." He took in a raspy breath. "Ta get the very book ya have now. But it all went awry, so it did."

"Did ya have a hand in her abduction?" Collins asked.

"I ordered it—it came dayn ta me from t'e higher powers of t'e IRA, but uders did t'e crime."

"Because of the book?"

"Sure and she was writin' abayt t'e O'Connely woman—" another long, raspy inhale— "and how it were a mistake, too. She knew names dere. She was gettin' ready ta send it ta some American newspaper."

"How did ya know that?"

"Some neighbors of t'e O'Connelys got wind o' it. Ms. MacCauley was pretty incensed abayt how it all came dayn for dat family and was ventin'." Bodach lit up another cigarette and took a long pull. "She was suspected of bringin' a transmitter ta t'e apartment. She had ta be stopped."

"Who carried out the kidnappin'? Who shot Eoin and killed Anna?"

"T'e Unknowns."

"Who are they?"

"T'e woman in charge—she were a tough one. Her name was Brigid Sullivan. She came from a long line o' tough women." He went into a coughing fit. Collins waited patiently. "Dey told me she was gettin' ayt o' control. It were her dat shot Anna."

"Do ya know where I can find her?"

"It ain't worth yer time no more."

"Why is that?"

"She overdosed—died—t'ree years ago. She divorced her husband, left her kids, couldn' handle the guilt o' all she done."

"What about the others involved in Anna's death? And the neighbors at the Divis Flats?"

"I can give ya names, but most are eeder dead or in prison by now and if they ain't, dey're livin' with t'e same guilt—" More coughing. "T'e same guilt as the rest o' us."

Collins sat with Eoin at a pub and filled him in on the recent arrest of Bodach and the remaining people who had a part in the abduction.

"Does it help, Eoin?" Collins lifted his coffee to his lips, watching Eoin's reaction to all that he'd just revealed to him. He could see that the young man was processing everything.

Eoin nodded and took a sip of his own coffee. "Aye, Collins, thanks."

"But does it truly help ya? An' will it help yer family ta know this?"

"It helps ta know the woman who shot Ma suffered fer her sins and is dead and gone and can' hurt no one else. An' I would rather be on this side of the tragedy than Bodach, or Brigid Sullivan, or any of the others. I cannae imagine livin' with that guilt. I'll tell the rest of the family about it. I already told them about Ma's journal but I'll let 'em know how accurate she was and that that's what they were after. I will leave them all ta digest it each in their own way, ya know?"

"Sure an' those are wise words."

"Workin' with families of the Disappeared has helped me understand and see the many different reactions of family and how ya cannae force anyone in the family ta feel any certain way. We all have ta live with what happened and move on from there." Eoin took another sip of his coffee. "What about ye? Ya see all this mess o' trouble all the time. How do ya stay sane?"

"Ach, I'm doin' fine, though I'm always lookin' o'er me shoulder. Other RUCs haven' been so lucky."

"So I've heard. Have things calmed down at all since the agreement?"

Collins pursed his lips and shook his head sadly. "Not so much."

"What now?"

"Did ya hear about the Orange Order and their parades?"

"Some of it."

"They weren't allowed ta march along Garvaghy Road in Portadown."

"The McGilroys were privy ta that one, bein' it's their town."

"The Catholics don't care fer—well, hate is a better word, so it is—they detest Protestants marchin' through their towns struttin' their stuff, beatin' their drums, playin' their bagpipes, and celebratin' William of Orange's victory over the Catholics once again. We've tried ta ban their marches through hostile areas but they continue ta march. There's been riotin' and Catholic churches have been attacked after we banned the march at Drumcree."

"Why can't all of the fightin' stop, Collins? When will it end?"

"Maybe when yer generation teaches the next generation ta love their neighbor no matter their race, religion, or political preference. And maybe when the past is left in the past. Irish have too good of a memory. It's time ta ferget and move on."

"So it is, Collins."

CHAPTER 31

Ed sat with his folks on the old white wicker furniture on their large wraparound porch. As a child he used to sprawl out on the love seat with the comfy blue-striped cushions and fall asleep to the sound of the trees swishing and the blue jays squawking. It was one of his favorite places growing up. Fall was just around the corner and now September teased off and on with warm, sunny days and then rainy, windy ones. It was raining now, but the roof overhang protected them from getting wet.

"Have you thought about what we've offered you, Ed?" Fred asked.

"I have." Ed nodded. "Did you talk to the others?"

"Yes. Your siblings are more than happy to let you take over the dairy farm here. Carrie and Keith are content with living in town near the church and Peggy is permanently moving to Africa to minister and use her nursing degree there. None of them want it."

"I'll send them their inheritance money from it, for sure."

"They know that and they trust you to follow through," Fred said.

"Will Gareth be able to get help with the boarding business?" Alma asked.

"Yes," Ed said. "Some of the men we hired when we were in Northern Ireland proved to be good workers and he's going to hire them on full time when I leave."

"Have you thought about wheh you'll live? You know you're welcome to live heh in this big house with us."

"I know, Momma, and I appreciate that, but I really long to have a home of my own and maybe start a family someday."

"Are Maisie and Erin in those plans?"

"I don't know. We're not communicating as much as we used to. It's tough being from two different countries so far away from each other. I told her I was going to take over the business here during our last phone call and it grew quiet on the other end. I wasn't sure what to make of her silence. Meanwhile, I've been looking for a place close by so that I can run this business adequately."

"What will you do if Maisie doesn't evah want to come over heh to be with you, Ed?" Alma looked troubled.

"I don't know, Momma. Maybe it just wasn't meant to be. Meanwhile, I need to find a place of my own, earn a living, and be the rich uncle to Benny and my friends' kids."

***

Callum came to see Brodie at the cottage. They sat down at the kitchen table and Brodie put the tea on.

"So, what's up, broder? What brings ya here today?"

"Is Maisie around?"

"She and Erin took a taxi and went shoppin'."

"Good. Because I came ta tell ya that Paul was dragged out of his house last night and beaten up pretty bad. Sure and Joe and a few of his old paras did it. I didn't want Maisie ta hear it."

Brodie let the filled teapot clink down heavily on the stovetop. "So, Joe is out?"

"Aye."

Brodie looked down. "This isn't good. Is Paul okay?"

"I don't know."

"I need ta go see him."

"Don't. Ya shouldn't show yer face around there."

"What is goin' on? Why'd they beat up Paul?"

"The paramilitaries are calling it 'punishin's.'"

"What's that?" Brodie poured hot water into a china teapot and let it steep.

"After the Good Friday Agreement, paras on both sides are suddenly findin' there is nothin' much ta do. No fights ta fight. This is all they've been doin' fer so many years, they don't know what else ta do and they want ta keep on fightin'. So now, many have been seekin' vengeance on past wrongs within their own groups."

"Ya mean the Provos are attackin' their own people, too?"

"So they are. And I'm concerned about ya, broder, now that Joe is out. He'll certainly be seekin' vengeance on ya fer puttin' him away. In fact, I shouldn't have even come out here. Anymore, I'm so suspicious of anyone followin' me."

"I'll be fine out here. I'm too far removed from anythin' out here."

"Don't tell Maisie. Youse'll just worry her."

"No worries. I won't."

"I wish she and Erin would've gone with Ed ta America, then I wouldn't have ta worry about them so much."

"Ya just worry yerself about Molly and yer kin. In fact, ya ought ta move out here and get yer family away from the city. I'll take care o' Maisie and Erin."

"Ya know I can't do that. We're settled where we are. And I'm countin' on ya keepin' our sister and her baby safe."

Maisie and Erin came in the door with arms full of groceries. The brothers got up from the kitchen table and helped her haul them in and put food away.

"So, what brings ya here ta us taday, broder?" Maisie asked.

"Just comin' by ta see how ya were doin'."

"We're grand. How are Molly and the kids?"

"Grand, so they are."

"So, ya coulda just called ta find that out, broder. Why are ya really here?"

Callum looked at Brodie. "Um, just had some bad news ta give Brodie about a friend of his in hospital. That's all. Is there anythin' else out in the car ya want me ta bring in? And then I best be gettin' back ta the family."

"I'm good—"

"Goodbye, then," Callum said and scooted out the door as quickly as he could. Brodie tried to disappear quickly up the stairs but Maisie stopped him.

"I'm not an eejit, Brodie. What's goin' on?"

"It's Paul who's in hospital, Maisie."

"Paul? Is he goin' ta be okay?"

"I don't know."

"What happened?"

"He got beaten up."

"Who did it?"

There was no getting around it. Maisie could sniff out deceit and lies like no one. Especially with her brothers. Brodie gave up trying to hide anything.

"By Joe and his close associates."

"Joseph Campbell? He's out? He's comin' after paras?"

Brodie nodded. And then he waited for her to put it all together.

"Callum was comin' here ta warn ya, so he was!"

"He was."

"Yer the one who put him away."

"I am that."

Maisie sat down. "Do ya think he'll find ya here?"

"Nay."

"How can ya be sure?"

"Maisie, there's no way he could find me here," Brodie said.

But deep down, he feared there might be a way. So, after Maisie and Erin were in bed, Brodie left the cottage. He placed a note on the kitchen table saying not to ask where he was, that he was in a safe place and that she was better off not knowing where until things quieted down. And then he instructed her to burn his note.

Brodie was right. Joe did learn where he was living. The only reason Paul wasn't killed the night before was because Joe finally got Paul to tell him.

Two nights later, Maisie was washing the dinner dishes and Erin was playing with her dolls in the sitting room. Erin heard the noise of an engine outside so she got up and moved the curtain to see who it was.

"Ma, there are some men getting out of a car. Sure and I don't know who they are," Erin said.

"Get away from the window, agra!" Maisie ran from the kitchen, turned out the lights, and peered carefully out the window. She recognized Joe Campbell right away. The men carried bats, iron bars, and broken boards toward the front door. Her stomach turned. *God help us!*

"Erin, go upstairs and lock yerself in the bedroom!"

"Why? Can I take my—"

"Only what ya can carry in two hands!"

"Aye, Ma!" Erin grabbed what she could and ran up the stairs.

Maisie ran to the kitchen and called the police, but she was so far out in the country she didn't think there was any chance they'd make it in time to rescue her and Erin.

"Brodie!" Joe yelled just outside the front door. "We know yer in dere! Come out and we won't do yer sister no harm!"

"He's not here!" Maisie yelled back on the other side of the door and grabbed the steel poker from the fireplace.

"An' I'm supposed ta believe ya, lass? If yer lyin' ta me ya've got anoder thin' comin'."

"Ya have no choice but ta believe me, do ya now," Maisie spat back. She hated this man who killed her Michael and now tried to bully her about her broder.

"Let me in an' I'll do ya no harm. Just let me see fer myself dat yer broder isn't here."

"I'm no eejit. One woman against five men. What do ya take me fer?"

Joe started to pound hard on the door. Minutes later the glass from a window crashed onto the carpet of the sitting room. Another glass pane crashed in the kitchen. Maisie ran upstairs with the poker in hand and got Erin to open the bedroom door for her. Then she locked herself back inside with her daughter. They curled up in a closet and waited. Erin shook and whimpered in Maisie's arms and Maisie tried to quiet her.

"Ma, sure an'—fear is on me. Are we goin' ta die?" Seeing her daughter so frightened, Maisie's memory stirred to those minutes when she hid, shut up in the wooden chest in the old barn of her home, afraid and wondering who those men were who talked so harshly in the barn. Then she thought of how Michael died at the hand of this man, Joseph Campbell, leaving her a widow and her daughter without a father. Suddenly, anger swelled up in her bosom and the urge to fight flowed through her with a different kind of adrenaline she'd not felt before. She was tired of these people scaring her, scaring her daughter, making Ed leave her and ruining their lives!

She got up and told Erin to stay in the closet and to not come out until she came to get her. She left the bedroom wielding the poker and started yelling at the top of her lungs. "Ye better get yerselves out o' me house before I kill ya all, ya dirty hallions!" Her stare was as icy as the wind that swept the North Channel and the veins in her neck pulsated.

"What do we have here? A crazy banshee?!" Joe laughed at the foot of the stairs.

"Get ye out of me house, Joseph Campbell! Ye killed me husband and I'll not hesitate ta run this through ya!" Maisie shouted.

"What are ya, daft, lass? Yer outnumbered." The men gathered behind Joe, humored by the scene at the top of the stairs.

"It's Brodie's feisty little sister!" one said and the others laughed.

"Michael's wife!"

"She's a grand woman now," Joe said. "Just put dat down now, we'll not hurt ya."

"I'd trust a pig before I'd trust any o' ya," Maisie said.

Suddenly, there was the sound of feet trampling through the back door. Maisie's heart pounded at the idea of more paras ganging up on her. Surely her life and Erin's was over. That is, until she saw Paul's brother, William, amongst the newcomers. He gave her a nod as his men started fighting Joe's men.

"What are ya doin'? We're on the same team!" Joe's voice was heard amongst the clamor.

"Not anymore," William said. "Not when ya started killin' innocents, Joe, beatin' up me broder and now threatenin' Brodie's sister and her child!"

When Maisie understood that William's group had come to defend her home, she backed up and disappeared into the bedroom to be with Erin. As she cuddled with her daughter, they listened to the threats made, the cries of pain, cracking of furniture breaking, weapons clashing together. She heard someone yell, "It's t'e peelers! Away with ya!" And then it grew eerily quiet as sirens were heard in the distance. Maisie and Erin stayed huddled in the closet. Erin was so quiet that Maisie feared she was in shock.

"Laurelvale police!" a strong voice echoed through the house. "Hello? Ma'am? Anyone here?" the same voice called out politely. "Laurelvale police, ma'am."

Mother and child exited the closet. Maisie unlocked the bedroom door and yelled, "We're up here." She and Erin came down the steps cautiously. There were men in uniform looking around at the destruction in the house. Furniture was tipped over, shattered glass was everywhere, and Maisie instantly picked Erin up to protect her from cutting her bare feet. One policeman pulled a man out of the kitchen who was just reviving from a blow he'd suffered. The police put him in cuffs and took him outside. There was another man lying outside.

"Do ya know who these men are?" the officer asked her.

"Aye. These two were with Joe Campbell. They're from the UVF. Five of them came ta my door tonight and tried ta break in."

"We've dealt with these lads before. What were they doin' here?"

"Well, ta be honest, officer, they were lookin' fer me broder, because he quit the group years ago when he put Joe Campbell away. The Good Friday Agreement freed Joe again."

"It's a frustratin' business, it is. Where is yer broder now?"

"I honestly don' know, sir. When he heard Joe Campbell might be comin' after him he left without tellin' me a thing, ta protect me—hopin' ta keep me safe."

"Sure and that didn't work, now did it?"

"No, sir."

"But who beat these men up?"

"Some heroic men," she said, unwilling to give out William's name. "I was upstairs when the others came so I hid with me daughter, sir."

"Is there anywhere safe ya can go fer the rest of the night?"

"Me cousin and his wife are just north o' here."

"Do ya need an escort?"

"That would be grand."

Maisie and Erin packed up a few things quickly and left for Eoin and Tonya's place. They didn't have time to call, but fortunately, when they pulled up with a policeman behind them, a light was on downstairs. Seamus was having trouble sleeping so Tonya had brought him down to cuddle for a while. She had just put him back in his crib upstairs when she saw the car lights shining from the road. She woke up Eoin and told him that Maisie's car and a police car had just pulled up. He went downstairs immediately and let them in. Erin went into Eoin's arms and Maisie went into Tonya's while the officer explained what happened. After he left, Tonya put on the kettle and gave Maisie and Erin tea and biscuits. While they ate she fixed up a place for them to sleep on the sofa. Eoin and Tonya walked up to their bedroom to go back to bed, listening to Maisie sing Erin to sleep. It sounded like a song they'd heard Ed sing before.

CHAPTER 32

Eoin and Tonya sat up in bed, discussing the events of the night.

"Now that Brodie has put Maisie in harm's way, will she feel safe anywhere here?" Tonya asked as she curled up against Eoin.

"I doubt it," Eoin answered as he drew his arm around her shoulders. "I'm not feelin' a bit happy about Brodie right now."

"Me either. And I want to send Maisie to Wisconsin to be with your father and Ed."

"Is that right?" Eoin smiled at his wife's motherly tone. "It's not that easy, Tonnie. So many people here have ta just live with this kind of thing." He took her hand and played with her fingers.

"But do they?"

"Ya hear the people talk that we visit with, ya know? They're still waitin' on gettin' news about their loved ones—especially now that some of the political prisoners will be given the freedom ta reveal the locations of the Disappeared without trial. There are still dangers out there, but those people stay and wait fer answers. So many people here are hopin' for a better Norn Iron."

"I just wish Maisie could have a happier life—"

"Yer wishin' fer an American story, lass. Hers is an Irish story."

"I know. But still—"

"Yer not goin' ta give up on this one, are ya?"

"I don't think I need to, Eoin. I think Maisie would be happier away from here. And I think she belongs with Eddy. I don't get why they're still apart. Haley feels the same way as me."

"Ya lassies have it all figured out, don' ya?" Eoin chuckled. "This whole group of friends of yers—ya won't rest until everyone is happily matched up with someone."

"It's true." Tonya smiled. "We won't."

"Yer all one big family and I love it."

"By the way, I meant to ask you, do you know where Brodie is?"

"Aye. He's with George McGilroy's son and his wife."

"That's amazing how God used other paras to show up at the cottage and fight Joe's men."

"I'd heard that there were some paras who left the group when Joe was in prison. They were angry at Joe fer killin' that Catholic girl and so they took Brodie's side in the matter. Brodie was the only man who had the guts ta testify, and I think the rest of them respected him fer it. And after Joe beat up Paul, sure and his broder, William, suspected there would be an attack and showed up ta defend Brodie."

"Ah. That sounds like the most feasible explanation."

"I'll ask Callum tomorrow and I'll get him ta come down and help me repair the cottage. I'm not lookin' forward ta seein' what got destroyed."

"Do you think Maisie will go back there to stay?"

"I don't know. Even if she got the courage ta go back—would she make Erin return? Poor wee'un, she looked as if she were in shock."

"The look on her little face broke my heart." Tonya slipped out of Eoin's grasp quickly. "I'm going to call Haley."

"Right now?"

"Yes," she said as she put her slippers and her bathrobe on. "It's late here but only 9 p.m. there."

"I'm ready ta go back ta sleep." Eoin yawned. "But ya go ahead and call her here in the room. I'll have no trouble fallin' asleep ta the sound of yer voice. I love ya, Tonnie. I love that ya care about yer friends so much." He smiled as she came over to his side of the bed and took his hand. "And yer a brave lass ta stay here in my country with all this mess."

"It's my country now, Eoin. It's our country—yours, mine, and the twins."

They kissed goodnight and Eoin sank down under the covers. Tonya took the cordless phone, sat in the closet, and called Haley.

***

"That sounded like an intense phone call." Gareth put his book down when Haley came out into the living room and sat down beside him. "Was that from Tonya? Is everything okay?"

"Joe Campbell and his men came after Brodie tonight at the cottage."

"Oh, no, this can't be good." Gareth bit his lip. "What happened?"

Haley told Gareth the story of events. "They were terrified, Gareth. It's just awful. As if Maisie needed more drama in her life! Eoin is going to get Callum to come and help clean up the cottage and make repairs. Tonya says she doesn't expect Maisie to go back to the cottage now. I feel so bad for her. Tonya says Maisie should come here and I agree. She needs to be with—"

"I know what you're going to say, Haley, but you girls can't do any matchmaking with Ed and Maisie. They've gone their separate ways for now and you can't just bring her over here and put the two together."

"But—"

"Haley."

"Please?"

"They're adults. They'll work it out themselves. They don't need you girls orchestrating their lives."

"But will you at least *please* tell Ed what's happened?" Haley begged with the most pitiful face she could make.

"Well, when you look at me like that—what can I say? I promise, I'll tell him. Now—" Gareth stood and took Haley's hand. "Come to bed with me, my lovely, help-everybody-in-the-world-matchmaking wife."

When Gareth found Ed the following day, he was talking to one of the new workers hired for the boarding business. Gareth waited until their conversation ended and then pulled Ed aside to talk to him about Maisie.

"Hey," Ed said before Gareth could get in a word, "I found this house for sale down the road. It's a fixer-upper so it's going pretty cheap. I'm kinda interested. You want to come with me to look at it? The realtor is going to be there in about ten minutes."

"Sure," Gareth said. They got in Ed's car and drove down the street while Ed talked about all the positive things about the house. They passed the Wagners' home on the way.

Ed pointed. "See this? It's just beyond my folks' house so I'll be near the dairy farm, near you guys, and I could walk to work! I'm so excited about this possibility!"

"That's great, Ed, really great." Gareth tried to sound excited, but all he could think about was how upset and worried Ed would be when he told him about Maisie and Erin.

They pulled slowly into a drive with several potholes. "Yeah, the driveway would have to be filled in a bit." Ed chuckled. The house was a ranch home with weather-worn blue aluminum siding. There was a small cracked stoop for a porch that rested beneath the front door. The screen was ripped and the once white but yellowed door needed a paint job. When the realtor pulled in, he opened the lock box and got the key out. Ed and Gareth stepped inside and looked around.

Gareth scrunched his face at the smell. "I feel like I just stepped into a *barn*."

"I think they had a few animals in here," Ed agreed.

"A few?" Gareth said sardonically.

"The gold shag carpet and paneling from the '70s would probably need to be pulled up and torn out," the realtor said.

"Probably?" Gareth smirked.

"Yeah, it's definitely in need of work," Ed said.

"But it's all cosmetic," the realtor added.

"It seems to have good bones," Ed added.

"I do think it has possibilities." Gareth tried to be positive. "What are they asking for this place?"

"$52,000," Ed said.

"It has fifteen acres, a small barn, a chicken coop, and two outbuildings," the realtor said.

"Not bad."

"I'm interested," Ed said to the realtor. "I'll get back with you real soon."

The realtor left. Gareth knew he needed to fill Ed in on Maisie's latest drama, but Ed's mind was so focused on the house and he was in such a good mood, that he didn't want to tell him.

"So, what do you think, Gareth?"

"It's got some possibilities, Ed. I'll bet you could get the owners to come down in price a bit. It looks like all the appliances will need to be replaced, there seems to be seepage in the basement, and the water heater has seen its last days."

"True," Ed said as they got in the car. "Thanks for coming with me. It helps to have someone else see it and give me some feedback. I wish—" He stopped himself. "Well, it doesn't do any good to wish."

"You wish what?"

"Never mind."

Here was Gareth's opportunity to segue into the recent news about Maisie. "Are you wishing you had a wife? A partner in life to help you with this decision?"

"Yeah, you know me too well. So much for my signing off to be a bachelor for life, eh?"

"Ed, there's something I need to tell you."

"What? Is something wrong? Did something happen to Maisie?"

"Wow, you jumped to that fast!"

Ed drove down the country road slowly.

"First of all, she and Erin are *okay—now*. Last night, Haley got a call from Tonya. Turns out Maisie and Erin came over to Eoin and Tonya's late in the night with a police escort to make sure they arrived safely."

"A police escort? Why? What on earth happened? Does this have anything to do with Brodie?"

"You guessed it."

"I've always worried about him staying there. From the short time I got to see him and learn about him, he seems to bring trouble with him."

"So, remember Joe Campbell, the guy Brodie helped put in prison, but got out after the Good Friday Agreement?"

"Yeah."

"He came after Brodie at the cottage. Brodie was gone, but he and his men tore up the place a bit."

Ed pulled the car over, put it in park, put his head on the steering wheel, and groaned loudly. "How are the girls?" His voice cracked.

"They were hiding upstairs. Another part of that same gang came and fought them off. Maisie said she saw one of Brodie's old friends in the group that came to save them. And then the police showed up. They've arrested two of the men who attacked the place, but Joe is still free."

Ed lifted his head and pounded the steering wheel. "Brodie! What a troublemaker! Why didn't he take Maisie and Erin with him?! Especially if he *knew* those guys would be coming there looking for him? Maisie can't go back to that cottage!"

"I'm sure she'll figure something out, Ed. I'm sorry. I really didn't even want to tell you, but Haley insisted you should know."

"I'm glad you did. This is so frustrating! She's so far away. And she says she needs to sort things out on her own, so I feel like my hands are tied."

"Would you have her for your wife if she was willing?"

"In a heartbeat!"

"I don't know what to tell you, friend."

After Ed talked to Gareth, he talked to Haley who talked to Tonya who eventually talked to Maisie.

***

Erin sat on the floor playing with Seamus and Sammy. She helped them build a tower with blocks and then watched them knock it all down with glee—to her own amusement. Tonya brought out some tea and Maisie took a cup from her.

"Eoin called. He said, after surveying the damages, it looks like it will be a while before they get secure windows replaced and anyone would be safe staying there."

"I appreciate it."

"Do you want to stay here for a couple of nights, Maisie? You're welcome to."

"Thank you, sure and we'll stay with ya, but we'll go back as soon as it's cleaned up and fixed."

"Are you certain?"

"We'll have ta sooner or later, so we will."

"You're braver than I am."

"I don't have a choice, Tonnie. I'm grateful Uncle Ian has been so willin' ta let us stay there."

"But you do have a choice, Maisie."

"What other choice is there?"

"Eddy."

She shook her head. "I pushed him away. He doesn't want me now, not after I was as cold as the wind on a winter's night."

"I think you're wrong."

"I'm not. We don't write as much anymore and he's goin' on with his own plans in life."

"I think that's just Eddy being cautious. But he's still interested."

"How can ya be so sure?"

"Well, let's just say that I have a direct connection to the friendship hotline in Wisconsin and I'm telling you, Eddy would take you for his wife in a *heartbeat*. He's just waiting on you."

Maisie's eyes lit up. "Do ya think so, then?"

"Yes. Would you marry him if he asked you, Maisie?"

"I would. I know now that I would. I miss him so much."

Tonya smiled.

Carrie was right all along. Dear, sweet, perceptive Carrie.

CHAPTER 33

Callum stood outside the damaged cottage, arms crossed, shaking his head while Molly and the kids pointed out the cracks in the façade, the broken windows, the trampled bushes, and the door still swinging open.

"They're lucky no one put a torch ta the house," Tommy said. "They could've been trapped upstairs and burnt ta death."

"Tommy, let's not go there," Molly scolded.

"Where was Uncle Brodie?" Shannon said.

"Gone," Molly said. "Now, you two be off and workin'."

Seeing the dismay, the frustration, the worry, and the near tears on her husband's troubled face, Molly weaved her arm in Callum's and leaned her head on his shoulder. "We can thank God that Maisie and Erin are safe."

"No thanks ta my eejit broder!" Callum said. "Why did he run off and leave them ta fend fer themselves?"

"How was he ta know Joe and his crew would come find this place?"

"Don' make up excuses fer him, Molly, lass. He shouldn't have left the girls by themselves, so he shouldn't."

Eoin walked around the cottage shaking his head, his lips drawn tightly.

"I talked ta Collins this mornin'. They got three men in custody, but not Joe. When is this goin' ta end?"

"First they come ta our house lookin' for Brodie, scarin' Molly and the children, then this," Callum said. "I'm weary o' it, cousin." He ran his hand through his dark hair just beginning to show signs of early grey. "I'm weary o' payin' fer me broder's bad choices in life."

"I understand. Seems that gettin' Joe back in prison would be a step in the right direction."

"I knew that guy was bad news the day he took us in as kids. I got out o' his place as soon as I could, but he really sucked Brodie inta his agendas."

Molly swept up broken glass, Tommy and Shannon wiped the surfaces and picked up trash, while Eoin and Callum straightened up the furniture, repaired a broken leg on a chair, took the telly with a broken screen out to the trash along with furniture that was irreparable and cut wood to size and nailed it over open window panes.

After everything was as back to normal as possible and the house was secured, they sat down at the kitchen table while Molly put a kettle of water on the stove. Shannon brought in a basket of food with sandwiches, apples, crisps, and homemade biscuits. Tommy set the table and everyone took a seat.

"So, what is Maisie goin' ta do?" Molly asked as she poured the tea.

"Tonnie says she plans ta come back and live here after it's secured," Eoin said, pulling another crisp from a pile on a plate and popping it into his mouth.

"Sure and she can't live here alone with Erin. Not after this," Callum said. "My sister has lived with enough trauma. I wish—I wish—"

"That Ed took her back ta the US? Tonnie and I do, too."

"Me too," Molly said. The kids echoed her response.

Callum shook his head. "We can't afford ta send her—"

"I think if the Wagners knew Maisie was willin' ta marry their son, they'd ship her and Erin over ta America without a second thought!" Eoin said.

"Why can't those two get it together?" Shannon joined in. "Are they both daft?" Callum and Eoin laughed.

"Be nice, daughter," Molly chided.

"She's just sayin' what we all want ta say!" Eoin said and Callum agreed.

"Does Ed know yet what happened here?" Molly asked.

"Most likely. Tonnie called Haley and Haley said she'd get Gareth ta tell him. Those girlfriends are tryin' ta light a fire under Ed."

"Fantastic!" Molly said. "And Maisie needs ta encourage the flame!"

"Ach, all these women!" Callum said.

"But maybe a little urgin' wouldn't hurt this time," Eoin said. "Look, cousin, I think we all see it, but we don' all do a thing about it. These women on the other hand—their passion can't be contained. I'm ready ta let 'em have at it with Ed and Maisie!"

"Meanwhile," Callum said, "I'm goin' ta find me broder, let him know what happened, and give him a piece of me mind!"

"Maybe ya shouldn't, Callum," Eoin said carefully. "Did ya ever wonder if maybe some of Joe's men followed ya the other day ta find Brodie?"

Callum looked away. "Do ya think—?"

"I'm not puttin' it on ya, but maybe we should all just leave Brodie ta his folly and not lead anyone ta him. It seems they know who we all are," Eoin said. "Meanwhile, Collins knows that Maisie identified Joe as the leader of the pack last night. We can only pray they find him."

Molly shivered. She'd like to see Joe back in prison and locked up for good—along with the men who were here last night. If she were Maisie, she'd take the ticket and fly to America tomorrow!

***

Now that the weather was turning cold again, Haley and Gareth invited their friends over for a bonfire. Of course, there would be marshmallows and hot dogs to roast, but most of all they would enjoy chatting and laughing amongst old friends.

The conversation that evening, however, turned to more serious matters. Gareth explained the phone call from Eoin about finding the people responsible for Anna's death and the reasons behind it.

"My da and I had a moment chatting about it together. We didn't even weep. We agreed that it was more of a relief to close this door and move on—no more need to investigate, no more questions to ask. We both want to enjoy the life in front of us, we want to enjoy the people and the events that God has put in our daily lives now."

"That's awesome, Gareth," Ed said.

"We heard about what happened to Maisie and Erin," Penny said.

"Poor things!" Carrie said.

Ed stared hard into the fire.

"What is she going to do?" Keith asked. "Where will she live now?"

"She's going back to the cottage once they replace the windows that were smashed," Gareth said.

"Is she? I wouldn't." Carrie looked at Penny and Haley.

"I wouldn't either."

"Nor I."

There was a pause in the conversation. Suddenly Ed realized all eyes were on him. "What? What am I supposed to do?!"

"Get her to come here, Eddy," Carrie said and the other girls chimed in, agreeing with her.

Ed looked to Gareth for help. "I'm with the girls, Ed."

"It's not that simple. What? Do I just propose to her—ask her to marry me and to come over here to live with me? Just like that? I already asked her once and she said 'no.'"

Everyone nodded vigorously. "I believe you're outnumbered, brother," Keith said. "Look, we all get it. You've gone through some tough love-related disappointments—"

"What a way to put it, Keith. Haley is sitting right here," Penny said, straight-faced. There was a brief moment of awkward silence as Keith got a worried look on his face. Penny looked at Haley with an expression of mischief. Suddenly, Haley guffawed. And then the rest of the friends felt free to follow suit. Except for Ed, who was still deliberating over his situation with Maisie.

"What if she's not ready?" Ed shook his head. "I don't think I can handle rejection from her."

"Come on, Sergeant First Class Edward Wagner," his brother teased. "You were in the war. You can handle a little rejection!"

"I don't think that will be in the mix this time," Haley said.

"How do you know that?" Ed challenged.

"We just do!" the girls said in unison.

Ed went home that night and prayed about it. He pondered the idea a few days. He put it off a few more days. What bothered him most was that the longer he put this off, the longer Maisie would be living in that cottage alone with Erin. What if some of those men returned? And who were the men who came to her aid? Did he trust them?

Was it a matter of his pride—the fear of rejection that was important here? Or was it Maisie and Erin's safety and his desire to be with both of them? He needed to call Maisie and take a chance. One afternoon he sat on his bed with his cell phone in his hand and thought about what to say. Should he just feel it out at first? Ask her how she's doing? Tell her he missed her and see if she responded similarly? Should he—? He slapped his free hand on the mattress. Enough overthinking! He tapped number one, which had the number to Ian's cottage programmed into his cell phone. His stomach was doing flips as the phone rang. It was just Maisie, he told himself. No need to be nervous.

"Hello?"

"Hi. Maisie? This is Eddy."

"How's about ya?"

"I'm fine. How are you doing?"

"Ah, I'm grand, yeah. How's the weather there?"

"It's getting colder, but the trees have been turning beautiful golds and reds. How about over there?"

"Mizzle. Every day just about."

"Um-hmmm. So, I'm sorry you had such a scare last week. Are you and Erin doing okay?"

"Grand."

"Good, then. Well, I just called to see that you two were okay and to tell you I miss you girls."

"Ah, thanks. I'd put Erin on but she's already asleep."

Ed grew nervous. "So, um, please tell her 'hi' for me, will you?"

"I will."

"Okay."

"Okay."

"Well, bye, Maisie."

"Um, bye, Eddy. Bye."

They both hung up. Ed threw his cell phone on the bed. When he said he missed her she didn't respond as he'd wished so he chickened out. He was such a coward!

Maisie hung up the phone and sat down on the sofa. Why did she feel like crying? His call got her hopes up. Maybe he was going to come to Northern Ireland. Maybe he was going to at least say he loved her. And maybe, even better, he was going to ask her to come to America and marry him. He did say he missed her, but that was all, and she knew it was her own fault for pushing him away.

Ed sat on his bed, elbows on his knees and head in his hands. When his phone started to ring he jumped. "Maisie?" Ed asked, hopeful.

"No, this is Eoin." The voice at the other end was quiet. "I've been stayin' here the last few nights with Maisie and Erin fer their protection and until we're sure things are settlin' down fer them emotionally."

"Why are you calling me?"

"Well, first of all, don't tell the girls—*any of the girlfriend, includin' me wife and Maisie*—that I made this call—that's why I'm whisperin'."

"Okaaay?"

"You know how those lassies are, doin' all the matchmakin', tryin' ta push us lads ta do things and right now I feel like one of 'em makin' this call," Eoin said sheepishly.

"My word is my bond." Ed laughed slightly.

"Here it is. I was in the kitchen gettin' a snack when ya called a minute ago. After Maisie hung up from talkin' ta ya she looked pretty defeated. When I asked her what was wrong, she brushed me off and went up ta her room. What'd I say to get such a brush-off? What's goin' on, Ed?"

"I don't know. I just talked to her. It was a polite conversation."

"Hmmm. Just polite? Maisie was hopin' fer more than a short courtesy call from ya, so. From what Tonya has been tellin' me, I think she'd like somethin' more from ya, ya know?"

"Would she? But she told me to go home last time I was there. I'm confused, Eoin. Does she really want more from me?"

"Are ya a right daft eejit, Ed? She pushed ya ta go home because she cares about ya and wanted ya safely out of her country."

"I think I am daft," Ed said. "And a right *eejit*."

Eoin chuckled. "Ya've been around us too long, lad."

"I have, but I don't begrudge it."

"We don' either, friend. But ya oughta try that phone call again."

"You're right. Thanks, Eoin. I needed the push. I really needed that."

"Just don' tell—"

"I know."

They hung up. Eoin went back into the kitchen. Ed paused for a few minutes, framing his words. And then he made the call. Eoin answered.

"What the—?" Ed didn't expect Eoin to be the one to answer the phone.

"Ed, how ya doin'?" Eoin talked louder than before.

"Why'd ya answer—?"

"Sure an' I'll get Maisie. She's upstairs." Eoin set the phone down and went over to the steps and called Maisie's name quietly. She appeared shortly at the top of the stairs, curious. "Phone call fer ya. It's Ed." Puzzled, she came down and picked up the receiver. Eoin went into the kitchen and sat at the table with some tea and biscuits. He couldn't help but listen in.

"Hello? Eddy? What is it?"

"I forgot to say some things."

"Go on, then."

"I was thinking of buying a house close to my folks and I'd like your opinion of the place."

"Have ya gone crazy? How can I give ya an opinion way over here?"

"Why, I thought maybe you and Erin could take a trip to Wisconsin and help me make the decision."

"What are ya? Mad as a box of frogs? Now, how are we goin' ta do that?"

Ed laughed. "Yes, I'm mad as a box of frogs, though, truthfully, I've never seen a box of frogs get mad." Maisie chuckled and he continued. "But, I would like to buy you some plane tickets so you can fly over here. Would you do that?"

"Um, well, it's a lot ta think about, but, I suppose we'd love ta come over there again." Maisie smiled. "So's that what ya wanted ta ask?"

"That's part of it."

"What's the other part?"

There was a long pause at the other end.

"Eddy? Are ya still there?"

"Yeah. I am." He sighed. "I don't know why this is so hard to say."

"Sure an' I've made things hard fer ya ta say stuff ta me? An' I'm sorry. I shouldn'a pushed ya and sent ya on yer way home like I did. It were cruel of me. I just wanted ya safe and far away from here, Eddy."

"Is that really all it was?"

"So it was."

"I do appreciate your thinking of my safety, but at the same time, I doubted and thought you weren't interested in me so much anymore."

"That's so far from the truth—so very far from it. I wish ya hadn' gone and I wish ya were here with me now."

Ed relaxed. "I'm so glad to hear it. I've missed you."

"And I you."

"Maisie, I want you to know that I love you beyond words and that there are other things I want to say to you, but it would be so impersonal to say these things over the phone with you sitting way across the Atlantic. For now, will you come to America so that you and Erin can be with me and help me find a house that someday will be ours— together?"

A lump rose in Maisie's throat. "I will!" She let out a happy cry. "We will!"

An overwhelming feeling of relief rushed through Ed's lungs and he took in a deep breath of air. Suddenly, his adrenaline took over and his words flew out of his mouth. "I'll get started on the tickets and let you know what I can get for you and Erin. Will you be okay flying here—just the two of you?"

"Eddy, I—"

"Do you think you should fly out of Edinburgh?"

"Eddy, I wanted—"

"Heathrow? Dublin? Never mind, I'll talk to Eoin and I'll look into—"

"Eddy!" Maisie laughed. "What a craic!"

"What?"

"I'm tryin' ta tell ya somethin'—somethin' important that I've been needin' ta tell ya."

"What is it?"

"That I love ya, too, I do."

There was a pause at the other end. "You never said that to me before." Suddenly Ed's voice was subdued.

"An' I shoulda, but I'm needin' ta say it now before we make plans. I love ya so much an' I miss ya. I can' wait till we're tagether again."

"I'm so relieved to hear you say that. It'll be hard waiting to see you again—and Erin." When Ed hung up from the phone call, he jumped up and yelled out, "Hallelujah and praise God from whom all blessings flow!"

"Edwahd," Alma yelled from the foot of the stairs. "Should I make up Peggy's room for guests?"

"Yes!"

Alma smiled as she walked to the linen closet and took out fresh sheets.

CHAPTER 34

Erin, nine years old, was up and finished with packing her last-minute possessions before her mother. There wasn't a need for too many suitcases, most of their belongings having been lost in the eviction of the old apartment. Maisie's alarm went off and she was out of her bed before Erin could come in and wake her. She showered and finished last-minute packing quickly and then went downstairs to make a quick breakfast of bubble and squeak with toast, butter, marmalade, and plenty of tea. Erin was already standing at the stove putting on the tea.

"Ah, ya've beat me to it!" Maisie laughed.

"I'm so excited, I can' wait!" Erin giggled.

Maisie helped get the food on the table and they ate quickly, knowing that Callum would be by soon to take them down into the Republic of Ireland to the Dublin Airport. They were done eating in time for Callum's arrival and soon they were leaving the Laurelvale area and traveling south through Newry and then to the border. At the border they were asked a few questions and were left to go on their way. Callum commented on how easy it was to get across the border into Ireland now and that he was greatly relieved. They passed through Dundalk and drove along the coastline of the Irish Sea. They drove through Drogheda and on to Dublin to the airport.

But when they pulled up to the airport they were redirected away from the terminal and as they passed it they noticed emergency vehicles, patrol cars, the bomb squad, and a helicopter flying overhead.

"What's goin' on?" Erin asked. Maisie looked at her brother, her eyes betraying her worry. When they were at an acceptable distance, Callum pulled off the road, turned on the car radio, and flipped through the stations to listen for a news report. Finally, he found one saying a bomb scare had delayed all flights. Anyone with a flight scheduled today should call the airport for further instructions. Maisie's shoulders slumped.

Callum reached over and touched Maisie's arm. "It'll be okay, sis."

Maisie's stomach flipped. *O Lord, please let us fly to be with Eddy!*

"What does that mean, Ma? Uncle Callum?"

"We don't know, agra," Maisie said.

"No bother, Erin, sure and it'll all be fine. We'll find a phone, go sit at a pub, and see what kind of a wait we have," Callum said. "Maybe we'll get a grand lunch ta eat while we wait."

They found a pub, but the parking lot there was full from other travelers in the same situation as they, so Callum parked the car on the street. There were families sitting around tables, men and women in business suits, young couples who looked and acted newly married. Maisie and Erin took a seat at the only table left in the cozy room while Callum stood in line at the pay phone to call the airport. When he returned to the table his face looked grim.

"What, Callum?" Maisie said anxiously.

"All flights have been postponed until further notice. They said the bomb squad is lookin' fer a potential bomb. The flight attendants won't know any schedules until they've been given the all clear from the officials."

"So what do we do?"

"We wait."

"I hate waitin'."

"Me too."

"Me too," Erin said.

"You should let Ed know," Callum said.

"I wish I had a cell phone about now," Maisie said as she got up to go stand in line at the pay phone.

Ed was up early in the morning getting ready for work at the stables when Maisie called. He hung up and prayed that she wouldn't lose courage and decide not to fly to America. Why did it seem like things always got in the way for them to be together? And now this. He told Maisie to keep him posted and that he'd keep his phone in his pocket. And then he prayed.

It was a long day for those waiting for news about the bomb scare. The pub was hospitable and understanding as the guests waited for news about the airline—as long as they kept buying food and drinks. By three o'clock in the afternoon, Erin had fallen asleep, resting her head on the table while Callum and Maisie paid for cups of coffee, tea, and dessert just to show their appreciation to the pub owner.

"So, Callum, what's ta come of our broder?" Maisie asked.

"Ach, I don' know."

"Do ya talk ta him?"

"No. Eoin advised me ta leave him alone. He said that stayin' connected ta him is possibly bringin' the trouble ta me."

"I wish you and the rest o' the family could come ta America."

"We'll be fine, Maisie. Molly has her folks here. She couldn' leave 'em. Besides, they've become parents ta me, too. I'm hopin' that Ed's folks can be that ta ya there in Wisconsin."

"I think they will. They're very kind. And I'll have me Uncle Ian, cousin Gareth, and the Beckett lasses. They're all very kind people."

"I'm happy fer ya. I like Ed, an' ya have me blessin' on the union."

"Thanks, that means a lot, but, sure an' it's not confirmed yet—"

"Are ya daft, Maisie? A lad pays for a lass and her wee'un ta come ta his country and help pick out a house with him?" Callum laughed and Maisie smiled at the prospect.

Suddenly, someone in the back corner by the phone let out a yell of excitement. "T'e airport is open fer business!" A cheer went up in the room as people started gathering their belongings and headed for their cars.

As Maisie, Erin, and Callum drove back to the airport Erin kept asking, "But there's no bomb, right?"

"Aye, lassie, they checked the entire airport. It was someone tryin' ta scare everyone, so it was."

"Sure an' it's not a nice thing they do," Erin said.

"Yer right," Callum said.

They arrived at the airport and were let into the parking area. After they went to the desk and learned when their plane would take off, Callum helped them take their baggage to the proper station to load them.

"We have a few hours yet ta wait," Maisie said. "There's no sense in ya waitin' around here fer us. Molly and the children were expectin' ya home hours ago."

"Me sister is leavin' fer another country and I don' know when I'll see her again. The family can wait."

"Yer gonna make me cry with those words, broder."

"I'm gonna make me cry," Callum said and they both laughed at it. They sat and waited and chatted about childhood memories, playing in the barn, picking apples in the neighbor's orchard, and going to the seaside with their parents. There was no talk about the terrible things that happened to them. What good would it do? Finally, it was time to board the plane. Callum hugged his niece and fought the quick tears that surfaced. Then he stood and before he could even give his sister a hug, they both were in tears.

"God be with ya, dear sister," he said.

"And with ya, me dearest broder." Maisie's voice was hoarse and her cheeks were also wet.

"Maybe someday we'll see ya again."

"I think Eddy will agree ta bring me back ta me homeland fer a visit."

"He's a good man, Maisie. Yer fortunate and I'm that happy fer ya."

With that they said their last tearful goodbyes several times over. They waved back and forth as Maisie and Erin walked down the loading bridge to the plane until they were out of each other's sight.

It was dark when their plane finally took off across the Atlantic Ocean, veering slightly upward over Iceland and then down again toward the US and on toward Chicago. It was after midnight for Maisie and Erin, but in Chicago it was only after 6 p.m.

As Ed drove to pick them up, his mind reeled with so much to be said, and he tried to suppress some very passionate feelings. As he stood in the airport waiting for them, he swayed and bounced in anticipation. But when Erin and Maisie deboarded, he could see how exhausted they looked and he decided to wait to say or do anything for now except work on getting them home safely. He greeted them with a gentle smile. They hugged and shed some quiet tears amongst them, relieved to finally be reunited. Ed helped them get their luggage and haul it out to the car.

When they got in the car, Maisie scooted close to Ed and he covered her hand with his. She wove her fingers in his and he caressed the top of her hand with his thumb. Erin rested her head on the back of the seat and fell asleep on the drive home. Maisie found the comfort of Ed's shoulder and rested her head there.

"Sure and it's grand ta be here with ya," she said.

"I'm still feeling as if I'm in a dream," Ed said and then kissed the top of her head. "I just want to get you girls home. Then I think it will feel real!"

"That it will. Just don't speed."

Ed chuckled. "I'm trying not to, but I'm too excited."

When they arrived at the Wagner home, Fred and Alma greeted Maisie and Erin with open arms and tears of joy. Alma showed them to a nice big bedroom, with a large antique canopy bed covered with a purple dotted swiss bedspread with curtains, shams, and a canopy that matched. Some of Peggy's fancier dolls remained on the dresser and a Victorian-style dollhouse sat on the floor beside it. Erin's eyes were wide with pleasure at the richness of it all. Alma explained that this was Peggy's old room and she figured they'd sleep better for now if they were together. Maisie appreciated Alma's thoughtfulness. The weary travelers ate a late snack of Wisconsin cheeses, salami, crackers, cut-up apples, oranges, and bananas. When Fred and Alma excused themselves and went off to bed, Maisie helped Erin get dressed for bed and tucked her in for the night.

Ed sat in the living room, waiting impatiently, hoping Maisie would come back down to the living room to be with him a bit longer. He had something he wanted to say and he didn't want to wait another day. When he heard the creek of the old stairs he looked up and saw her descending. She had taken the time to take out her ponytail and brush out her hair. Now it flowed around her shoulders and after the refreshing snack and some cold water with soap, her countenance was brighter.

Maisie took in a breath at the sight of the man waiting for her. His familiar handsome form gave her joy and his loving eyes told her she was cherished beyond her comprehension. She moved a little quicker now as she came off the last step and went toward him without hesitation. He took her in his arms and she felt herself melt into his grasp.

Home.

This was home.

"I'm still tryin' ta believe we're here with ya." Maisie relished the feel of his strong arms and the warmth of his chest.

"We've waited a long time for this, Maisie."

"Aye, we have."

"No more waiting. Not another day," Ed said as he released her, got down on one knee, and cupped her hands in his. He looked up at her with unmistakable passion, took a deep breath, and said, "Maisie, I wish for you to be my wife, to be by my side together in this world—no matter what country—*forever*. I know we both had resolved to never give our hearts to another, but I'm more than ready to give my heart to you—no, I have already lost my heart to you. Are you willing to take a chance with me, my sweet Maisie? Will you marry me?"

Maisie trembled as she nodded. "Aye, I am and I will, fer always. Ya have me heart also, and I want ta be with ya forever, dear Eddy, so I do."

Ed felt her hands shake. He stood, slid one hand beneath her hair, gently touching the nape of her neck, and pulled her close. She lifted her eyes to his as he leaned down and placed his lips on hers. It was a long-awaited kiss for both of them, and now, when they were finally together and alone, it came freely and passionately.

CHAPTER 35

Before Maisie and Ed announced their engagement to any of the family or friends, they sat with Erin on the Wagners' front porch to tell her the news and include her in the new future family arrangement. Fall colors were at their peak. The abundance of maple trees in the yard filled the perimeter outside the house with scarlet red, burnt orange, and yellow ochre. There was a slight chill in the air, but Alma had plenty of old quilts and crocheted afghans draped over the seats for everyone's comfort.

"Erin," Ed said as he pulled a quilt over the three of them on the settee, "last night your ma agreed to marry me. But now I want to ask you if *you* will consent to my marrying your ma and you being my daughter?"

Erin's eyes lit up. "Have ya popped yer clogs? What else would we come here fer but ta be with ya, Eddy? Oh, an' so shall I call ya me da?"

Ed let out a laugh. "Please do!"

"Well then, *Da*. I give ya permission ta marry me ma." Erin smiled.

Maisie and Ed looked at each other and laughed freely. Ed hugged Erin tightly. "I love you, *lassie*."

"I love ya, too!" Erin said. "An' can I say, what took ya so long? I been waitin' fer donkey's years."

"Erin!" Maisie scolded.

"It's okay." Ed laughed again. "I fear the rest of our friends and family might say the same thing!"

"Let's go in and tell yer folks," Maisie said. "I think yer ma is suspicious anyhow."

"Women and their intuition!" Ed said, as they all got up, too excited to fold the quilt, but leaving it in a pile on the settee.

Alma was working in the kitchen making soup for lunch when they came in. When she heard them, she wiped her hands on a dish towel and turned to them as she smoothed out her apron and started talking excitedly.

"Well, I hope y'all are hungry for some homemade squash soup! It's an old recipe—"

"Momma—"

"Yes?" Alma stopped her chatter immediately and looked wide-eyed at Ed in hopeful expectation.

"We have some news to tell you. Where's Dad?"

"Frederick!" Alma yelled in a high-pitched voice, her hands moving nervously about her apron. Fred appeared from the study almost as if he were waiting for that cue.

"Yes?" he said, almost as if he'd practiced it.

"Momma and Dad, Maisie has agreed to marry me and Erin has agreed to be my daughter."

Alma started to cry with happiness. Ed went to his mother and wrapped his arms around her. Fred went to Maisie and Erin and hugged them. "Welcome to the family, girls!" He got down on his haunches and said to Erin, "And can we be your granddad and grandmomma?"

"Aye! Aye!" Erin jumped up and down. "Oh, this is grand! I've never had grandparents before! Ah! I have happiness on me, so I do!"

Alma went to Maisie and hugged her. "I'm overjoyed to have y'all in our family! Another daughter! And a granddaughter, too. I am surely blessed by God on this day."

Later in the evening, Gareth, Haley and family, and Ian and Phyllis came over for dinner. When Ed announced the engagement, more excitement followed and then plans began. Maisie and Ed had waited long enough. They had decided it would be a winter wedding. "Why not December?" someone asked. "Why not around Christmas?" someone else suggested. They all agreed to help get decorations, flowers, food, and other details together. Haley, Phyllis, and Alma got excited talking about taking Maisie and Erin for a trip into Milwaukee to look for proper fabric for dresses.

Later that week, Ed took Maisie and Erin to meet with the realtor again to see the rundown house that he was considering to buy.

"It's a grand big house!" Maisie said as she stepped inside the front door.

"This is actually small by American standards," the realtor said to Maisie in particular.

"Um, that won't be a problem." Ed explained. "They're not used to the size of homes in America."

"Oh? Where are you from?"

"Norn Iron," Maisie said quickly. The realtor looked puzzled.

"Northern Ireland," Eddy said slowly. Maisie smirked.

"All the land around it would be ours, too?" Erin asked.

"Yes." Ed smiled.

"The kitchen is grand." Maisie ran her hands along the old Formica countertops. "I could get lost in here. And the refrigerator is brilliant—and olive green?"

"We'll get a new one," Ed said.

"Why? It still works, doesn't it? And I like green." Maisie opened the refrigerator door and felt the coolness inside. "It's perfectly fine."

"But it's from the '70s," Ed said.

"So then it's still fairly new?" Maisie said. Ed tried not to laugh.

"This could be your room, Erin," the realtor said as he led them down the hallway.

"All of it?" Erin's eyes grew wide.

"Yes, all of it." The realtor chuckled.

"If me ma and me new da have more babies, the children could stay in here with me, so they could."

"Those are big bedrooms," Maisie said, blushing at Erin's comment. "I love the big windows. I can see much of the outdoors." She turned to the realtor. "This is a fantastic place, so it is."

The realtor looked at Ed, pleased to see such appreciation for such a humble abode by American standards. While Maisie and Erin roamed the yard and the outbuildings, Ed talked business with the realtor.

"I'll let the owners know you're interested. I'd put in a low bid. Nobody else has been biting on this one," the realtor said. "I'll get back with you." And then, he left.

On the way back to the Wagners, Maisie grew quiet.

"Something wrong?" Ed reached over and took her hand.

"It's all happening so fast. So much ta take in."

"Do we need to slow down? Because we can. Anything you want, baby. Don't ever be afraid to tell me what you want."

Maisie slipped her fingers through his. "No bother, I'll be fine. Ya just make me love ya more every day, Eddy. I'm not used ta so much happiness all at once."

***

When Tonya heard the news about the wedding, she sat down on the sofa and stared blankly at her sons playing around her feet.

"Tonnie?" Eoin sat down beside her. "Ya want ta be there fer the weddin' don' ya? Yer thinkin' about all yer friends bein' there and ya won't. Am I right?"

"Yes," Tonya leaned her head on Eoin's shoulder. "I'm so very happy for Ed and Maisie, but selfishly sad to not be there."

"If we could afford ta go—or even just ta send ya alone—I'd do it."

"I know you would."

"These things are going ta start happenin' more as the friends in the States have events like this. There will be special birthdays, graduations, weddin's—I suppose Ed and Maisie will have children, too."

"I know."

"Does it make ya have second thoughts of livin' here, Tonnie?"

"No. I knew I'd be missing things coming here, but I love Northern Ireland, Eoin. It's such a beautiful country. I still want to get out and photograph more of the countryside and the coast."

"Okay. I just want ta be tender ta yer feelin's."

"You are and I love you for that." Tonya reached up and kissed Eoin on the cheek. Eoin started to take her in his arms, but Seamus hit Sammy with a Hot Wheels car and Sammy retaliated by pushing him to the floor. Eoin and Tonya each picked up a child to comfort them and talk over what just happened and who was at fault.

***

Haley, Maisie, Carrie, and Penny met at Mullen's Dairy.

"We're so happy to have you here again," Carrie said to Maisie.

"I agree," Penny said. "And I'm buying today, girls. I got a raise in pay this week and I'm looking forward to a Christmas bonus, too!"

"The last of the big spenders!" Haley laughed as the girls ordered their milkshakes and sundaes and sat at a table together.

The girls all listened in awe as Maisie told them about the men who vandalized Ian's cottage while she and Erin hid in the bedroom closet.

"Is Tonya safe over there?" Carrie asked.

"Aye, she and Eoin don't have a connection to Brodie's paras and the IRA have backed off a bit because of the Good Friday Agreement."

"I wish she could come to the wedding." Carrie sighed and the girls agreed.

"Eoin doesn't make enough money ta send her over," Maisie told them. "Ed said that when he talked to him last, Eoin said Tonnie was pretty down about it. I wish she could be here fer the weddin', ya know? She's been such a grand friend ta me, so she has."

"Haley, you've been pretty quiet over there. Is your malt that good or are you deep in thought?" Penny teased.

"Deep in thought," Haley said. "I was just thinking."

"Oh, this could be dangerous," Penny said and Maisie laughed.

"What are you scheming now? Tell us!" Carrie said.

"Well—I was just thinking how Mr. and Mrs. Miller haven't seen their grandsons in a few years now and that maybe they might help Tonya and her family come to America at Christmas this year."

All the girls sat there silently thinking on the idea. How would they reach the Millers and who would put the bug in their ear?

Two days later, after a phone call from Haley, Mrs. Miller called her daughter.

"So, I hear that Edward Wagner is getting married, Tonya?"

"Yes, Mom, to Maisie MacCauley. You met her when you and Dad came up to see the twins, remember?"

"I do. She seems to be a nice girl."

"She is. We're good friends already. How'd you hear about it?"

"Haley told me."

"Oh? Why were you talking to Haley?"

"She called me. She was concerned about you not being there with the rest of the friends for the wedding."

"She was? That's sweet."

"Well, I bet you're pretty sad about not being able to go, aren't you?"

"Yes, I am. But I made the choice to move far away, so I guess this is the first of these kind of things—special events— that I'll miss."

"Well, it won't be the first one."

"What do you mean?"

"Your dad and I want to pay for your family to fly over there. If you and Eoin can take the time off to go, we'd like to pay for it. Do you think there'd be a place for you to stay?"

"Oh, Mom, that's really generous, but you guys don't need to do—"

"Look, Tonya dear, I know your dad and I haven't always been there for you and now we're missing out on seeing our grandsons. So, this is self-serving. We want to get you back to the States to go to Ed and Maisie's wedding, and then we'd like to see you, too. We're snowbirds now, so we don't want to come up to Wisconsin in the winter, but we'd like to fly you down here after the wedding to spend some time with us in Florida."

Tonya felt the butterflies in her stomach as she thought of the possibility of seeing everyone and seeing her parents play with their grandsons. "I'll talk to Eoin about it. I'm pretty sure he can take the time off from work for a vacation. Thank you so much, Mom! I love you."

"I love you, too."

Tonya talked to Eoin about it and the plans were set. They'd travel to Wisconsin for the wedding and then go to Florida. Eoin had never been in the sunny south of the US, so this would be another adventure he looked forward to.

CHAPTER 36

December, 1998. The Baptist church was all abuzz with Ed and Maisie's wedding plans for the Christmas season. The church had never been so marvelously decorated with lights, poinsettias, pine boughs, wreaths, a huge Christmas tree in the front of the auditorium, and a manger scene outside.

The wedding reception was to be held in the Wagners' spacious home. Alma wouldn't have anything lacking as far as decorations and food. She planned a delicious buffet and ordered a three-tiered wedding cake in town. She was beside herself to gain another daughter-in-law and ready to adopt a new granddaughter into the family.

Haley and Phyllis worked diligently on sewing dresses for the bride, the maid of honor, and the many little flower girls. Maisie learned the art of sewing quickly and was glad she was able to help. The men were reminded constantly to go to the tailor in town to get fitted with their proper suits. The day before the wedding, all the women were in the church auditorium, decorating the platform, the pews, and the lobby. All was finally set and they thought all the wedding garments were ready until Eoin called and said that they were coming! What a fun rush it was then to sew up a dress for Tonya and rent suits for Eoin and the twins.

It was a festive morning when the time for the wedding arrived. Ed stood beside the pastor, his very own brother, and listened as the processional started with "The Wedding Gift," written by Dave Panting and played by a special Celtic band that the Wagners' found and hired. There was an Irish flute, a fiddle, a guitar, a bodhran, Uileann pipes, and a Celtic harp.

Gareth and Haley, Eoin and Tonya, Penny and Scott walked down the aisle. When they were in place on the platform, Carrie directed all the children from the foyer: four young girls, Erin, Annie, Fiahd, and Angie Brannen wearing dark-purple velvet dresses with ivory lace, and six boys, Seamus, Sammy, Benny, Bobby, Liam, and Jonathan wearing black suits with dark-purple shirts and black bowties. The guests smiled at the parade coming down the aisle.

And then, when the musicians picked up the volume on the last verse, a beautiful young woman with flowing chestnut hair, wearing a dress made of Irish lace, glided down the aisle on the arm of her Uncle Ian. Ed, tall and handsome in his black tux, watched his beautiful bride and nothing else. When Maisie approached him, she took his arm and stood close. Her heart fluttered, feeling as if she were in a dream standing beside someone so good-looking, yet so loving and kind to her. She squeezed his arm and smiled up at him. He glanced down at her, grinned, and winked, hoping his brother would rush to the part about "you may kiss your bride."

Haley looked at Gareth with tears in her eyes, joy overflowing that her old childhood friend had finally found the love of his life. Tonya looked from Haley to Gareth and giggled with delight, while Eoin felt thankful for this day of celebration. There had been too many days behind them of sorrow, pain, and grief, he thought, and a joyous day like today was a healing to the spirit. After all, a merry heart does good like a medicine. The wedding ceremony finished and Ed finally could kiss his lovely bride. They exited down the aisle as the band played "Slip into Spring," by Bill Whelan.

The lunch reception flowed at the Wagners' home with guests, family, and friends. Ed and Maisie moved about, talking to all the guests. At one point they sat down together in a corner of the room.

"I'm knackered," Maisie said.

"I'd like to sneak out and get going on our honeymoon," Ed said as he took her hand.

"Me too," Maisie said, and they locked eyes. "But, we have so many here ta celebrate our day—"

"I know."

"I never would have ever expected all this." Maisie was continually grateful for everything and Ed appreciated that about her.

After the church family went on their way, the others sat around talking and laughing. In the midst of the conversation, Gareth stood in the center of the room and said, "Excuse me, everybody, but I'd like to say something." Everyone quieted and by the mischievous look on Gareth's face, Ed sat in anticipation, suspicious of what his old friend was about to say. Gareth grew serious. "I just have one final word to say to my beloved friend, Ed, and my dear cousin, Maisie." Gareth paused. Ed crossed his arms and shook his head. "Finally!" Gareth shouted, pumping his fists in the air as if he'd just won an Olympic medal. Laughter and applause erupted.

The back fields were covered in a soft layer of snow. The wedding party went outside for a photo shoot. Phyllis and Alma had crocheted matching shawls for the girls and the men and boys put on their suitcoats. A line of trees in the distance was stark against the grey-blue sky, their bare branches coated with a thin icing of snow. The deep purples, blacks, and whites of the wedding party contrasted and matched the setting behind them.

Tonya put her camera on the tripod, instructed everyone where to stand, set the timer, and joined the group. She wanted to get the best photos, so she took several—going back and forth from the tripod. Finally, she got everyone out of the picture except the bride and groom. Ed and Maisie looked at each other, sighed, and then laughed. They had waited so long to be together that by now, they were anxious to get away from everyone and be alone.

After some formal shots of the couple, Tonya said, "Let's get some pictures of you two walking in the field!"

"That's a great idea, Tonya!" Haley said.

"I love it," Penny added.

"Look at them. This is so romantic," Carrie said.

Tonya instructed Ed and Maisie to walk out into the field a short distance so that they could return, walking hand in hand toward the camera. The couple laughed and talked while Maisie held her skirts with her free hand. The others watched, chatting, enjoying the brisk winter air. The pictures were perfect but Tonya was a perfectionist. After she made the couple go back into the field and walk toward her again, she asked them to do it once more. "One more time, guys. I promise. The sun is just beginning to set so this would be a perfect shot!" Ed and Maisie sighed together but then Maisie got a mischievous look on her face and mouthed something to Ed. He nodded. They started to walk out in the field but instead of turning around, they walked on and on, amidst Tonya and the other girls' shouts to come back. Out into the frozen field they walked, toward the row of trees, over 120 yards, more than the length of a football field. The guys began to laugh. Tonya looked at the others, threw her hands in the air, and said, "I give up."

"Honey, you got a lot fantastic shots of them walking into the sunset!" Eoin said, laughing at the newly married couple's escape. But they all understood. Ed and Maisie wanted to be alone. They felt like two children escaping their parents' eyes as they tucked in between the line of trees, finally out of sight of everyone. Ed turned Maisie toward him and pulled her close.

"I love you, my sweet Irish lass," he said as he pushed strands of her hair away from her face and then cupped her cheeks, rosy from the cold.

"I love ya, too, farm boy—*me farm boy*." She giggled as she rested her face in his warm hands.

"If we stay out here long enough—" He leaned in closer. "Do you think they'd all eventually go back inside and we could sneak to the car and take off on our honeymoon without being seen?"

"Why, Edward! Yer ma wouldn't appreciate that, so she wouldn't! And neither would *our* daughter!" Her eyes danced.

"Then kiss me long, now," he said, winking, "and that will hold me over until tonight!"

And she complied.

CHAPTER 37

In April of 1999, the Independent Commission for the Location of Victims' Remains (ICLVR) was established by the United Kingdom government and the government of Ireland in order to locate the Irish and British people who were referred to as "The Disappeared." The MacCauley family was excited to see this new establishment go forward toward discovering where the bodies were buried. Eoin and Tonya were able to rejoice with other families as some bodies were found and funerals were able to take place.

In June of 2000, two years after the Good Friday Agreement, Nationalists (those against British rule) attacked the Protestant homes in the north and the west of Belfast. Then, in August, because of Loyalist feuds, 160 families living in the Shankill area were rehoused. It was good timing that Callum's family moved into Ian's cottage south of Lurgan. With the help of Eoin, Brodie, and the McGilroys, Callum began to rebuild his father's old cottage. Soon, Eoin and Callum would be neighbors again, living in the homes they were each born in.

In May of 2001, Joe Campbell was shot and killed in a scuffle. Brodie left the area and went to live with the McGilroys in Ballantrae, Scotland. He decided to remain there to avoid any lingering trouble or "punishings" with paras.

In August, 2001, three republicans from Northern Ireland, suspected of belonging to the IRA, were arrested in Colombia, suspected of training FARC rebels and narcoterrorists.

Then, on September the 11th, 2001, the US suffered multiple fatal terrorist acts affiliated with Al-Qaeda. The Islamic terrorists highjacked four airplanes in a suicide attempt to bring the planes down in strategic places. Two planes took down the twin towers in New York City, killing and wounding thousands. One plane crashed into the Pentagon and another failed in its mission to attack the Capitol, but crashed instead in a field in Pennsylvania. Almost three thousand lives were lost altogether. It was the deadliest terrorist attack in human history. Because of this, security was heightened at airports worldwide and continued into the following years— especially for international flights.

In December of 2001, Gerry Adams, affiliated with the IRA and a member of Sinn Fein, visited Cuba and met with Fidel Castro. It was no surprise that the Bush administration of the US highly criticized his activities.

Ironically, because of the heightened security in the airports, the MacCauley and Wagner families felt it safer to fly from Wisconsin to Northern Ireland. In 2002, they made the long-awaited trip to County Armagh, Northern Ireland. The MacCauley families looked forward to reuniting. Ian was excited to see his nephews, Callum's family, and the old homesteads rebuilt, housing a new generation of MacCauleys. Phyllis, Haley, Fred, Alma, and the children were excited to take the trip and see another country, but especially the place from where the MacCauleys hailed.

After resting a day from a long flight, the travelers visited both homesteads. Ian was emotional, but happy. The following day, the family took a trip to Waterfoot Beach. They had a very surreal, but good moment at the beach, and then enjoyed a lunch at a pub in Waterfoot with Brodie and the

McGilroys, who came across the North Channel. The family was glad to meet a relative of the McGilroys to whom Brodie was engaged. Her name was Isla and she was a very quiet, serious lass. Everyone agreed that she was a good match for Brodie.

The following day, a trip was taken to Lurgan and ended with a sweet visit at George and Margaret's house. The expressions on the old Scottish faces were priceless. Margaret asked that they all sing "Auld Lang Syne" before they left even if it wasn't a holiday, because, she added, "We'll not be gettin' any younger here!"

On the last day before returning home, Eoin and Tonya hosted a big family dinner with the entire MacCauley/Wagner family. There were a few new faces to add to the mix: Siobhan, Eoin and Tonya's little girl, and Erin's new little brother, Sean. The children all sat around the floor of the sitting room to eat their food and let the little ones get into the toys. The adults crowded around the table in the kitchen.

"Do you think there's ever going to be peace here? Can we ever move on from the past?" Gareth asked.

"It's hard ta say," Eoin said.

"We had hoped the peace process would've moved along more smoothly," Callum said.

"Brodie still struggles with the past." Maisie looked at Ed. He rested his hand on her shoulder lovingly. She put her hand on his and nodded. "All right, I still struggle a wee bit, too."

"I don't think any of us can forget what happened here ta our families," Eoin said.

"Some people believe our country is destined ta continue in conflict and uncertainty," Callum said.

"But there is always hope," Ian interjected, and at his tone, everyone grew silent. "We have ta live in hope, ya know? If we let all the prejudice, the tensions, the violence, destruction, and death get ta us, sure and we'll be no better than those who came before us. We need ta pray every day fer our country and its leaders and trust God ta guide them. We have ta teach our children ta love God, love others, love their country, and hope that they contribute ta a better world in the future." The older children were curious as to why it was only their granddad speaking in the kitchen and, sensing the seriousness, one by one they came in quietly to listen, putting the wee'uns in the laps of their parents. "These problems we have seen in our country have been embedded in the hearts and attitudes of the people here fer centuries and they've passed it on ta their children.

"Hundreds of years ago, the Catholics persecuted the Baptists and drowned them. Just over a hundred years ago, Britain's government starved the Catholic communities in the west of Ireland during the Great Famine and suppressed them—keepin' them from equality of jobs and housin'—until we had the Easter Rising and then the Troubles. Back and forth this has gone fer thousands of years. That has ta change. It shouldn't matter if yer Catholic, Anglican, Presbyterian, Baptist, Methodist, Hindu, Islamic, et cetera, et cetera. Sure and it shouldn't matter where ya came from or how ya worship. We can all live together in peace. It's time ta break the old patterns of hatred and prejudice. I hope and pray youse can teach yer wee'uns a new way so that the Irish can finally *be at peace*." Ian's voice cracked as the emotion finally got to him. "I pray—I pray that me grands and someday me great-grands can grow up and live in this beautiful country peacefully, with no hatred fer their neighbor and with no fear."

When Ian finished, the room was silent and there was hardly a dry eye in the room—even amongst the older grands.

The new generation understood what he was talking about.

And they would never forget it.

AUTHOR'S NOTE

As of 2023, out of the seventeen people who were "disappeared" in the 1970s and '80s by the Provisional IRA, thirteen had been discovered. There are still four families waiting for answers and closure. All seventeen who were "disappeared" were Catholic and suspected of being touts—informers to the British. Only one was a woman, Jean McConville, who was taken from her apartment in the Divis Flats in 1972. Her husband had passed away the year before, so when she was abducted, murdered and buried secretly, she left behind ten children to fend for themselves. Her body was found in 2003.

There are also hundreds of other families in Northern Ireland dealing with injuries and trauma that still linger.

Yet, if one were to go visit, one would see the beauty of the island, hear the lively, uplifting Irish music, and experience the welcoming smiles and voices of the people. I have been there and I have witnessed it! There is strength in the survival of these people. This is the way of the Irish.

Glossary of Words and Phrases

Irish

Ballies—balaclavas (ski mask)

Foundered—cold

Jumper—sweater

Knackered—Tired out

Langered—drunk

Loch—lake

Mollycoddlin'—pampering

Punts—Pounds in currency

Runners—tennis shoes

Sinn Fein—Translated"we ourselves,"it is an Irish republican party

Stook—Someone predisposed to idiocy

Scottish

Braw—fine looking

Bampots—foolish, annoying

Doolally—crazy

Dinnae ken—don't know

Dreich—damp,wet and miserable

Goin' a stoat—going for a walk

Peely-wally—pale or unwell

Tae—to

A Pronunciation Note from the Author

In trying to imitate a significant authentic sound in the Northern Irish accent I used "ay" instead of "ou" or "ow" in the normal spelling, but only for small character parts, as this is a very hard transition for the reader who is not Irish to hear in their ear. (E.g., ayt instead of out, draynin' instead of drowning, dayn instead of down, abayt instead of about.)

In trying to imitate the Scottish pronunciation for the very same sound "ou" or "ow" I used "oo" (e.g., aboot instead of about, hoose instead of house). For words with the "ay" I used "ee"(e.g., dee instead of day).

Irish Political Acronyms and Initials:

DAAD—Direct Action Against Drugs

ICLVR— Independent Commission for the Location of Victims' Remains

IRA—Irish Republican Army

IRD—Information Research Department

PIRA—Provisional Irish Republican Army

PPS—Public Prosecution Service

RIC—Royal Irish Constabulary

RUC—Royal Ulster Constabulary

UVF—Ulster Volunteer Force

UDA—Ulster Defense Association

VWCU—Victim Witness Care Unit

WAVE—Widows Against Violence Empower

Political and Religious Names, Nicknames/Slang:

Fenian—an Irish Catholic, Roman Catholic

Loyalist—mainly Protestant

Paras—Paramilitary

Prod or Proddy—a Protestant

Provos—Provisional IRA

Republican—mainly Catholic

Taig—a Catholic

Dear Reader,

If you have enjoyed this MacCauley saga, I would ask you kindly to please leave a short review on Amazon in order to help the algorithm, and to push this series forward to other readers. It can be as short a sentence as this, "I enjoyed this book!"

Also, if you're interested, click on "Follow the Author" in Amazon and you will be notified when future books are published.

Thank you,
Jannis DeGraw Buhr

The MacCauley Trilogy

More Than a Brother

Book One, *More Than a Brother*, covers the years 1974-87. Gareth MacCauley, a "Child of the Troubles" in Northern Ireland, finds refuge on the Beckett's farm in Southern Wisconsin, USA. Haley Beckett is a happy-go-lucky young girl whose peaceful farm life is interrupted by his arrival. Why is he here? Edward Wagner lives down the road on his family's dairy farm. He's known Haley from birth and has always loved her as his own sister. Both young men are falling for Haley and she loves them both. But who is truly more than a brother to Haley? And, when Gareth returns to find his family in Northern Ireland, will he find them? Will Haley ever see him again?

Anna MacCauley's Legacy

Book Two, *Anna MacCauley's Legacy*, picks up where *More Than a Brother* left off and spans the years 1987-92. The story answers more questions about those who have gone missing, while continuing to develop new relationships between the MacCauleys, the Becketts, and the Becketts' friends. Meanwhile, Northern Ireland continues to struggle to gain peace and find answers for the families of those who have disappeared.

The Lost Cousins of County Armagh

Book Three, *The Lost Cousins of County Armagh*, spans from 1992 into the 21st century while Northern Ireland continues to seek a peaceful agreement amongst its people. It is during this time that the Ian MacCauley clan and their friends learn that there are MacCauley cousins still living in Northern Ireland. If the two families unite and piece together their past, they might find answers and final justice from when the families were torn apart. Meanwhile, an unexpected romance sparks, tying the two countries together once more. But will these MacCauley families ever unite? Will there be satisfaction in seeing people pay for their crimes against the clan? And will Northern Ireland ever find peace?

Made in United States
Cleveland, OH
24 November 2024

10922552R00233